Paul Simon .

Paul Simon

THE POLITICAL
JOURNEY OF
AN ILLINOIS
ORIGINAL

ROBERT E. HARTLEY

Southern Illinois University Press
Carbondale

12 11 10 09   4 3 2 1

Library of Congress Cataloging-in-Publication Data
Hartley, Robert E.
Paul Simon : the political journey of an Illinois original
/ Robert E. Hartley.
      p. cm.
Includes bibliographical references and index.
ISBN-13: 978-0-8093-2945-8 (cloth : alk. paper)
ISBN-10: 0-8093-2945-X (cloth : alk. paper)
1. Simon, Paul, 1928–2003. 2. Legislators—United
States—Biography. 3. United States. Congress.
Senate—Biography. 4. Illinois—Politics and
government—1951– 5. Illinois—Biography. I. Title.
E840.8.S544H376 2009
328.73′073092—dc22
[B]   2009000537

Printed on recycled paper. ♻
The paper used in this publication meets the minimum
requirements of American National Standard for Information Sciences—Permanence of Paper for Printed
Library Materials, ANSI z39.48-1992. ∞

To A.J., for superb book designs and tech support
And to the journalists, past and present, who tell the stories of Illinois politics

Contents

Preface

Paul Simon decided not to run for reelection to the United States Senate in 1996. He preferred to end a forty-year career in politics on a high note and exit the national stage a winner. Instead of a life of semileisure in which he might spend time reflecting, traveling, writing, and enjoying a slower pace, he chose to continue what appears now to have been a race against the clock. He formed a public policy institute and began pursuing ideas and issues with all the energy he could muster.

People who had followed his political career were not surprised. They could not imagine a "retired" Paul Simon, and many of them were eager to help him build further on the legacy of a man determined to bring people together in the name of solving problems. He gathered present and former state and national public figures to the institute's headquarters at Southern Illinois University in Carbondale, Illinois. Simon gave them a stage on which to address their favorite subjects in hopes of enlightening audiences and encouraging action. Initiatives reflecting Simon's long-standing interests, promoted by institute programs, inspired public policies including Illinois campaign finance law.

Those years might have been his finest hours. No longer did he have to wait on legislative colleagues and reluctant office holders to address his ideas. He could set the agenda, and he did. It seemed the perfect capstone to a life of advocacy. But this phase of his journey lasted just six years. On December 9, 2003, Simon died after surgery at a Springfield, Illinois, hospital.

The immediate mourning of Paul Simon occurred in two phases. First came the obituaries, testimonials of public officials and citizens, and newspaper editorials in the days immediately after his death. To say the least, he was well remembered. The second phase happened a week later at his funeral service in Carbondale. With as many as 6,000 people gathered to pay tribute, his longtime friends, associates, and family members offered what can only be called grand testimony to Simon's productive life. He asked not to be the center of attraction at the funeral, but he must have known the wish could not be granted.

The outpouring was appropriately one-sided, devoted to what made the man great in the eyes of many. The image that endeared Simon to friends, politicians, voters, and those who may not have always agreed with him was presented by an array of media.

These comments extolling the virtues of Simon after his death invite a deeper look at the man and his careers:

"He connected so well with people. He spoke with candor and they trusted him more than their own instincts."

"He will be remembered as a political leader who was never afraid to tell you something you didn't want to hear."

"Mr. Simon was uniquely able to mix idealism with practicality to accomplish much for the people of Illinois—and always with his integrity intact."

"He was never contentious or strident, but instead used calm and reasoned arguments to make his points. He was a good man."

Newspaper headlines left these capsules of a carefully crafted image:

"Illinois' honest man."

"Paul Simon, public servant."

Individual statements offered additional material for this book:

"Idealistic in a cynical age, honest and forthcoming in a state whose political climate perfected the secret deal and secret riches."

"Paul Simon had that quality of moral courage in abundance. He couldn't have cared less about the games of politics; that's why he was successful in politics."

There was much more, but the impression is clear: high praise, warm sentiment, and good feelings. It was the stuff of a positive image. Getting behind the image is the objective of this book. The outpouring raises these questions for exploration: How did this image happen? What did he do to earn such respect? Was it an accident or part of a careful plan? Was it something he did, or something others did for him? What were the critical decisions and when did they occur? The book explains how he became a successful Illinois politician, and how his image worked and when it did not work.

The emphasis is on his years in Illinois government. The impressions of the Paul Simon many came to know from media accounts and election campaigns arose from his time as a journalist, state legislator, and lieutenant governor. His years as a congressman from southern Illinois and in the U.S. Senate hold no less importance as he strived to build a national image on an Illinois reputation. This segment deals mostly with how the image played out in a national setting, and how he worked to live up to his own expectations as a man of ideas, principles, and action.

This is a political story. However, since politics was life to Paul Simon, it tells us much more about him than what can be found in headlines, statistics, and election outcomes, or what might be the case with a politician who served one or two terms in office. Because Simon was a complex person, his forty-year journey in public office contained triumphs and failures. They are part of an intriguing Illinois story, and should help us better understand Paul Simon.

Acknowledgments

As background for the Simon story, I sought conversations with people who knew Paul Simon at critical moments. There are not many people around today with personal knowledge of Simon from 1948 to 2003, the span of his public life. His brother, Arthur, is one, and he provided important details. Simon's daughter, Sheila, has encouraged me whenever I launched a project involving her father. For the newspaper days and the early political times, Ray Johnsen and Elmer Fedder had front-row seats. They were generous with reminiscences. I called on former Sen. Alan Dixon, Gene Callahan, and Sen. Richard Durbin to cover the political years. They spoke candidly about their friend and colleague. As a journalist, political operative, and Simon's partner in the public policy institute at Southern Illinois University, Mike Lawrence offered his observations of Simon across the decades. Staff people and colleagues, such as former Sen. Alan Simpson of Wyoming, helped define Simon's congressional years. I am indebted to everyone for impressions and recollections of Simon and his times.

Many others contributed to this project. At the beginning of my newspaper career, I benefited greatly from associations with Bill Boyne and Charles Stewart at the *East St. Louis Journal*. They taught me about the crime culture of the region and inspired my search for details. I called on longtime associates David Kenney, D. G. Schumacher, and Fletcher Farrar Jr. for their editing expertise and familiarity with Simon's performance. I leaned heavily on Cheryl Schnirring's familiarity with Simon material from the Illinois years under her care at the Abraham Lincoln Presidential Library. Skilled researcher Claire Fuller Martin is an expert at developing resources in Springfield, and I am grateful for her many contributions to this story. Walter Ray of the Morris Library Special Collections Research Center at SIU-Carbondale sorted through the huge Simon collection for details of the congressional years. As on many previous occasions, Steve Kerber and Amanda Bahr of the Bowen Archives at SIU-Edwardsville responded capably and promptly to my requests. Working with Southern Illinois University Press editor-in-chief Karl Kageff was a pleasure.

When it came to images of Simon to complement the text, I called on old friends Charles Brown at the St. Louis Mercantile Library, Heather Moore at the U.S. Senate Historical Office, Bill Tubbs at the *Journal of Illinois History*, and Mary Michals at the Abraham Lincoln Presidential Library. Also contributing was Walter Ray at SIU's Morris Library. Book ventures are always a team effort, and it was a pleasure to work with those who assisted on the visual side of this project.

I am grateful for the personal experiences with Paul and Jeanne Simon. Of many encounters, an evening at their Makanda home in February 1998 ranks at the top. For hours they shared stories of their long and turbulent relationship with Paul Powell and their time together in the state legislature. Thank you, Paul and Jeanne, for that, and much more.

And a special note of appreciation for Mary Hartley: listener, editor, critic, and most of all, patient partner.

Part One

Newspaper Years, 1948–55

A Youthful "Ink-Stained Wretch"

In the 1940s and 1950s, many a young man with journalistic yearnings believed that ownership of a weekly newspaper offered the opportunity of a lifetime. Who could pass up a chance to be his own boss and write editorials and columns about worldly subjects?

Weekly newspapers existed then in most towns with 500 or more inhabitants, and often could be purchased for a modest amount of money down and a contract for the balance. A weekly newspaper career could begin for $20,000, most of it debt. By today's standards, the amounts paid in the mid-twentieth century look unbelievably low. In many cases they were, even when considering inflation and cost of living.

Many owners willing to sell had reached an advanced age with no one in the family standing by to take over. The buyers usually were individuals, sometimes married couples, and invariably were new to the community. Sellers usually wrote an article introducing the buyers and recounted the decades of their ownership and family lineage. The article asked readers and advertisers for patience with the newcomers. There was more than friendliness behind this approach as former owners held a contract that new owners had to pay off.

What a new publisher received for that offering of cash and contract might have dampened enthusiasm had there been full disclosure. Office space often barely accommodated furniture and equipment, and smelled of dried printer's ink and overheated machinery. The aroma of old or newly brewed coffee never left the place. The clatter of equipment and voices could be deafening, and the stale cigarette and cigar smoke nauseated nonsmokers. Equipment on hand cannot be imagined by people who produce weekly papers now with computers and quiet running presses operated by push-button controls. New owners took over equipment that had not been upgraded in decades and in some cases dated to the early twentieth century.

The operation usually came with an itinerant typesetter who could keep a cranky old Linotype machine grinding away day and night, setting the lines of type that would be tightened in a page form and placed on a decrepit press. Not too many years earlier, type for a complete edition was handset and printed one page at a time. A typesetter's work habits could be unpredictable. He might not show up for work on the new owner's schedule, forcing the young publisher to decode the typecasting machine and start the hunt for a new, mostly sober, mechanical wizard. Someone always seemed to be available. Amazingly, many weekly papers hadn't missed an edition for decades, finding ways to publish through floods, fires, illnesses, and in spite of stubborn creditors.

Regardless of these conditions—larger weekly papers often had better equipment and more employees—there always seemed to be a willing buyer, ready to work night and day to eke out a living. In the century's mid-decades, the classified advertising section of *Editor and Publisher* magazine, the weekly chronicle of the newspaper business, contained a lengthy list of papers for sale. Although tempted, most young men came to their senses, put the dream of a weekly paper on hold, and headed off to be a reporter on a daily newspaper where the hours were more regular and pay looked good in comparison.

If someone succumbed to buying a rural weekly, he (and often a spouse) struggled to keep the dream from becoming a nightmare. A publisher had to collect from slow-paying customers and advertisers to pay bills and maintain a positive cash flow. An alert publisher kept the local banker's phone number handy. Hard-working and dedicated publisher/editors were living proof that one could sell as few as 400 newspapers a week and remain solvent.

This was the weekly newspaper tradition that drew Paul Simon at age nineteen away from completing a college education to become editor and publisher in Troy, Illinois.

As a teenager in Eugene, Oregon, Paul Simon got his first smell of and feel for newspaper journalism at the daily *Register-Guard*, owned for decades by the Baker family in that city. Then, as now, the paper has continued as one of the finest in the Pacific Northwest. Simon followed in the footsteps of many journalists of his generation who found work in sports departments where they caught the addictive bug of reporting the news.

Simon's early years took shape in Eugene, where his father, Martin, served as pastor of Grace Lutheran Church and published religious materials.[1] Martin and his wife, Ruth, arrived in Eugene after years as missionaries in China. During a civil war, they left aboard a ship from Shanghai. They were asked to return to the United States for safety reasons. Late in 1928 they arrived in Eugene, a month before the birth of son Paul on November 18. A year and a half later, a second son, Arthur, was born. The two boys grew up in a household attuned to religion. Martin and Ruth were devout Christians who insisted on devotions at dinnertime. Arthur, who became a Lutheran pastor and later in New York City spent a career involved with Bread for the World, a citizens' lobby on hunger, remembered long discussions with their father about the meaning of life. "Dad used to say whatever you choose to do in life, the important thing is to do it for God," Arthur said.[2]

Perhaps young Simon's choice of newspaper work had its first urgings as far back as age eight, when he was in elementary school. At least that is the recollection of his brother.[3] While that sounds a bit like candidates for U.S. president recalling how they decided on that vocation at their mothers' knees, those also were the years when youngsters wanted to be nurses, policemen, and firemen.

After graduation from high school at age sixteen—Paul skipped a year of grade school because of an excellent scholastic record—Simon went to work as a part-time sports writer and general helpmate on the *Register-Guard* for sports editor Dick Strite. Demonstrating early dependability, the youngster put together sports pages with local articles, wire service stories, columns, photographs, and his own stories. He wrote headlines and decided the play of news. Most of all, Simon learned the news business from the ground up working with Strite, a fairly typical newsroom habitué of the times. Simon described his first newspaper boss this way: "Dick Strite wrote good stories and expected the same of me. He also had the affliction of most journalists in that day, a love of whiskey and smoking. His top right-hand drawer had a fifth of whiskey in it, which he made clear I should not touch."[4]

Simon's mother had a favorite story about her son's first newspaper job. She told a reporter:

> Whenever the daily papers would misrepresent facts of a game, he wouldn't hesitate to write up an accurate account of what happened and take it to the sports writer, bawling him out for inaccuracies. He kept calling their hand on stories until one of the sports writers came out to our place one summer. He said, "Any boy with the gumption to come down and tell the editor he's wrong would be worth having on the sports staff." And this fellow was instrumental in Paul's landing as reporter for 14 months on the Eugene (Ore.) Register-Guard.[5]

During those years, Simon also discovered politics with a progressive twist. His father believed the two greatest politicians were Abraham Lincoln and Robert LaFollette, a Wisconsin progressive who eventually became a Republican. Simon traced his early political interest to his father's support of men with a strong social conscience and a reputation for financial conservatism. Martin's political interests made a huge impression on his son Paul, who heard of Lincoln's virtues at home long before becoming a resident of Illinois.[6]

For many who had a similar opportunity on sports staffs, addiction to the newspaper world came quickly. For others, it served only as one of several part-time jobs leading eventually to a career in another field. Nonetheless, learning to write quickly and well paid off in many lines of work, such as politics, where a gift for communication paid healthy dividends.

Looking back at his youth, Simon believed he had a "calling" to newspapers. Many a young journalist, including Simon, found a hero to worship while pursuing a career. For Simon, Walter Lippmann and William Allen White filled that role. White owned and operated the Emporia, Kansas, *Gazette* during the first four decades of the century, reaching audiences around the world through his editorials and magazine articles. For young people hoping to work in community journalism, White was the icon.[7]

Lippmann, one of journalism's stars from the early years of the twentieth century until his death in 1974, held an envied position when Simon started his journalistic career. Lippmann helped start the *New Republic* magazine, became editor of the *New York World,* and worked on the *New York Tribune.* He wrote books and became one of the nation's most influential syndicated columnists. By the 1940s, his column *Today and Tomorrow* appeared in hundreds of newspapers across the nation. Presidents of the United States sought his counsel and endorsement, and listened to his advice.[8] Simon set his sights high as the sky, but the road to a career in journalism took several jogs before fully developing.

Simon began college at the University of Oregon in his hometown. During the first year, he worked almost full time at the *Register-Guard* while carrying a class load and studying. The same year he was elected president of the Oregon Walther League, a Lutheran youth organization, the youngest district president ever to be elected by that international organization. He might have continued to graduation at the university if his parents had not decided to leave Eugene. They settled in Highland, Illinois, a community about thirty-five miles east of St. Louis, where Martin continued publishing religious magazines. Simon transferred to Dana College in Blair, Nebraska, a liberal arts school influenced by Lutheran and Danish cultures. He remained at the small college from 1946 to 1948, enjoying a life and activities not experienced at the University of Oregon. He worked on the student newspaper and yearbook, but had no professional journalistic experiences.

Simon remembered the years at Dana fondly for the spirited discussions among student friends, singing in the college choir, and participating in campus politics. He was elected student body president in his sophomore year and became an active member of the National Association for the Advancement of Colored People (NAACP). Reflecting the political leanings of his father, Simon organized the Dana chapter of Young Republicans and met frequently with county and state leaders. In 1948, he actively supported Harold Stassen for the nomination against Thomas Dewey and Robert Taft in Nebraska primaries, demonstrating a willingness to back someone with whom he agreed rather than someone who could win. In all, Simon recalled the time at Dana as typical for students in the post–World War II world. He concluded, "Dana College was good to me."[9]

That statement covers more than just the academic experience. At Dana, Simon made the acquaintance of Ray Johnsen and his brother Paul, also students. Simon played on an intramural basketball team organized by the Johnsen brothers. He commented later, "We won few games but we enjoyed ourselves."[10] The friendship between Simon and Ray Johnsen lasted a lifetime, through years as weekly newspaper and political partners. Johnsen served on Simon's Illinois lieutenant governor staff and later on his congressional staffs. Simon said, "Ray Johnsen, who worked with me in the newspaper business, headed our bookkeeping efforts to make sure nothing amiss happened."[11]

Simon might have completed studies at Dana and gone on a career route similar to other students at the college. However, that prospect ended with a telegram in 1948 from father Martin to son Paul, then age nineteen, about an opportunity to own and operate a weekly newspaper to serve the 1,200 citizens of Troy, Illinois, not far from his parent's home in Highland. The publisher and owner of the *Troy Call*, Ben Jarvis, who had operated the *Call* for fifty years, was seriously ill and had stopped publishing the paper.[12] Jarvis asked $3,600 for the equipment. People in town, realizing the importance of having a newspaper, began a search for someone to take the challenge.

Troy's history was common to small towns that dotted the Illinois prairie. The first settlers of the area, Jacob Gregg and a Mr. Moore, arrived in 1803 and 1804. John Jarvis, a native of Virginia who moved from Turkey Hill near Belleville, Illinois, arrived in 1806 and began the family legacy attached forever to Troy.[13] Jarvis Township, in which Troy is located, is named for John. In 1816, two years before Illinois became a state, Jarvis erected a tavern and gristmill, the first business enterprises in the region. The tavern became a gathering place for travelers on the emigrant trail westward. John Jarvis died October 29, 1823.

In 1819, Jarvis sold ten acres of land for $10 per acre to James Riggen and David Hendershoot who mapped a community known as Columbia. Soon Riggen renamed it Troy, which had a population of about 120 people. The town grew slowly, with a post office added in 1833. In that year, a mercantile store was the only business; citizens organized the first church in 1842. Construction of the National Road—which later became U. S. Highway 40—extended east of Vandalia in 1843, then the capital of Illinois. The road never reached Troy, although surveys were completed.[14] Meanwhile, Troy became a destination for stages running from St. Louis to Terre Haute, Indiana. After departing from St. Louis, the stages made a lengthy first stop in Troy for fresh horses. One history of the town stated, "The arrival and departure of these stages was the great feature of the day."[15]

Troy became an incorporated town by special act of the legislature in 1857. Growth picked up at that point with the addition of farms, industry, and shops. Mining and agriculture provided employment opportunities, while churches and schools made the community more attractive to prospective residents. Troy's first newspaper, the *Commercial Bulletin,* owned by James Jarvis, a descendant of John Jarvis, began operations in April 1872. In May, he changed the name to the *Troy Bulletin.*[16] On April 12, 1882, the town became a city, with a population of about 1,000. By 1900 population had increased to 1,080.

In 1948, Troy had a population of 1,200 and was on a major highway, U.S. 40, which continued from New Jersey to California. George Stewart, in his history of the national highway, said of the stretch from Vandalia to St. Louis two years after Simon's arrival, "This section is one of the poorest on the whole transcontinental reach. Although much had been relocated as a wholly new highway, even in 1950 other sections remained narrow and poorly paved. In that year travel-services were routing Indianapolis-St. Louis motorists by way of Springfield over highways 36 and 66."[17] Eventually, the route became Interstate 70, assuring Troy of attention as a rest stop for cross-country travelers.

Simon inquired of the weekly newspaper opportunity in Troy and with his father talked to the owner and members of the Troy Lions Club. Based on their recommendations, a local bank loaned Simon $3,500 to buy the paper. He changed the name from the *Call* to the *Troy Tribune* and began publishing a four-page paper on June 24, 1948.[18]

Those first days and weeks, maybe months, at the helm of a newspaper eagerly anticipated by residents of Troy quickly took Simon beyond the dreamy, high-minded expectations of being the proprietor/editor. Single and full of energy, Simon devoted his days and nights to the *Tribune* because in large part if he had not, there would not be a *Tribune.* He described losing twenty pounds while working seventy-five-hour weeks during the first months of publishing.[19]

Joining him in the work on the initial issue was his brother Arthur. Between them they had scant experience, just the understanding gained from having worked with their father in a small print shop. Years later Arthur's impression of the paper's office had not dimmed. "The print shop was small and dingy. The equipment was caked with dust. Type was handset. The Linotype needed repairs constantly. The press was built in 1879, and clanked when it ran."[20] Here is how Paul Simon described getting out the first edition, an event that the high school band prepared to serenade with the mayor in attendance:

> We wanted to have that initial newspaper ready for the band and Troy's hopeful citizens. We finally got everything into the forms and loaded the type onto the old press, started the noisy motor running and we prepared for our masterpiece! Unfortunately the gelatin-type rollers that ink the type had not been used for six months [when the former owner stopped publishing] and when we started the presses the rollers crumbled into uselessness. I had to go outside and with great embarrassment tell the waiting band and small gathering of citizens that the newspaper would not come out for another week.

Each week afterward the chore became more routine and less troublesome, but unique for the uninitiated. Ray Johnsen, who taught school after graduation from Dana College, joined Simon that first summer, an eye-opening vacation from the rigors of a classroom. Simon and Johnsen stayed together with other roomers at the home of Ann Kueker in Troy. After working through the Wednesday nights to get the paper out Thursday, the two young men walked into Kueker's house for a "night's sleep" about 8 A.M. the next morning.[21]

Also helping the young editor and publisher from week to week was his mother, Ruth Simon, who came to Troy from her home in Highland to pitch in. She filled the positions of typist, bookkeeper, Linotype operator, and "all-around flunky" at the *Tribune*. Simon's parents hoped the *Tribune* would be the first in a chain of Christian newspapers, with Paul's younger brother Arthur also in the business.[22] Arthur became a Lutheran pastor instead.

The life of a weekly publisher quickly put an end to Simon's plans to finish his college education. He contacted Washington University in St. Louis about taking classes while publishing the *Tribune,* but it never happened. Simon eventually served two terms in the United States Senate, taught at universities, traveled the world, and was author or coauthor of twenty-three books, but he did not finish college. He received more than fifty honorary college degrees before his death in 2003.[23]

Simon found the expectations of readers and the realities of a small staff meant a tough daily grind. Citizens of Troy wanted a weekly chronicle of local news: city government, schools, births, deaths, weddings, divorces, crime news, street repairs, and so on. Almost anyone who spends time editing and publishing weekly newspapers tells stories about the routine of wedding notices, petty crime news, items about travels of local residents and visits from relatives, all the while beating on doors for subscribers and advertising. Writing later about newspaper life, Simon added his affirmation: "People in a small town want to read in their weekly newspaper the stories about a family visiting their friends in New Orleans, about a birth, about an automobile accident, about the myriad of small things that never make the news of a metropolitan newspaper but are the lifeblood of a community of 1,200."[24]

Residents of Troy got their wishes, but they also got a strong editorial voice. In a few months, *Tribune* readers knew the young publisher and editor, if not from meeting him on the street or at community meetings, from his photograph and an editorial column he named "Trojan Thoughts."[25] (Everyone who hailed from Troy was referred to in the *Tribune* as a Trojan.) Throughout the paper, his ideas sprouted every week. Rarely constrained in his opinions, Simon gave the publication a personal touch and the impression that the *Troy Tribune* covered all the important news. His exploits as well as his cheery personality had full run of the paper. While the column often began on a serious note, it almost always included local names and happenings, a thank you or two, and notable comings and goings. In its best promotional voice, the *Tribune* brushed up its own image and expressed pride in the community. By 1949 Simon had increased circulation and boosted advertising, although by his own admission gains were hard won.[26]

It did not take Simon long to see that Troy needed a sewer system and a public library. He badgered city officials constantly in a campaign for sewers and finally succeeded years later. The library idea took even longer. A special election for a library, strongly supported by Simon, failed. Later, momentum generated by volunteers ignited enthusiasm for a library that opened in 1964. Simon summarized those early years with this comment on his campaigns: "Most of my editorial efforts, while commendable, caused few ripples outside our newspaper." For those efforts that did yield results, Simon said, "A newspaper can be a powerful force for good, even when operated by someone with almost no experience."[27] Perhaps reflecting his wishes for the community, the *Tribune* ran its motto on page 1, declaring "A Progressive Newspaper in a Progressive Town."

As Simon settled into the fabric of Troy and the paper prospered, he became aware of newspaper wars being waged against organized crime in the Illinois counties of St. Clair and Madison, which included Troy. The primary newspapers that challenged the criminal element and called for reforms in law enforcement were the *St. Louis Globe-Democrat*, the *St. Louis Post-Dispatch*, and the *East St. Louis Journal*. Other papers in the region, including the *Alton Evening Telegraph* and the *Collinsville Herald*, joined the fight periodically. Until mid-1949, Simon had not commented on gambling and prostitution because they seemed remote from his community. One incident in Troy changed his mind and started the editor on a crusade that lasted for years and elevated him from small-town publisher to a voice with an audience well beyond Troy.

Crusader and Politician

Simon told the story frequently of his first encounter with the acceptance of gambling among citizens and elected officials. It happened less than a year after he began publishing the *Tribune*.[1] One day Simon had lunch at a small restaurant in town. On the counter were punchboards. For a small fee, maybe a nickel or dime, a customer could push a metal device into one of the many holes on the board. A piece of paper emerged telling the player how much money he or she had won. The payoff might be $3 or $5, or nothing.

Simon asked the proprietor how much he paid for a board. He was told the price was $3. Total board sales were $90 and paid out $30 in prizes, for a profit of $57. However, that was not the way it worked in Madison County. He had to buy punchboards for $30 each from an individual with connections to the Madison County sheriff's office. If he did not buy from this man, a deputy sheriff would call on the owner and confiscate the punchboards on the grounds that gambling was illegal. The proprietor took a smaller profit to avoid tangling with the sheriff. After a tour of shops in Troy, Simon discovered thirteen businesses that operated in that manner.

Under Illinois law and in Simon's eyes, punchboards were illegal. The sheriff's office did not respond to Simon, and on June 23, 1949, a year after starting the paper, he wrote an article about punchboards for the *Tribune*. He received responses from a number of readers. Officials continued to ignore Simon, but newspapers in Madison and St. Clair counties paid attention to Simon's columns and stories. After that introduction to minor graft, Simon launched the crusade that became his signature achievement as a newspaper editor, an account of which appeared in almost every biographical article about him thereafter.

As Simon learned, the metropolitan area in Illinois across from St. Louis had a firmly entrenched culture of lawless activity dating to the mid-1800s.[2] Newspapers from the nineteenth and early twentieth centuries told story after story of union strife, prostitution, gambling, unsolved murders, illegal sales of liquor, and official corruption.[3] Living with organized crime had been the rule since the early 1920s when the Shelton gang ran roughshod over law and order in southern Illinois. The notorious brothers used East St. Louis as a base of operations for years.[4] During Prohibition, the Sheltons prospered by establishing stills in the woods of Madison County. One of the small-time hoodlums who joined the Shelton gang was Frank Leonard "Buster" Wortman, who began his life of crime in the mid-1920s. In the 1940s, Wortman became mob boss in St. Clair and Madison counties.

Wortman started building his rap sheet of criminal charges in 1926. He avoided conviction until an episode in 1933 near Collinsville. Whether he was picking up a delivery at a still or in charge of liquor production never was clear. However, federal agents raided the still and Wortman resisted. Officials charged Wortman with assault for beating a federal agent. Found guilty and sentenced to ten years, he served first at the U.S. penitentiary at Leavenworth, Kansas, and later at Alcatraz, "The Rock," reserved for prestige gangsters and dangerous characters. Al "Scarface" Capone was one of the inmates at Alcatraz with Wortman.[5] When released in the early 1940s, Wortman returned to the East St. Louis area and began assembling a gang to challenge the fading Shelton influence and any others who wanted to control gambling in the region.

After bloodshed eliminated the competition, Wortman became the principal agent in St. Louis and southern Illinois for the criminal syndicate once headed by Al Capone of Chicago.[6] At one time or another, Wortman and his associates owned or controlled gambling establishments, a racing news service, handbooks, nightclubs, taverns, restaurants, a loan company, a stable of racehorses, real estate companies, and a trucking line. They distributed slot machines, jukeboxes, and pinball machines. By 1948, Wortman had consolidated his control of the rackets and established headquarters at the Paddock tavern in East St. Louis. In that year, Simon's first in Troy, gambling casinos, handbooks, slot machines, and lotteries ran wide open in Illinois. Wortman's rackets empire extended throughout Madison and St. Clair counties.

The reality of organized gang activity was that law enforcement officers and public officials in St. Clair and Madison counties turned their backs on illegal operations. As long as violence did not become excessive and gambling operatives knew enough to close down temporarily when newspapers turned up the heat, local officials were willing to ignore gambling.[7]

Against such forces, ordinary citizens refused to get involved. As long as open gambling did not directly corrupt or interrupt their lives, they let the criminal action continue. Many viewed gambling as harmless. The resulting apathy became the handmaiden of corruption, and the combination produced a political culture in Madison County that recognized illegal activity as an acceptable way of doing business. This is what stunned Simon as he tried to rally citizens against corruption.

The larger newspapers of the St. Louis metropolitan area had lived with and chronicled gangster activities for decades. They focused much of their attention on sensational incidents, such as large heists and murders. Gangs reached into all corners of the communities and cultures, defying reform and spending much of their energy fighting among themselves for a share of graft and rackets. Too much corruption money flowed to elected officials for any long-term remedies to stick.

In the years immediately after World War II, returning veterans, restless with the status quo among public officials and frustrated with visible influences of racketeers, inspired grassroots reforms by electing people to local government who refused to knuckle under to crime bosses. This encouraged newspapers to dig deeper into the examples of illegal activity. As Paul Simon began publishing the *Troy Tribune*, the *Post-Dispatch* and the *East St. Louis Journal* devoted major resources to digging for and exposing the causes of crime. The papers backed up reporters' efforts with editorial campaigns that pulled no punches.[8] As sordid details of criminal activity received prominent play in daily papers and Simon discovered the trail of corruption in Troy, he began to see himself in the image of famous crime reporters. He couldn't afford to hire a crime reporter, so if the *Tribune* were to take on related issues in Madison County, the editor would do the job. Whatever Simon lacked in experience, he made up in chutzpah.

The *Post-Dispatch* and the *Journal,* despite significant differences in circulation and staff resources, competed for decades investigating organized crime and haunting racket bosses and their associates. The *Post-Dispatch* star crime reporter was Theodore C. (Ted) Link. In East St. Louis, his counterpart was Charles O. Stewart.[9] Other papers had crime reporters, but these two worked with an intensity that separated them from the crowd and inspired the young Troy editor.

In the late 1940s and early 1950s, news about crime from across Illinois provided a backdrop for Simon's growing awareness of gambling in Madison County and complicity among law enforcement officials. On a statewide scale, Adlai E. Stevenson, candidate for governor in 1948, turned his focus on gambling and caught Simon's attention. Stevenson accused incumbent governor Dwight Green of allowing commercial gambling to flourish.[10] His rhetoric accelerated when newspapers divulged that Green had received campaign donations for the 1944 gubernatorial race from people known to have associated with gambling.[11]

Newspapers from Chicago to St. Louis joined the battle on behalf of Stevenson and helped catapult the challenger to victory over Green by a plurality of 572,067 votes.[12] Stevenson was barely inaugurated when he warned local governments to end gambling or the state would do it for them. Previously, no governor had so openly threatened to usurp local law enforcement authority. But Stevenson dragged his feet when it came to action. He hoped county officials would decide on their own to crack down on gambling.[13] That was wishful thinking, as Simon learned.

Stevenson's election victory and thrust at gambling bolstered Simon's courage and brought the two men together philosophically in spite of their age difference. Stevenson was twenty-nine years older. Shortly after his discovery of punchboard graft, Simon corresponded with James W. Mulroy, executive secretary to Governor Stevenson. Over six weeks starting in July 1949, Simon wrote three letters to Mulroy and received two responses, none of which was published.[14] Simon repeatedly urged state action in Madison County. He related conversations with the state Republican party chairman regarding the lack of action by Stevenson and quoted editorials in the St. Louis papers on the gambling issue. To Simon's urgings, Mulroy initially repeated the Stevenson line that the administration had conducted quiet conversations with law enforcement officials and that the governor hesitated to usurp local prerogatives.

Simon searched for other ways to push the case. He asked Mulroy to send Madison County officials letters requesting them to inform the governor of action taken against gamblers. He also suggested Stevenson appoint a committee of "responsible men" to study the situation and make recommendations. Simon nominated Irving Dilliard, editorial page editor of the *Post-Dispatch,* who would become a mentor and close friend to the youthful editor. Mulroy wrote back that he would discuss the committee idea with the governor.[15] Simon's suggestions apparently did not inspire the governor, but the editor's faith in the governor appeared unshaken.[16] Simon wrote to Mulroy on September 3, "I was among the political independents who did some fighting for Governor Stevenson prior to November. I feel he has served the people most ably so far, but the gambling situation is not gaining him any friends."

During the letter exchange, Simon decided to take the initiative in the *Tribune,* becoming his own version of Ted Link and Charles Stewart. Simon noticed an announcement from Madison County sheriff Dallas Harrell and state's attorney Austin Lewis that they had closed two houses of prostitution on Highway 40, just a few miles from Troy. Shortly after the announcement,

Simon noticed the businesses had reopened. He decided to make a personal call on the establishments. The description of his visits appeared under the headline, "Prostitution Houses Again Operating; Tribune Editor Visits Spots Near Collinsville." The provocative article opened with these words:

> The houses of prostitution along Highway 40 known as the Plamor Inn and the Club 40 which were "closed" by the sheriff in cooperation with the state's attorney's office are now operating in full swing again—except that no liquor is being sold over the counter as it formerly was.
>
> I know. I was there.[17]

Simon described how he visited the Plamor Inn and asked for a Coke. He was the only customer. After serving the drink, the waitress asked, "Do you want a girl?" Simon answered, "Not tonight," but inquired about the cost of services. "Depends on what you want," she answered. "It starts at five dollars." He left the Plamor and went to Club 40, starting with the same Coke routine. Simon noticed more male-female activity. This time the bartender, a "very good looking lady," wasted no time propositioning the young editor. She came around in back of the counter, picked some lint from his suit coat, stroked Simon's back, and said, "Say, if you're interested in entertainment I suggest we go out to one of the bedrooms and talk things over. They won't let us make propositions at the bar."

Simon went to the bedroom with the woman and asked, "How much is it?" The woman replied, "Five dollars for once and ten dollars for twice. For ten dollars I can give you a nice long party, honey." Simon began looking for a way out, saying that five dollars was "a little much for me." Applying pressure on the prospective client, the woman responded, "Listen honey, for five dollars, I'll give you a good long stay and arrange for some drinks for both of us on that, too."

Simon asked if she would be available later in the week. He wanted out before anyone recognized him. "No honey, this is my last night. Won't you give me just a little satisfaction tonight? We'll have a nice long party in the bed and then if you don't have quite enough money we can settle up afterwards." Simon headed for the doorway, and "some much-needed fresh air."

Addressing his readers, Simon stated, "I walked out of the place with a still lower opinion of the activities of our county sheriff, Dallas Harrell, and the state's attorney, Austin Lewis." He closed the article with a tactic he used frequently to get the attention of the media and increase leverage with public officials: "For the information of my readers, a copy of this issue of the Tribune will be sent to the sheriff by registered mail."

A week later Simon continued the drumbeat on prostitution under the headline "Vice Organized in Many County Spots."[18] The article included this notice: "Readers of The Tribune may be interested to know that a 'for sale' sign is again hanging on the Plamor Inn. However, it has appeared at other times when pressure has been brought on the place." In another story, Simon wrote, "What was the general reaction to the publication of the headline story in last week's Tribune? some have asked. Reaction was mixed. Principally, however, it was divided into two groups: 1. Those who were shocked at actual conditions which exist in the county, and 2. Those who were indifferent to conditions but were shocked that The Tribune would print a story telling of conditions in the county."

Simon used his "Trojan Thoughts" column that week to expand on the "shock" aspect of the story, and offered his justification. "A newspaperman has the responsibility to bring you the news—particularly when it concerns possible corruption on the part of public officials. If it shocks you I'm sorry but that's my business: to bring you the news." He concluded, "Of one thing you can be certain—however much you may have disliked our publication of the story, there were county officials and 'business men' near Collinsville who disliked it much more than did you."[19]

The November 3 issue of the *Tribune* carried the first reactions of other newspapers to Simon's adventure. The *Mounds Independent* declared its support, adding, "It reads like something from Erskine Caldwell's 'Tobacco Road,' but it puts over its point like an air hammer. . . . There is no excuse for an official who does not fulfill his obligation to decency." The *Highland Journal,* published where Martin and Ruth Simon lived, showed little sympathy for the article. "If that was his [Simon's] idea of courageous, crusading journalism, he'd do better grinding out stuff for the 'true confession' type of publication rather than a weekly newspaper for the consumption of the entire family."[20]

Simon mentioned other critics in his column. One letter "accused me of writing the article to buildup my sales and that I sold the extra issues for one dollar each! Since publishing the article I have heard a lot of rumors of what was going to happen to me, what prompted the story, etc., but that one of selling the issues for one dollar each was a new one on me."[21] In spite of the rhetoric, Simon had results to report, indicating that public officials had taken notice. "On Friday morning the sheriff received a copy of the story in the Tribune and Friday afternoon he again decided to make a raid."

Pressure built on Governor Stevenson to take action against gambling interests—his most supportive paper, the *Post-Dispatch,* had joined the cry.

In November, Stevenson called Madison County "an obstinate problem." Simon quoted Attorney General Ivan A. Elliott as saying the governor and he "stand ready to help to the extent of the state's power and resources," if local officials fail to enforce the law.[22] Still, nothing happened.

The *Tribune* reported that the 200 Club in Madison, west of Troy near the Mississippi River, operated again "in defiance of the governor." Mulroy, the governor's executive secretary, issued a statement when word reached Springfield. "Gov. Stevenson is handling this matter in accordance with the law, and there will be no spectacular activity. But you may be certain the matter is being investigated and proper action will be taken. The challenge has been accepted."[23] Simon said the inability of Sheriff Harrell to cope with the 200 Club "is giving Madison County a black eye from one end of the state to the other." Taking aim at the sheriff and the state's attorney, Simon added, "Laws should be enforced or changed—not enforced according to the whim or pocketbook of our officials."[24] In the December 1 issue, Simon noted that Sheriff Harrell had raided Club 40 and Plamor Inn and made eight arrests.

While crime news and the editor's involvements got top play in almost every issue of the *Tribune* through the end of 1949, Simon departed from current events in the December 1 "Trojan Thoughts" for a personal note that added new meaning to his campaign to clean up Madison County law enforcement. He registered to vote upon turning age twenty-one in November and declared himself a Democrat.[25] "This column is going to 'shock' a great many of my friends this week," he acknowledged. "I have been for a positive Republican party which is not a party which fights for big business alone, which fights for civil rights and the rights of all laboring men, which is fully aware of the need for international cooperation. But I have come to the belief that that party does not exist with the exception of a few men like Senator [Wayne] Morse of Oregon and Senator [George] Aiken of Vermont."

Simon provided four reasons for his decision:

1. The most important problem existing today is the problem of establishing world peace. As I see it this involves recognition of the necessity of our shouldering a responsibility in the world situation. While the Republican party has followed this line, it has done so reluctantly. If there would be a swing in public opinion I feel many a GOP congressman would be happy to switch from an internationalist vote to a stand of isolationism. Probably more important than this for world peace is the necessity of striving for a genuine world free trade. This is essential to world peace and will not be

a lever for the lowering of American standard of living as so many falsely have stated. Even if it would, free trade is very basic to world peace and world peace is essential to the future of civilization. The Republican party has been the party of the high tariff and the Democrats of the low tariff. I cannot conscientiously side with the former group on this stand.

2. The question of "civil rights" is a major problem in the United States today and will be for some time to come. While both parties officially are for it, the Republicans in the last session [of Congress] did not stick to their guns with few exceptions. The GOP-Southern Democratic coalition defeated the proposal which would have made possible the passage of civil rights legislation.

3. The problem of the working man and woman is one which will be a real problem for much time to come. Extreme legislation on either side must be avoided. I believe that the Taft-Hartley act is an extreme and an indication of Republican sentiment generally. While I do not agree with President Truman that it should be repealed in its entirety, I do believe that it does contain sections which harbor a real danger to the working man when economic conditions are not as favorable as they are now.

4. Affiliation in the Republican party in Illinois would mean backing men who are nothing more than stool-pigeons for Chicago's Colonel [Robert] McCormick [owner of the *Chicago Tribune*]. I want to affiliate with a party which will put up men for whom I will be proud to pound the streets and ring doorbells. I don't want to do that for a [Everett] Dirksen or a [Dwight] Green or a [former senator C. Wayland] Brooks. Many people say that there are two things in which they never take an active part: politics and religion. These happen to be two things in which I feel I must take a very active part. The Democratic party is the party with which I more fully agree. It is the party for which I will be willing to ring doorbells.

Simon declared independence within party ranks, saying he would not blindly support a Democrat, whether able or not. "If I feel a Republican is more able than a Democrat, I shall be proud to support him with my vote and with my newspaper."[26] He pointedly made exceptions for the party in Madison County. "My affiliation with the Democratic party in Madison county does not mean support of [political machines]. Personally, I don't believe either group is headed for immediate sainthood." These statements set the stage for future clashes with Democratic party officials in Madison County, and later with fellow Democrats in the state legislature.

He concluded, "I am not a socialist nor do I believe in deficit spending except in times of real national emergency such as a depression. I do believe that the government should see that all men get certain basic needs, but should avoid anything which might eliminate incentive from our national picture." Simon received so many requests for the *Tribune* issue that he had to print another 1,000 copies of the editorial.

One of Simon's newspaper neighbors, James O. Monroe, founder of the *Collinsville Herald,* responded to the announcement with a letter. He emphasized points that must have made the young editor's head swell. Monroe said, "Congratulations, not on your becoming a Democrat, but on your becoming an intelligent Democrat, or on becoming a Democrat intelligently. Your four basic reasons are eminently sound. Your reservations in local matters are equally logical. I welcome you not as a potential precinct captain but as a kindred intellectual spirit."[27] Democrat Monroe served as a state senator from Madison County for thirty years, concluding with the 1962 General Assembly. Upon Monroe's retirement, Simon ran for senator and was elected.

Simon's foray into Democratic politics began before he publicly announced the decision about his allegiances. Speculation had begun in the fall of 1949 about the U.S. Senate contest a year later. The incumbent senator was Democrat Scott Lucas, who also held the position of senate majority leader. His Republican opponent was to be Everett Dirksen, a former member of Congress. However, Lucas's trip to the general election was muddied by poor relations with elements of the party in Illinois. For example, Governor Adlai Stevenson remained distant from the incumbent, the result of a clash of personalities rather than any specific incident.

Rising from this and other party arguments was a rumor that Benjamin Adamowski, the boy wonder of Chicago politics in the early 1930s, was preparing a primary election challenge to Lucas. Adamowski, first elected to the General Assembly as a protégé of Chicago Democrat leader Anton Cermak in 1930, served five terms in the House. In 1938 he broke with the organization of Edward J. Kelly and began a career of waging battles with the party establishment. Stevenson, a virtual unknown in 1938, campaigned for Adamowski, and the two maintained a friendship for years. Adamowski ran for lieutenant governor on the 1940 ticket with gubernatorial candidate John Stelle and lost.

Stelle, still a political powerhouse in southern Illinois by 1949 and no friend of the Chicago political machine, supported renegade Adamowski against Lucas. When that failed to materialize, Stelle supported Dirksen. In the midst of this party wrangle, the young editor in Troy, who later would have relationships with all the principles in this saga, volunteered to work for Adamowski. Simon made the offer in a letter dated November 21, 1949.[28] After acknowledging Adamowski's possible challenge to Lucas, Simon wrote, "I consider myself an independent Democrat and frankly am not too enthusiastic over the candidacy of Scott Lucas for renomination. If you are qualified for the job, and everything I have heard indicates you are, I would like to encourage you to seek the senatorial nomination on the Democratic ticket. I know of a great many others who feel as I do who would be happy to support you if they felt you were qualified for the position." Although there is no explanation for Simon's attitude toward Lucas, it may have resulted from an incident during the 1949 session of Congress. Party liberals blamed Lucas for allowing a successful filibuster by southern Democrats and Republicans against President Harry Truman's civil rights bill.

Without any foreplay, Simon volunteered to help Adamowski. "I would be happy to volunteer my services to do whatever I could in the Southern Illinois territory for you, if I feel you are qualified for the job." He concluded, "If you can at all live up to the rumors which have preceded you downstate I know you could rally a great deal of support to yourself for the nomination." Adamowski did not run in the primary against Lucas, and there is nothing in Simon's papers to indicate a dialogue between the two. However, the letter demonstrated a boldness that characterized Simon during his newspaper days, and his desire to be labeled as an "independent Democrat."

Early in January 1950 during a radio address mentioning issues facing Illinois, Stevenson reviewed his first year in office. He said commercialized gambling had been the "biggest headache."[29] However, Stevenson continued to speak about the importance of electing "conscientious, vigorous officials and insist that they enforce the law." Jumping on the governor's comments, the *St. Louis Globe-Democrat* acknowledged Stevenson's concern about encroaching on local jurisdiction but did not accept his speech as the final word, stating, "Even more dangerous, however, is the continuance of wide-open gambling with its 'attendant corruption and corroding disrespect for law.'"[30] Newspapers across the region echoed those words.

The *Tribune* continued its watch over Madison County gambling operations. In the March 2, 1950, issue, Simon wrote, "It was also reported this week that Buster Wortman, East St. Louis hoodlum and jukebox distributor, has invaded Madison county and has placed one of his machines in a county tavern on State Route 111 near Horseshoe Lake."[31] The article also mentioned other Madison County activities: four smokeshop bookie operations in Granite City, the 200 Club horse race betting parlor in Madison, two bookies at the Hyde Park Club in Venice, and scattered poker and blackjack games in the back rooms of saloons and pool halls. "While the Hyde Park and 200 clubs are for the present confining their liveliness to horserace betting, it is reported that the owners are preparing to re-open dice games after the April 11 primary election," the paper concluded.

Stevenson could not get the antigambling pressure to diminish. The media drumbeat gathered momentum early in April with two articles in *Collier's,* a magazine with national circulation, in which the author accused Stevenson of failing to make good on campaign pledges to rid the state of commercialized gambling.[32] Simon jumped into the fray with a letter on May 2 to Stevenson aide Mulroy. Simon sympathized with the governor's plight, saying, "It seems to me your extremely able administration should not be hindered by attacks of failing to act in the gambling situation. . . . I am not suggesting what action should be taken, only that it should be taken."[33]

The response to Simon's letter from Mulroy in May 1950 gave the editor a clear exclusive for the *Tribune.* Mulroy repeated the often-told story that Stevenson and Attorney General Elliott had spent more than a year meeting with law enforcement officials in an attempt to convince them to go after gambling. Then Mulroy provided a news flash: "I am told that Madison County is still open in some respects but I am of the considered opinion that in a comparatively short time the better known gambling places in your county will be closed either due to action taken by your own authorities or by some other type of action which might have to be taken in the future."[34]

Even a young editor could read between those lines of bureaucratic talk. The next issue of the *Tribune* shouted from page one: "Big County Gambling Places to Be Closed," ahead of an article that quoted from Mulroy's letter.[35] Within days, state police, directed by Stevenson and Elliott, raided the 200 Club in Madison and Hyde Park Club in nearby Venice, launching an intense effort to intimidate gamblers and their sympathizers throughout Illinois.

When Stevenson finally decided to act, it happened in Paul Simon's backyard. On May 12, 1950, about fifty state policemen, mostly new officers from throughout the state, conducted the surprise raid.[36] Officers arrived in unmarked state cars to confront stunned patrons. More than 500 people at the Hyde Park Club were busy with racing forms and receiving results from racetracks over a public address system. About 300 people were engaged in similar gambling activities at the 200 Club. Police arrested forty-eight workers at the clubs and confiscated gambling paraphernalia. Simon went to the state's attorney's office that evening and stayed until about 3:30 A.M. when state officials filed charges. He wrote of the time spent with prosecutors, defense attorneys, and state police as "a hectic evening. One I won't soon forget."[37]

Harry Curtis, state police chief, said the raids were calculated to "put the fear of God" in Illinois gamblers. The *Post-Dispatch* editorial page pointed the finger at apathetic citizens. "Had the business men of Madison County required State's Attorney Austin Lewis to do his duty these raids would not have been necessary. And the next complaint of the same business men against 'socialization' in Washington would have had a less hollow ring."[38]

Simon cheered from "Trojan Thoughts." He wrote, "Governor Stevenson is to be commended for taking action. Personally I feel it is too bad he didn't act a little sooner, but that he did act is commendable." With the war against gambling now on the ground, Simon became an unflinching cheerleader for the governor. Within a week of the Madison County raids, the governor responded by inviting Simon to Springfield for lunch and a talk.

Under the headline "Governor Has Hour-Long Talk with Troy Tribune Editor," Simon said the two discussed "policies of state government, the politics of state government and the Madison county political situation."[39] Obviously impressed with the governor and with being invited to the state capital, Simon added, sounding a bit obsequious, "Beyond any doubt the man is giving the state of Illinois an unusually high type of government. He is a man of real integrity. The Democratic party is fortunate in having him in that position and the people of the state of Illinois are fortunate." A sentence in the article clarified Simon's political role. "Simon has no official connection with the state Democratic organization but is secretary-treasurer of the Illinois Democratic Editorial association."

Mingled with his campaign against gambling, Simon continued to build a stronger, more profitable *Tribune*. In a postscript to his "Trojan Thoughts" column of July 30, 1950, he noted the paper had passed its second anniversary since resurrection. He wrote, "Although we're still creeping toward our goals it's not hard to see that we've come a long way since those agonizing first months of existence—to use the term very freely." He said advertising was better than a year earlier, and "mechanically our shop is in better shape than it has ever been."[40]

Circulation had reached 1,600 a week, much higher than any previous Troy newspaper. (Another source stated that advertising revenue reached $200 a week and the paper was in the black.)[41] Simon thanked readers for their "courtesy and cooperation." On a personal note, Simon said that people "have gradually become accustomed to the idea of having Paul Simon in the driver's seat—although I'll admit that's a hard thing to get used to. I'll know I'm really accepted as soon as our very efficient county clerk, Eulalia Hotz, starts calling me Paul instead of 'Mr. Simon.' While I'm about that I might as well make my annual plea to be known as Paul. If I ever become 200 years of age maybe I'll be old enough to be called Mr. Simon but until then it's just Paul. I'm on record as detesting titles."[42]

While pleased with Stevenson's action against Madison County gambling houses, Simon took no vacation from his war with county officials who he believed continued to dodge responsibilities for upholding state gambling laws. Simon raised the ante with Sheriff Harrell and State's Attorney Lewis. On page 1 of the *Tribune* for June 15, 1950, Simon wrote a signed editorial challenging Lewis to discharge his duty against a new wave of slot machines in the county promoted by Democratic party officials and political friends of the prosecutor.[43]

Simon wrote that Lewis "is the man standing in the way ... Strong political pressure will be on him and pressure is on him in other ways. I'm hoping Austin Lewis has the guts to stick to his guns; but guts it will take." As an aside in the editorial, Simon acknowledged that he had fought Lewis on many issues, "although liking the man personally. . . . He deserves my support and the support of every citizen of Madison County in his attempt to keep the county clear of a wave of slot machines."

Simon received a letter of support from Governor Stevenson's aide James Mulroy for his challenge to Lewis and for urging the state's attorney to do his duty. Mulroy wrote, "I am in no position to commit myself as to the capabilities or sincerity of Mr. Austin Lewis. However, I do know that your editorial urging him to stick by his guns and show 'guts' is a worthwhile effort to bring about the type of enforcement in your county which all counties in the state of Illinois certainly need."[44]

By fall, Simon appeared to have lost patience with the two officials. Harrell, whose term as sheriff neared an end, felt the sharp point of the editor's pen in a November column. Responding to a query about previous criticisms of Harrell, Simon said, "To assure any doubting souls let me take the time to say in my mind there is no question but that he [Harrell] is the gangster-type. Maybe not as rough and crude as the bank robber, but just as effective."[45] Simon accused the sheriff of getting a payoff on punchboards, accepting money from professional gamblers for "the favor of letting them rob us," and "at least one person in the sheriff's office has gotten money from the men along Collinsville Road who deal not only in dollars but in women. In my mind that's gangsterism at its worst—official corruption."

Simon threw down a final challenge to the sheriff. "If the statements above weren't true Dallas Harrell could sue me for every cent I've made or ever hope to make. But if he would sue, you can be certain the case would never come to court for an open hearing." Harrell did not sue Simon, and the editor took note that the sheriff had not replied to the accusations.

Rather than just a continuing harangue at the county law officers, Simon had an objective that he announced two months later. The plan launched on

Tuesday, January 23, 1951, stunned readers and fellow editors alike. Simon took legal and professional steps against Lewis and Harrell. In a letter to an official of the Illinois Bar Association, also published in the *Tribune*, Simon requested disciplinary proceedings against Lewis.[46] He criticized the state's attorney for failing to eliminate the "flagrant abuse of the law in Madison County" by gamblers. He accused Lewis of practicing "common sense law enforcement," meaning that gamblers brought to court by Lewis and given nominal fines soon continued operations. "The procedure followed by Lewis brought the legal profession into ill repute and made a farce of legal procedure by his failure to mention that the defendants were guilty of more than one offense. There is no question but that his actions brought the courts of Madison county into disrepute."

Coinciding with the letter complaining about Lewis, Simon filed a complaint with the state's attorney asking the next session of the county grand jury to indict former sheriff Harrell for "palpable omission of duty" in failing to prevent wide-open gambling in Madison County.[47] In a list of accusations, the editor said during the years of 1949 and 1950 Harrell knew that professional gamblers operated openly in Madison County. Simon wrote that Lewis assured the editor of cooperation in bringing the matter before a grand jury in two months. Quoting himself in the article, Simon said, "If this can in any way help clear the air of political corruption which has hung around Madison county, then it's well worth the effort."

In a curious comment at the end of his letter about Lewis to the bar association, Simon apparently wanted to make sure no one thought his actions were personal. "This is in no sense caused by personal animosity or political motive. Today I also am filing a complaint asking the next session of the grand jury to indict our former sheriff, Dallas Harrell, a Republican. Austin Lewis is a Democrat. I am on personally friendly terms with both men." Simon's assurances must have struck Lewis and Harrell as peculiar after requesting punitive action.

The actions prompted extensive newspaper and magazine coverage, spreading Simon's name and the *Tribune* across the nation. The *Tribune* bragged, "Troy probably received more publicity as a result of the complaint filed by Paul Simon, *Tribune* editor, than the city of Troy ever has received."[48] The *Post-Dispatch* carried a two-column front-page picture of Simon with a lengthy article. The *St. Louis Globe-Democrat* reacted a little less excitedly, but still ran an article on page 1. Radio news broadcasts throughout the day provided details. Television stations featured Simon's picture with the story. The Associated Press, United Press, and International News Service carried stories across the state. A correspondent for *Newsweek* magazine visited the *Tribune* plant.

Charles Klotzer, who had joined the *Tribune* as an advertising salesman and columnist, provided in his weekly column a number of comments from citizens of Troy and Collinsville. They ranged from outright pride in Simon's actions to hopes that he could back up the accusations with proof. A few wondered if Simon might have put his life in danger.[49] In subsequent issues, Simon filled the paper's columns with letters to the editor and editorial comment from other papers. The *Post-Dispatch,* already a fan, said, "Paul Simon, editor of the weekly Tribune at Troy, Ill., is only 22 years old. But he is far more courageous than many citizens of Madison County who are much older, much better established and much better equipped in resources to stand out for law and order."[50] Simon's editor friend at the *Mounds Independent* wrote, "Paul, who is ordinarily a peace loving man, says that he's got the goods on the sheriff and is going to present it to a grand jury."[51]

Simon acknowledged the landslide of bravos. "Reaction so far has been overwhelmingly favorable. I've received worried telephone calls and letters from people concerned about my safety. This somewhat surprising reaction is appreciated but I'm not too worried. Even more surprising to me was the fact that no less than three salesmen tried to sell me life insurance." He thanked fellow newspapermen for generous comments, saying, "It is a satisfaction to know that men I have never seen are willing to cooperate in the fight for better government."[52]

At the *East St. Louis Journal*, editor Tom Duffy spent an entire column giving advice to his young compatriot.[53] After calling Simon's actions a case of "raising a lot of hell," Duffy talked about the culprit in the shadows. "He'll sneak around holding up his hands to his friends and preaching a holier-than-thou sermon of outraged dishonor . . . Punctuating it with barks at the newspaper for daring to retard the progress of 'our home town' by 'raising a lot of hell' . . . He'll try to bribe you. He'll write you nasty letters . . . He'll pry into your personal life . . . He'll telephone you . . . He'll call you names. But there is one typically despicable characteristic he has . . . He'll do it all anonymously."

Drawing on years of campaigning against corruption, Duffy identified the culprit for Simon. "Another thing, Paul . . . You might keep in mind the fact that it isn't the professional gunman or thief or gambler who gets ideas about trying to scare newspapers . . . The professional criminal knows what he is doing and he expects attacks from newspapers as well as police . . . It's the crooked politician who gets those ideas . . . His greed for the easy dollar is an obsession." Duffy signed off by characterizing the corrupt politician: "He hasn't any guts."

Bill Boyne, an editor at the *Journal* who later served a stint as managing editor of the *Southern Illinoisan* in Carbondale before returning as editor of the *Journal* in 1961, wrote at length in the paper's January 28 issue under the headline "Troy Publisher's War on Gaming Keeps Him Busy." For readers who may not have heard of Simon, Boyne recounted many of the crusades and controversies of Simon's two and half years at the Troy newspaper. In one portion, Boyne caught the flavor of Simon's mixture of content for Troy readers. "The paper has considerably more scope than the births, deaths, marriages and social notes which usually make up a small town paper. Almost every issue includes a book review by the editor or a reader. Editorials and open letters admonishing public officials often are splashed on the front page and there is frequent use of correspondence from friends of Simon in this country and elsewhere."

Boyne described the youthful editor:

He looks as if he should be worrying about putting the glee club's picture in the high school yearbook—not taking on the ex-sheriff in a legal battle. He's young and he looks younger. He wears a snappy bow tie, his hair won't slick down and, although he undoubtedly shaves, it isn't apparent.

When he sits at his old fashioned roll-top desk in the Tribune office, he has to use a big book of Linotype faces—about the size of an unabridged dictionary—to bridge the gap between the seat of his pants and the seat of the swivel chair. He has a youthful grin, laughs readily—often at himself—and goes about a man's work with a youngster's enthusiasm . . . Simon is not a sensationalist. He is an aggressive editorial campaigner. Besides fighting gambling and vice, he has been prodding the Troy city council to go ahead with a sewer construction project.

Boyne gave a glimpse of Simon's future. "Some day, he'd like to run a number of newspapers . . . He also has plans for going into politics one of these days. If his editorials are any indication, he'd make a drastically honest and independent candidate."

The *Newsweek* contact with Simon in Troy produced a major spread in the weekly magazine.[54] In its Press section covering two-thirds of a page under the headline "Simon Pure," the article, with a photograph of Simon at his typewriter, blended the story of acquisition of the *Tribune* with the editor's adventures in his crusade against organized crime. Meanwhile, well into February the *Tribune* published letters to the editor mostly in support of Simon's efforts. In his February 22 column, Simon noted that the widespread publicity had prompted requests for him to investigate everything from murders in the 1930s to dice games in East St. Louis. Simon responded, "I frankly know nothing about the truth of these charges and I'm afraid I don't have the time to investigate . . . I would love to . . . But unfortunately I have to work to eat."[55]

With the grand jury appearance of Simon in his case against Harrell pending until March, Simon prepared for another publicity opportunity on the subject of crime in Illinois. For two days in February, Senator Estes Kefauver of Tennessee brought the U.S. Senate Special Committee to Investigate Organized Crime in Interstate Commerce (the Kefauver Committee) to St. Louis for televised hearings and testimony by a number of elected officials from Illinois.[56] Kefauver focused his investigation on gambling that crossed state boundaries. However, the senator questioned city and county officials about gambling of all kinds, with special attention paid to bookies that received racetrack results by telephone wire.

Simon testified at the hearing. Prior to reading a prepared statement, he answered questions from Kefauver, as follows:

KEFAUVER: You seem to be quite a young man.
SIMON: I am, unfortunately, or fortunately.
KEFAUVER: How old are you, sir?
SIMON: Twenty-two.
KEFAUVER: And what is the name of your paper?
SIMON: The *Troy Tribune.*
KEFAUVER: And you are the publisher?
SIMON: Yes, sir: publisher and janitor.
KEFAUVER: And editor?
SIMON: And editor; that is correct.
KEFAUVER: How long have you been a publisher and editor and general mogul of your paper?
SIMON: It will be three years in June.
KEFAUVER: And you have been carrying on an editorial crusade for a better government all alone over there in Madison County?
SIMON: Well, we have been fighting for it anyway; yes, sir.
KEFAUVER: Well, that is very admirable. Has it hurt your newspaper business?
SIMON: No; we lost one advertiser, but that was very minor; I mean, actually, it has helped the paper.
KEFAUVER: That is very encouraging, to see young men like you interested, who have the courage and the fortitude to stand up and take an open position in matters of this sort.

Simon's statement added a personal touch to testimony about gambling conditions in the county.[57] He said, in part:

I have been publishing a newspaper for almost 3 years—and those 3 years have been an eye opener for me. I consider myself neither a crusader nor a blue-noser—but as an honest, responsible citizen this has become very apparent to me: The big-time gamblers and others who would violate the law have formed an unholy alliance in our county with those charged with the responsibility for enforcing the law. I have little respect for the gentry of the gambling profession and the hoodlums they bring with them. But I have even less respect for men in our county who have prostituted public office and betrayed the public for a few dirty dollars. This has been particularly true of the office of sheriff and state's attorney.

Simon related how gamblers contributed heavily to political campaigns and to the treasuries of both political parties, giving them considerable power with elected officials. "Aiding their cause is the fact that the citizens of our county have had no real leadership to fight this situation." He lamented how lax law enforcement encouraged prostitution, permitted an unlawful lottery to operate in Alton and allowed gambling of every kind including dice, bookmaking, and punchboard rackets.

"The former sheriff of our county [Harrell] only allowed a certain type of punchboards to appear. When the wrong kind appeared, tavern and restaurant owners were told 'punchboards are illegal.' The kind the sheriff's office allowed—even though illegal—cost many times their ordinary price. When I accused him editorially of having a punchboard racket, he made no reply." Simon called on the committee to recommend legislation that would restrict interstate transmission of racing news for gambling purposes, and he asked for increased appropriations for the Treasury Department to investigate income tax evaders.

Simon painted a dismal picture of Madison County law enforcement but also said the situation had improved, beginning with state police raids under Stevenson. He mentioned a number of violations of the law that public officials overlooked and ignored. "What I have mentioned to you are little pieces of a powerful picture—a picture of vice and corruption. Thanks to a good governor and a gradually awakening citizenry the situation is temporarily improving. Good government can only come when there is an alert citizenry. Your important part in helping to awaken our people deserves the praise of citizens for generations to come."

Harrell testified in an appearance that featured angry exchanges with Kefauver.[58] The committee subpoenaed Lewis to appear, but he was not called, causing Simon to write, "Biggest disappointment to Madison county residents who knew what was going on was the fact that Austin Lewis was not called. The committee was prepared to ask him some very embarrassing questions. When it appeared that Lewis would not appear, I talked with Sen. Kefauver and urged him to call Lewis. He sounded as though he wanted to but the idea evidently was vetoed by his assistants over the lunch hour."[59]

Kefauver's hearings in St. Louis encouraged newspaper editors and reporters in the metropolitan area, and especially in Illinois. The prominence of television and huge newspaper headlines shed harsh light on criminal activity. The hearings awakened the public and sent racketeers scurrying for cover. Testimony given under the persistent questioning of Kefauver and commission members exposed law enforcement officials as virtual associates of gangsters. Racketeers stayed out of sight for months but began operations again when they thought the heat had passed. Organized crime continued for more than a decade in the region, but its grip on the populace and public officials loosened. Eventually the organizations crumbled.

While the Kefauver Committee had a positive impact locally, the senator's efforts to raise awareness on a national level failed. No corrective federal legislation passed as a result of the hearings, and some believed the effort was a publicity stunt by the senator whose presidential ambitions were well known.

Approaching his day before the Madison County grand jury, Simon took more than a column of space in the *Tribune* for a signed article to provide the essentials of his case against the former sheriff.[60] He recited the examples of the high-profile gambling operations at 200 Club and Hyde Park, the proliferation of punchboards during Harrell's term, rampant prostitution in the county, and the accusation that Harrell "permitted petty gambling to continue and also allowed big-time gambling to operate." Concluding, the editor wrote, "My main contention is that he is very obviously guilty because of the wide-open operation of the Hyde Park Club and 200 Club. If the grand jury will have the courage to act they can do much to keep the county clean for generations to come. Madison County needs it desperately."

Simon wanted readers to take him seriously, so frequently he took time and newspaper space to explain his actions. Before the grand jury appearance, Simon claimed that he bore no personal ill will toward Lewis and Harrell. "What I am very much interested in is killing the system which existed in Madison county prior to the governor's raids on May 12 of last year . . . I believe in the principles of good government and I intend to fight for them."[61]

Simon recognized his comments stretched believability. He wrote,

Some people think it's strange when I tell them I like Dallas Harrell and Austin Lewis and others whom I have attacked. I personally don't think it's strange at all. I disagree violently with some of the things for which they have stood in the past, but I can't help liking the guys. Will Rogers once said, "I never met a man I didn't like," and while I am a long ways from being a Will Rogers or anything near to that, I find myself in the same situation. There is something about everyone you can admire. I hope I can always be able to find that and get along with everyone—even those whom I feel obliged to attack now and then.

That was easy for Simon to say because he had little at stake on a personal level, other than the prosperity of his newspaper. Lewis and Harrell had plenty at stake, personally and professionally. While neither of the officials publicly responded to Simon's attack on their job performance, they most likely did not consider Simon a friend. They knew it rarely paid to argue in the media with newspaper editors.

Shortly after Simon presented his case, the grand jury dismissed the charges. The *Tribune* made this comment on the verdict: "The only partial victory gained was a statement issued by the grand jury, believed to be unprecedented in county history, in which they ordered the state's attorney and sheriff to enforce the gambling laws and send letters to all law enforcement officers asking them to enforce the laws."[62] Simon wrote in his column, "Did you ever hear of a jury which condemned a murder but let the murderer go free? Sounds crazy, doesn't it. Yet essentially that is what the grand jury did which let Dallas Harrell . . . go free."[63]

As if 1951 had not been active enough with Simon's war against corruption, he literally went to war as a part of the U.S. Army. Initially he joined an Army Reserve unit in St. Louis and trained as part of a unit designated to take over temporary operation of the government in the northern part of Korea. The mission changed with the Chinese invasion of North Korea. Still, Simon wanted to complete his military obligation. In 1951 he and two friends from Collinsville, Elmer and Wally Fedder, enlisted for twenty-one months, hoping they would serve the time together. (Reserve time of three months was added to make two years.) The Fedder brothers were assigned to Japan and Simon to Germany, upsetting those plans. Simon trained as an agent for the Counter Intelligence Corps after basic training, and in March 1952 arrived in Germany, his first trip outside the United States.[64] While in the Army, he also spent time in England, Spain, and France. In the years ahead Simon would make frequent trips abroad and write of his travels for readers of the *Tribune* and other newspapers interested in his opinions of world events. These trips helped form his strong opinions on foreign policy.

While in the Army, Simon might have worried about his investment in a newspaper operation just barely three years old, but he seemed satisfied that others could carry on. He convinced Dana College chum Ray Johnsen to quit his teaching job in Nebraska and take over operations of the paper although Johnsen had never held such responsibility.[65] Johnsen's move to Troy set in motion a decades-long association with Simon, the *Tribune,* other newspapers they eventually acquired, and politics. Simon signed a power of attorney agreement that gave Johnsen full authority to make any necessary decisions at the *Tribune* in his absence, ranging from news coverage to financial matters. One such decision occurred in August when the *Tribune* company purchased a new printing press and accessories with a down payment of $1,300 and a contract calling for payments until August 1958.[66]

In his absence, Simon put Elizabeth Murphy in the position of managing editor, "an Irish bit of Boston who combines mental capabilities with good old-fashioned gumption." Before Simon returned, she left to work on a newspaper in Mascoutah, Illinois, and Johnsen assumed editor responsibilities. Working in production were old hands Art Benz, "an unusually capable Linotype operator," and Eldon School, who operated the press and wrote an occasional science column for the paper. In his final promise, Simon said, "I'm still going to keep in very close touch with things in Troy and in Madison County."[67]

The winds of change increased beginning in the summer of 1951. Simon experienced the release of responsibilities in Troy to his good friend Johnsen, and time would tell if he could turn away from the hands-on experience of the first three years. By the time he returned from the military in 1953, Simon had considered leaving journalism for politics, but doing it was quite different from thinking about it.

Frequently a "Trojan Thoughts" column showed up from a distant Army base in the United States or in Europe. Friends at the *Tribune* kept Simon supplied with clippings from which he could make a timely commentary. Simon kept a watchful eye on Lewis, refused to relent against Harrell, and maintained his stout defense of Governor Stevenson. In answer to an editorial in the nearby *Wood River Journal* stating that Stevenson had displeased the Democratic party rank and file, Simon stated, "Stevenson may not be the shrewdest politician in the world, but the reason a lot of people who are 'the small boys' dislike him is because he didn't pass out a lot of soft jobs as his predecessor did. I'm hoping Illinois will stick with good government."[68]

With time to reflect on the personal battle against crime and corruption, Simon discussed the accomplishments in a column about his tussles with Lewis and Harrell. He preceded his list of achievements with an overall thought: "When you do something which you think is right, you shouldn't expect results all the time. Doing what is right is the thing to do, results or no results."[69] (There may be no better description of Simon's motivation in journalism and later in politics.) The five outcomes, in his words, were:

1. Even though right now the county is slipping into its former status somewhat, still we are a long, long way from being there. We're bad, but not as bad as before pressure was put on.

2. For a while gambling and corruption in Madison County were at an all-time low. This alone was worth the fight.

3. A Madison County grand jury which I have some reason to believe was stacked against me was pressured into an unprecedented statement condemning gambling and asking county officials for action.

4. It made known to more people the conditions in the county, and being for good government suddenly became politically wise—a strange thing in Madison County. It reached such a stage that State's Attorney Austin Lewis even preached a sermon to the county ministers in which he told them how he was going to fight gambling.

5. It let people know that you can fight corruption and crookedness in officials and gangsters who go with them and live.

"So I have no regrets for having made a fight," he concluded, "I didn't score a knockout in that round—but figuring points I think I took the round."

Back in Troy on a furlough, Simon discovered backsliding in the war on gambling. He wrote, "I found evidence of published reports in several newspapers that gambling is on the rise again in our county."[70] He visited one gambling club and found it wide open and prosperous. He commented, "While conditions today are still considerably better than they were before the heat was put on the boys at Edwardsville [the county seat] still it makes me sore that stuff like that goes on."

During the 1950s, daily and weekly newspapers on the Illinois side of the St. Louis metropolitan area reported on crime and criminal activity in almost every issue, often with information provided quietly by agents of the Federal Bureau of Investigation and the Illinois State Police. The bureau monitored suspicious behavior, and Director J. Edgar Hoover placed Wortman on the national "top hoodlum" list. The Internal Revenue Service had a special team of agents searching for violations of tax laws by criminal suspects, and state police conducted periodic raids on gambling houses outside incorporated cities in St. Clair and Madison counties.[71] In two trials on federal charges of conspiracy in the early 1960s, Buster Wortman and associates were acquitted. However, the details of his operations revealed in testimony helped to erode Wortman's control, accelerating his decline and authority in the rackets.

The initiative against gambling by Stevenson and hearings in St. Louis and Chicago by Senator Kefauver and his crime commission elevated public interest in exposing organized crime. Completing the picture were demographic, racial, and cultural changes occurring in the urban area and a gradual improvement in the quality of local police, prosecutors, and judges. Eventually, this concentrated effort had impact. Criminal activity continued, but organized racketeering diminished under the assault.

This perspective is important when assessing the influence of editor Simon in the fight against criminal behavior. His strong voice in the chorus, with an occasional solo, must be acknowledged and importance attached to his consistent effort. The personal dividend from self-promotion and impact on newspaper profits cannot be overlooked. The resulting name recognition launched a forty-year political career and put the *Troy Tribune* on the map, increasing demand for the paper well beyond anything that could have been generated in the community. Simon did not personally cleanse his part of Madison County, but he contributed to a regional effort that bore fruit over the years and encouraged independent politicians to step forward. Public awareness, clearly achieved by Simon and the *Tribune*, had to occur before the cleanup could begin.

Elective Office Beckons

Heading into his second year as a soldier in Germany, Simon continued long-distance editorial writing on local and state subjects. The articles did not have the ring of passion that resonated before he entered the military, probably reflecting that he could not pick up a telephone and call a source or friend in the newspaper business to get details of reports. The criminal incidents seemed less commanding compared to the days of 1950 and early 1951. But two things did not change: his intense dislike for corruption and crime, and a fondness for Governor Stevenson.

Simon came to Stevenson's defense from Germany in a column on May 8, 1952, addressed to Vernon L. Nickell, Republican state superintendent of public instruction.[1] At issue was a speech Nickell gave criticizing Stevenson. Specifically, the superintendent said that Stevenson had delayed action against downstate gambling too long. Simon wrote, "Your speech was a collection of half-truths and misrepresentations, which do neither you nor your office any great honor. . . . It so happens that before the governor acted I was among those criticizing him for not taking action. But when the governor saw that local officials did not and would not act, he moved decisively and courageously. Madison County, for example, has been much cleaner ever since, largely as a result of his action." He noted that Nickell failed to mention former governor Green's friendliness with gamblers.

Nickell also stated that graft among state employees had been uncovered after Stevenson became governor. Simon replied, "But you fail to mention that he put those responsible out of office. When we have a Governor like Adlai Stevenson who is trying to do a good, honest job (and is nationally recognized for doing it brilliantly), then you lower the boom." Simon concluded, "It seems to me a bit inconsistent that you should support the teacher who won't let little Johnny shoot spit-wads, while you throw mudballs at our Governor."

Simon again rose to support the governor when Harold O. Gwillim of Alton, a candidate for Madison County state's attorney, implied Stevenson had not fought crime in the county because elected officials were Democrats. Drawing on his experience contesting the elected establishment in the county as well as racketeers, Simon tried to set the record straight by recalling the 1950 raid on gambling clubs. "The Governor took this action in a county where the state's attorney, Austin Lewis, was a Democrat. Not only was he a Democrat, but at that time Austin Lewis was chairman of the county Democratic organization, the third most powerful Democratic organization in the State of Illinois [Cook was first, St. Clair second]. What Governor Stevenson did then took real courage; you know that as well as I."[2]

Simon added that Democratic and Republican county officials opposed his fight against gangsters. "For a longtime I was alone in that fight. What I was able to accomplish, an attorney could have accomplished much easier—but I know of no attorney who took up the fight early in the battle, not even an Alton attorney named Harold Gwillim." Simon promised to return from the military and continue the fight against the state's attorney if Gwillim was not "making a decent fight on gambling."

Not long after returning from service in May 1953, Simon became embroiled in a gambling issue, demonstrating his touch for finding a high-profile subject and exposing it in the *Tribune*. The paper's involvement began with a guest column on August 20 by Charles Klotzer, a former *Tribune* staff member. After reading an article in the *Post-Dispatch* about gambling at Club Prevue on Highway 40 not far from Troy, Klotzer paid a visit. In a lengthy explanation of his evening at the club, Klotzer described action by 200 patrons at two roulette tables, three dice tables, and one blackjack bar.[3]

Two nights later, Simon and Ray Johnsen and his wife Nancy went to Club Prevue in hopes of getting past guards and bouncers to the gambling action. Simon wrote in "Trojan Thoughts" that the Johnsens quickly got into the room where "they saw big-time gambling in operation."[4] Simon went a different direction and failed to get past the bouncers, although he identified Gregory "Red" Moore, a former owner of the Hyde Park Club and reportedly an owner of Club Prevue. Moore had close relationships with Wortman and Capone operatives. Simon left without witnessing any gambling.

The following day Johnsen and Simon tried to call Sheriff James Callahan and State's Attorney Fred Schuman but were unable to reach them. Two days later they went to Edwardsville and called on Schuman. The prosecutor told Simon he opposed gambling but had too many things on his agenda to go after Club Prevue. "Ray and I were asked whether we were ready to sign a complaint against the Club Prevue operators and we said we were." Schuman said he would prepare the complaint, and the newspaper people left for Troy.

Within days, Club Prevue stopped gambling operations. Simon did not take credit for the closure but quoted the *Post-Dispatch* that "newspaper pressure" had impact.[5] Simon wrote a letter to State's Attorney Schuman saying, "Since the Club Prevue is now no longer in the gambling end of things, Ray and I are frankly somewhat less interested in signing a complaint. Our purpose was to eliminate that county eye-sore, and that purpose apparently already is accomplished. However, should you wish to prosecute, we are ready to sign a complaint and/or to serve as witnesses in any such prosecution." A few days later, state attorney general Latham Castle sent orders to Sheriff Callahan and Schuman ordering them to stop gambling in the county—at the Club Prevue in particular—or his office would be forced to take action. Daily newspapers in the region gave full accounts of Simon's aggressive efforts.[6]

The Club Prevue triumph was a convenient prelude to Simon's announcement for public office—not totally unexpected—in the *Tribune* of December 17, 1953. Simon planned to run for nomination as a state representative from the district that encompassed Madison and Bond counties in the April 1954 Democratic primary election.[7] The announcement listed his accomplishments since resurrecting the *Tribune* and tied that record to achievements of former governor Stevenson. The announcement stated, "During Adlai Stevenson's term as governor, Simon worked with Stevenson on matters of law enforcement in this area of the state." Simon pledged that all campaign contributions and expenses would be made public following the primary, whether he was elected or defeated.

The declaration received prominent display in newspapers serving Madison County. The *East St. Louis Journal,* long a booster of Simon, called him the "youthful publisher and foe of the underworld in Madison County."[8] The article repeated the well-known journalism résumé of Simon and noted his interest in politics.

Simon credited his time in the Army with providing an opportunity to plan his career move. He wrote, "I could more likely effect real change through public office than through my journalistic efforts. I also recognized that I would never become a Walter Lippmann. In addition, I wanted to show that someone with my beliefs could not only physically survive in Madison County, but actually have a chance to win."[9]

Simon presented his case for the turn to politics in "Trojan Thoughts":

It is my first—and perhaps my last—venture into the field of politics as a candidate. My father was probably as interested in politics and government as any minister when I was a child, so I imagine I inherited that interest from him. Politics always has seemed somewhat exciting to me. In 1936—I was eight years old at the time—I can remember listening excitedly to the Republican convention which nominated [Alf] Landon. To me it was—and is—much more exciting than any baseball game could be. I can remember the Model "A" my dad had for 18 years. For many of those years we carried a big red, white and blue "Roosevelt" sticker in the back window. So one reason I am entering the political field is that I was reared liking it, and I haven't changed in that respect. But more important, the field of politics is an opportunity to be of service to your fellow human beings as are few fields. It's been my impression that too often staying in office has been the motivating power for actions of office holders. My advice to myself as I start a somewhat new phase of activity is to make my goal service, not staying in office. I hope and pray that always will be my goal.[10]

The district covering Madison and Bond counties elected three members of the Illinois House of Representatives, as did each House district in the state. Law prescribed that of the three members elected, two must be from the majority party and one from the minority, regardless of how many candidates entered from each party. In Simon's district, with Democrats dominating, two members represented the Democratic party and one represented the Republican party. Consequently, Simon's candidacy forced a contest among three people for two positions. The other two candidates were incumbents. The two with the highest vote totals would advance to the general election.

The peculiarity of the system—called cumulative voting—was that each voter had three votes. A vote could be cast for a single candidate, thus giving the person three votes; or one vote could be made for each of two candidates, giving them one and a half votes each. A final choice was to vote for three candidates, in which case each received one vote. Giving one vote—in effect three votes—to a candidate was called "plunking." Simon's strategy was to get enough of the single votes to overcome the incumbent advantage. Voters in 1980 changed the constitution and established single-member House districts with one vote per person.

The two Democratic incumbents—Lloyd "Curly" Harris from Granite City and Leland Kennedy from Alton—provided a formidable obstacle for Simon. Harris had been a representative since the 1937–38 session, and Kennedy since 1947–48.[11] The powerful Madison County Democratic Central Committee endorsed each for reelection. In fact, the party made its decision a day after Simon announced for the office. That did not surprise Simon. He knew the battle was drawn, and the incumbents had an initial advantage. He decided early not to attack the individual incumbents, "because I like both of them personally."[12] His battle was not with the officeholders but with the party that tolerated corruption throughout the county and chose its favored candidates without consulting party members.

Simon campaigned on the issues and spoke anywhere he could get an audience: clubs, labor organizations, fraternal societies, sewing circles, and church groups. Before them he stated his beliefs: "That the State of Illinois should operate each year on an economically sound basis, and that the state should give cities and counties the same opportunity to operate on a financially sound basis. That, insofar as possible, party politics should be separated from higher judicial offices. No man can serve two masters, and justice, not party bosses, should be the master of our judges. That legislation regarding law enforcement officials needs to be re-examined."[13] He reminded everyone of the crusades against gambling and corruption that he began in 1949.

The underdog candidate operated on a meager budget, relying on volunteers to distribute literature and speak in his behalf. His brother Arthur, then a student at Concordia Seminary in St. Louis, went to dormitories throughout the seminary of 600 students for volunteers to go door-to-door throughout the district to hand out brochures on Saturdays.[14] Representative Alan Dixon of Belleville, who had an easy reelection campaign of his own, spent time working for Simon. That launched a friendship that lasted fifty years.

Only a few precinct workers agreed to work for Simon, as most were beholden to the party apparatus. No one worked harder than Simon, who turned operations at the *Tribune* over to Ray Johnsen for the duration of the campaign. On election day, Paul and Arthur went out early to watch the polls. Arthur remembered, "By dawn the streets were alive with workers paid by the organization to bring people to the polls. We were sure the machine had overwhelmed us."[15]

Simon rented a hall in Troy for family and volunteers to hear election results. Arthur said, "We were in a somber mood. Then as the returns came in, precinct by precinct reported Paul running way ahead. We could hardly believe it. Before long one committeeman after another showed up, and soon the hall was filled with excitement. Clearly a lot of the workers paid by the organization had been bringing a lot of Simon voters to the polls, some of them no doubt putting in a good word for Paul."[16] Paul Simon had pulled a major upset. He received 30,141 votes, Harris 20,684, and Kennedy 18,584.[17]

Regional newspapers gave Simon top billing on front pages. The *East St. Louis Journal* reported, "Paul Simon, 25, publisher of a Troy weekly newspaper, upset experienced politicians and forecasters to lead in the race for the Democratic nomination for state representative from Madison and Bond counties."[18] The *Alton Evening Telegraph* proclaimed under a large banner headline "Paul Simon Is Nominated in Upset," and stated, "Paul Simon, crusading young editor of the *Troy Tribune,* scored a sensational upset when he won one of the Democratic party's two nominations for state representative. The newcomer who wasn't supposed to have a chance toppled two veteran vote-getters to lead the field of three."[19] The Alton newspaper identified Simon as "the candidate with the bow tie." Simon said later, "I've worn one ever since."

Simon's total expenditure for the campaign came to $3,852.18, a figure he made public. His largest contribution was $100.

The *Post-Dispatch* especially enjoyed Simon's victory. An editorial, probably written by Simon's good friend Irving Dilliard or one of his colleagues, stated:

> The professional politicians in Madison County said Paul Simon didn't have a Chinaman's chance. They said he wouldn't even get to first base. If the young editor of the Troy (Ill.) Tribune wanted to run for the Democratic nomination for state representative, why, that was his business. It would be his money and time spent, and that of his friends who tried to help him. He would learn. It would be a little rough, but that is the way it is with idealistic young amateurs in politics . . . Just about everybody joined the professional politicians in thinking that the young fellow from the little town of Troy didn't have a chance. Just goes to show that the voters don't know their own strength and how they can do things they don't even expect to do. At the courthouse in Edwardsville they will talk about Paul Simon's nomination for a long time to come.[20]

Winning the primary made his election to the General Assembly almost automatic. The large majority of Democrats in the district meant Simon and Harris would be chosen, along with one Republican. With the political hurdle cleared, Simon assembled a team to manage and operate the *Tribune* while he spent time in Springfield during legislative sessions, and began foreign travels.

Ray Johnsen's position as managing editor and chief operator was assured based on his performance during other Simon absences in 1951–53 and 1954. The paper showed steady gains in profitability, which gave Simon additional confidence in his friend. Gross revenues for the period November 1952 through October 1953, six months of which Simon was in the military, amounted to $15,566. From November 1953 to October 1954, a period that included Simon's campaign for the legislature, gross revenues increased by

14.6 percent to $17,843. As the principal stockholder, Simon took a personal withdrawal in 1953–1954 of $4,893.[21]

The newspaper balance sheet showed an income tax paid in that year of $650. That left an after-tax figure of about $13,750. Simon's equity in the company amounted to $8,205 after the subtraction of $5,545 in debt. Simon stated Johnsen's equity at $3,145. Much of the debt was for the press and equipment. Johnsen loaned the company $1,000 on the press debt and received about $40 a year in interest.

Another of Simon's friends—Elmer Fedder—joined the *Tribune* operation at the beginning of 1955. Fedder described his duties as "printer, typesetter, ad work, and I took some pictures, etc."[22] A graduate of Collinsville High School and a former student at Washington University in St. Louis, Fedder served briefly with Simon during the Korean conflict. In the three years he worked in Troy, Fedder held the title of assistant editor.

Among documents in the Simon collection at the Abraham Lincoln Presidential Library in Springfield, Illinois, are a draft of proposed policies and a draft of an agreement for future operations and executive pay at the *Tribune* company.[23] While details might have changed before the agreement went into effect before 1955, they provide insight about the shape of operations after Simon became a member of the legislature. Officers of the formal organization were Simon, president; Fedder, vice president; and Johnsen, secretary-treasurer, and they formed the board of directors. On the newspaper's masthead Simon was listed as editor and publisher, Johnsen as managing editor, and Fedder as assistant editor.

The draft agreement said a minimum of $55 a month would be set aside for capital investment and could be adjusted upward upon agreement of stockholders. Any capital expense over $100 had to be approved by two of the three stockholders. An emergency fund would be started with $10 a month invested in a savings and loan stock. The annual dividend policy established a minimum of 5 percent of profits and a maximum of 9 percent for an employee who worked a minimum of 1,250 hours. It read, "At the end of the year all employees who have worked at least one full year for at least 30 hours a week will receive a division of 10 percent of the accumulated surplus. The remaining accumulated surplus may be divided three ways among the three original major stockholders." These decisions would be subject to approval by the stockholders and the plant manager.

The manager of the Troy operation could look forward to receiving 50 percent of the net profit after expenses, capital investment, savings and loan deposit, depreciation, and taxes. This distribution applied to any other papers purchased by the stockholders. Regarding hourly pay, the statement read, "The manager and Paul Simon will receive the union scale for time put in."[24] It listed a separate hourly pay scale for Fedder with increases each year. The agreement established a sick leave policy and two weeks vacation with pay for all employees who had worked a year or longer full time.

One of the documents included a list of "long-range goals." They included:

- Enter the offset press field. [The *Tribune* had letterpress equipment.]
- Go union. The next full-time person hired should be a union person. [Simon was always a union member.]
- Expand the job printing business end of things and also get other newspapers.
- Finally, we must constantly keep in mind that our ultimate goal is service to our Savior and our fellow man. Sometimes we will have the choice between being of service or making money. As much as possible we'll do both, but sometimes we will have to do the former.

With those operational and long-term goals, the *Troy Tribune* marched confidently into the future beginning January 1, 1955, with its editor and publisher embarking on a new career.

The benefits to Simon's political ambitions of his six-year stint in journalism were obvious. He became a media star by attacking what he believed to be the root causes of gambling and corruption in Madison County. Simon was not a flash in the pan, either. He proved the importance of writing frequently on the same issues. Single editorials may win a newspaper contest but rarely move a mountain. Simon had a "nose" for news. Brother Arthur said it this way: "Paul had the instincts of an investigative reporter."[25]

He pulled off a public relations coup more than once, displaying a fine sense of timing and a willingness to take risks. There is no better example than his nighttime visit to the houses of prostitution on Highway 40. He took the fight directly to the sheriff and state's attorney, virtually shaming them to silence, even if his challenges failed. How many newspaper editors can be named who called the sheriff a gangster and then dared him to file suit? It is little wonder that an admiration society of editors and publishers verbally lifted him on their shoulders in triumph.

Simon had no apparent political or journalistic wizard in the background pulling strings or whispering in his ear. He may have consulted with close associates such as Ray Johnsen before his adventures, but nothing in Simon's writing, correspondence, or public pronouncements gives any hint of backroom string pulling. He saved his bragging for comments in "Trojan Thoughts" where they seemed less vain. He did not lay claim to doing things he hadn't done. That may have been a part of his appeal to fellow journalists and a growing crowd of citizen admirers. The payoff came when he won the 1954 primary election.

If big city journalists or crime reporters depreciated Simon's achievements, they kept quiet. He looked impossibly youthful. His writing lacked polish and suffered from not having an editor with a sharp pencil. However, none of the gaffes made him sound or look like a bumpkin, especially when he relentlessly pursued the bad guys and they hesitated to fight back.

His admirers had substantial credits of their own. Bill Boyne and Tom Duffy at the *East St. Louis Journal* had few peers in the long-distance run against crime, gambling, and corruption in the region. They attracted talented reporters and editors and provided leadership on dozens of issues. Paul Cousley, publisher of the *Alton Telegraph*, a mild-mannered man who gave praise cautiously, developed as one of Simon's cheerleaders. Charles Klotzer served an apprenticeship in Simon's shop and went on to start the *St. Louis Journalism Review*. He raised Simon's flag high on many occasions. With few exceptions—maybe some who were jealous or felt the need to express counterpoints for political reasons—fellow weekly editors praised his courage and gave frequent pats on the back.

As time allowed during his duties as editor and publisher, Simon made the rounds of professional groups in St. Louis and Illinois and joined the tight-knit group of newspaper editors. He maintained active membership in the Illinois Press Association, a group consisting mostly of representatives from small weekly and daily newspapers. Simon belonged to the St. Louis chapter of Sigma Delta Chi, the professional journalists' organization, but also attended meetings of the southern Illinois chapter. He established a close relationship with Howard R. Long, chairman of the Southern Illinois University Department of Journalism, who also ran the National Conference of Weekly Newspaper Editors. Simon made several appearances before student groups at SIU, always attracting large crowds. In an exchange of letters with H. R. Fischer of Granite City, an SIU trustee, regarding higher-education legislative issues, Simon took the opportunity to praise the SIU journalism program as offering a curriculum "more practical than some of the larger schools, and I personally believe much more sound."[26] These professional activities brought Simon in continuous contact with other editors and publishers and produced his journalism network.

Among the acquaintances and friends, one journalist played a singular role in encouragement, advice, and counsel. "Mentor" is the word that comes to mind with the name of Irving Dilliard of the *St. Louis Post-Dispatch*. Apparently without strings attached, he extended the hand of friendship to the young editor precisely when needed. Timing is everything when it comes to being a successful advisor and counselor.

Dilliard began work as a correspondent for the *Post-Dispatch* while in high school at Collinsville, Illinois.[27] After graduation from the University of Illinois in 1927, he joined the paper full time, a career that ended with his forced retirement. A year out of college, Dilliard joined the paper's editorial page staff, where he worked for the rest of his time at the paper. He maintained a residence in Collinsville. An intellectual with a knack for research, he specialized in writing about civil liberties and constitutional law. He wrote extensively in magazines such as the *New Republic* and the *Nation,* both noted liberal publications. He often focused on stories of people whose civil rights had been violated.

A close friend of Adlai E. Stevenson, Dilliard directed the paper's editorial support for the 1948 gubernatorial campaign, and in 1949 he became editorial page editor of the *Post-Dispatch.* Dilliard was criticized inside and outside the paper for urging Stevenson to enter the presidential race in 1952.[28] Before the Pulitzer family, owners of the paper, decided to endorse Stevenson, Dilliard directed the use of positive articles about the governor and negative articles about Republican candidate Dwight D. Eisenhower. Labeled by his biographer as liberal, doctrinaire, and rebellious, Dilliard eventually angered Joseph Pulitzer III, grandson of the founder, to such an extent that the publisher removed Dilliard as editorial page editor in 1957.[29] However, during the 1950s when Simon and Dilliard formed a mutual admiration society, the encouragement of Dilliard weighed heavily with the young editor.

Correspondence between Simon and Dilliard began in June 1949, a year after Simon revived the *Tribune.* In that first contact, Simon offered congratulations for Dilliard's promotion to editor of the editorial page. Simon wrote, "Although I have never had the privilege of meeting you, I have talked with many who have and also have read many a story with the Dilliard name as the by-line."[30] He enclosed copies of the last two issues of the *Tribune* "to give you a little on what our newspaper (I use that term cautiously) is doing re Lewis and Harrell. The Harrell story, by the way, might make something worthy, a paragraph or two, in the *Post.*" He also urged Dilliard to put editorial pressure on Lewis and Harrell. Simon pursued a personal meeting with Dilliard and invited him to Troy.

Dilliard, at one-time president of the Illinois State Historical Society, invited Simon to attend a meeting of the society in Springfield.[31] Simon soon shared Dilliard's enthusiasm for the state's history. Letters from Dilliard to Simon during 1950 reveal a continuing dialogue, with Simon sending tear sheets of the *Tribune* and offering suggestions for redesign of the *Post-Dispatch* editorial pages. Simon showed chutzpah in comments about a part of the paper that had so much history behind it. Dilliard accepted Simon's idea for a "rearranged editorial page," promising to circulate it among his associates. Dilliard added, perhaps to indicate the page's reach into the past, "If my information is correct, the Letters column was put in its present place some 40 years ago. The purpose was to show how highly we regarded the opinions of our readers."[32]

Two undated handwritten notes among Simon's papers may have been sent by Dilliard during the high-profile efforts to thwart Madison County rackets. One, addressed to "Dear Paul," said, "Thanks for the tear sheet on sheriff [Harrell]. You're doing a courageous job. Hope I can get something in about it. Space is so short and there are so many things to write about. Stop in Collinsville and see us." The second, addressed the same, said, "Congratulations on your courage. There should be some red faces in Madison County!"[33] Coming from someone who Simon courted and admired, Dilliard's encouragement provided motivation for the editor's continuing efforts. While the *Post-Dispatch* editorial pages and news coverage remained separate in terms of coverage and commentary, the newsroom's attention to Simon and support for his work must have been influenced to some degree by Dilliard's devotion.

In the correspondence, it is apparent that Simon had begun drafting articles for magazine publication in addition to his writing for the *Tribune*. In one letter, Dilliard commented on an article Simon sent for publication on the goals of higher education. "It is at least three or perhaps four times too long for the space under the cartoon, which is the only spot on the editorial page available for reprint or original contributions. I, of course, do not want to try to chop it down to that size and I think, as a matter of fact, that would be ruinous to the article."[34] He suggested sending it to the editor of the Sunday editorial section, which ran longer articles. Dilliard obviously thought Simon's chances for publication would not be helped if Dilliard did the internal legwork. Dilliard added a paragraph of advice for future efforts by Simon, which may have inspired the young editor. "Magazines like the *Yale Review, American Scholar, Atlantic, Harper's, The Survey, The Progressive, New Republic* and *Nation,* all print pieces from time to time on this subject."

During 1951, one of the most active periods for Simon's anticrime work, he thanked Dilliard "for everything you did for me recently." Simon also wanted to assure Dilliard he had not done anything unethical or unlawful in a telephone conversation with the editorial page editor. "After talking to you on the phone about two weeks ago, I happened to think that possibly you thought I was violating an oath when I told you what Austin Lewis asked and said in the grand jury room. Under oath, I said I would not tell what questions the grand jurors asked me or what they said, which I have not done. That is as far as I went, because I had reason somewhat to anticipate the type of questions Lewis would ask and I hope to use them in the case before the state bar association."[35]

Apparently, during the proceeding Lewis asked Simon about meetings he had held with Dilliard. Simon wrote to his friend, "Through his questioning he attempted to indicate to the grand jury you and I were in some kind of cooperation on this thing; that we 'plotted' it. I felt honored that I was in on a plot with you, but these questions and other equally absurd charges and questions were discouraging, to say the least." At the letter's end, Simon wrote, "For your defense of justice in one small part of America, my sincere thanks, Irving."

Once in the state legislature, Simon continued to confide in his friend. During the 1955 session, Simon's first, he sent Dilliard a column he wrote regarding a bill proposed by Senator James O. Monroe, who owned the *Collinsville Herald,* and an ally of Simon on many Madison County issues. Monroe intended to submit a bill preventing state police from entering a county jurisdiction on a criminal investigation, the tactic Governor Adlai E. Stevenson had used in 1950. Simon had applauded Stevenson's action in the face of Madison County officials who balked at closing down gambling businesses. In the letter to Dilliard, he wrote, "The results of such a move [Monroe's bill], of course, would be a boon to the gambling gentry and to a few money-hungry officials."[36]

Simon commiserated with Dilliard upon reading of his "retirement." Noting the length of their relationship, he said,

> I was sorry because in so many ways you have always symbolized to me what the P-D can and should stand for. I am sure it will continue to be a great newspaper; but I am also afraid an era in its history may have ended . . . Most important, I shall always be grateful to you for sharpening in me an awareness of the constant need to protect our basic liberties. I've always been interested in this field but your writing and conversation awakened and deepened that interest in me and I know that at least a few sentences of the Illinois statutes today are a reflection of your influence on me.[37]

Simon concluded with his comment to wife Jeanne: "I have never known a finer man."

Perhaps the greatest testimony to Simon's newspaper career was that he did not fail in resurrecting a publication for Troy. Without experience or a bottomless cash box, he scrambled to demonstrate that he could run a business as well as write an opinion column. Against the odds, the paper moved into the black soon after being started, and it continued to make money during Simon's ownership. He may have had good and loyal help, but Simon provided the mission, the drive, and commitment. The six and a half years at the helm, off and on, day and night, provided Simon with knowledge of the weekly newspaper business that he shared with many others.

Part Two

Climbing the Political Mountains, 1955–66

Racetrack Runaround

Never one to hesitate when it came to making his mark, Paul Simon began his legislative career in 1955 with banners flying. How else would anyone expect a freshman member of the House of Representatives in Springfield to be noticed? As the session began, Democrats found themselves in the minority in both houses and out of the governor's mansion. Even if one of the seventy-four Democrats in the House could get the votes of all his fellow party members for a bill, Republicans could kill it in a minute.

Instead of confronting those odds, Simon announced initiatives he could control. He said he would make public an annual financial statement that included all sources of his income and assets. Such disclosure made him an exception to virtually every public official in the state, past and present. Others revealed that kind of information only to the Internal Revenue Service, and then because it was the law. He did not intend this as a one-year stunt. In fact, Simon provided annual financial statements as long as he served in public office. This gesture constituted an opening salvo on the subject of full disclosure and openness in government, which he preached regardless of the level of public service. One of his primary objectives was to pass an open meetings law, which occurred in his second term with bipartisan support. He also pledged to make public his costs of campaigning for office. Illinois did not then have laws requiring such disclosure.

In January, he began a commentary called "Sidelights from Springfield," which he wrote almost weekly during every session of the legislature until 1969 when he became lieutenant governor. The legislature met for six months from January to July every two years in the odd numbered year. He wrote simply, in short sentences and with easily understood words and usage.[1] He preferred to write about one subject at a time, rarely mixing topics in a way that might confuse a reader or leave someone asking, "What did he say?" If he wrote on more than one subject in a column, he clearly separated them. He was not bashful about proclaiming his position on issues but did not use the column to mention every legislative initiative he sponsored. Simon spoke directly to readers of all education levels and stations in life.

The columns appeared in the *Tribune* and he offered them to weekly and daily newspapers across the state at no cost to taxpayers or newspapers. He had a mailing list of 200 papers at the beginning. By 1961 that number had increased to more than 300 newspapers. Thus began the statewide reach of this little-known legislator from a town of 1,500 residents in a county where many of the Democrats in power did not care much for him.

In appreciation of his audience after his second legislative session in 1957, Simon thanked the 260 newspaper editors who requested his column that year. His comments captured the importance of the column to editors and readers but, more importantly, to the growing audience in all corners of Illinois. He said, "I want to thank the newspaper editors who have been good enough to let me use their valuable space to express my opinions. This does not reflect its value as much as the editors' interest in presenting views from Springfield. For this they deserve your appreciation. Many who read the column have written in agreement or disagreement. Some have visited me in Springfield and others have generously (and perhaps dangerously) asked me to speak at various functions. The thing that has been most encouraging is that more people seem to be taking an interest in their state government. If I've been able to help that trend at all, it's been well worth the effort."[2]

Did this mean that Simon had eyes on running a statewide campaign anytime soon? There are no early documents in which he stated such an ambition. But when he began publishing and editing a newspaper in 1948, he gave no indication of wanting to run for office either. Simon wanted his opinions on state issues, and matters beyond his legislative district, to be seen and read by a large audience. The column seemed the most natural way to accomplish that objective. Again, Simon struck a chord as one of a kind. When he began the "Sidelights" column, no other member of the legislature offered columns so frequently to so many newspapers in Illinois, and written on his own typewriter.

For at least two years, until the next election, Democrats remained a minority in the state house and senate. He learned early that serving in the minority could be tedious and boring, so he decided to do more than sit in meetings and listen to Republicans. Regardless of the Democratic party status, Simon pursued his open government agenda from the outset, and he scored a major success in the 1957 session.

In 1955, his first legislative session, he sponsored a "right to know" bill requiring public agencies to hold open meetings. Simon said he got the idea from a reporter for the *Illinois State Journal* who wrote him about a law in California. Using that information, Simon drafted a bill and began looking for support. He received help from the Illinois School Board Association, Sigma Delta Chi, the professional journalists' organization, and the Illinois Press Association, but municipal governments opposed the idea as hindering effective administration. Simon said one reporter stated he was "heading uphill on roller skates."[3] The bill caught the fancy of newspapers across the state, earning editorial page support. Simon learned that open government had low priority among state legislators unless prompted by external forces, such as media.

To requests from leadership, Simon made adjustments to the bill, but they were not enough. The proposal stalled before the session ended. He reintroduced the bill in the 1957 session after spending time rounding up support among colleagues. Joining as co-sponsors were Representative Alan Dixon, Representative Anthony Scariano, Representative Abner Mikva, and Representative Jeanne C. Hurley of Wilmette.[4] Representative Hurley became Simon's wife in 1960. Simon defended the bill in a "Sidelights from Springfield" column in which he wrote, "The general proposition that public business is the public's business is important and it is sound . . . In a democracy the people have a right to know not only the final decision reached by the elected officials, but how they reached that decision." The House and Senate quickly approved the measure, and Governor William Stratton signed it.[5] Simon had his first major legislative success.

The "right to know" bill brought together young and new legislators who quickly formed what they called a Democratic study group. Other legislators called them Young Turks. Most were Democrats, with a few Republicans participating on specific issues. No matter the name or group, they shared liberal beliefs and aligned themselves against the prevailing party establishment in the General Assembly. They first began meeting just prior to the 1957 session when Scariano, Mikva, and Hurley began their legislative careers.

Scariano explained how the group functioned. He said, "We went about studying the issues and preparing for the legislative session and trying to get placed on committees that would be appropriate to our interests. The Democratic study group kept up, I would say throughout our entire tenure in the House. Membership changed, but we always had a Democratic study group."[6]

In the 1955 session, Simon became a seatmate with fellow Democrat Dixon from Belleville. The two remained seatmates in the house and state senate until 1969. They shared a friendship, personal and political, that lasted until separated by death.[7] The relationship covered a half century, including forty-two years in public service. While they had some common interests as a result of being from adjoining districts, that did not provide sufficient reason for the basic relationship. From the outset, they established a kinship on issues facing the legislature, and they respected each other's ethics and honesty.

The Simon and Dixon friendship was tested frequently, but it survived. U.S. Senator Richard Durbin, who worked with both men, observed, "Matters never got petty or personal between them."[8] They trusted each other in careers where trust is hard earned and often lost. Dixon said, "We never in our lives had a serious falling out."[9]

Dixon started his state political career with election to the state House of Representatives in 1950, representing the district covering his native Belleville and St. Clair County, across the Mississippi River from St. Louis. He had been in the House two sessions before Simon won the 1954 election. Dixon made his way to the legislature by defeating the Democratic party machine's candidate, and thereafter had the party's blessing. That gave the two men something in common. Dixon knew of Simon's activities as editor just a few miles away. Dixon remembers, "During the campaign [1954] I heard about Paul raising hell with politicians in Madison County. He was viewed as a 'young devil' by the party people."[10]

During those early years in the House, they developed personal and political styles that changed little over the decades. Dixon preferred hanging out with fellow Democrats at Springfield bars during the evenings, and Simon chose his apartment and issue discussions. During the day, they ended up back in the House next to each other where they worked together at forging alliances and comparing insights. The relationship might have helped convince Dixon to remain in public office. Dixon remembered that in 1952 after his first session there were no Democrats holding state office. "I talked with fellow Democrats about resigning and going home to work because it looked like Republicans would rule forever. We were the minority party more or less in that era, and I was never a mover or shaker."[11]

They worked together with other mavericks. "We appealed to anyone who had independent thoughts," Dixon said, and "there were not many."[12] They often had breakfast together while in Springfield, but that routine did not extend to nighttime activities. Simon did not drink, smoke, or swear. Some colleagues remembered seeing him with an occasional glass of red wine. Dixon on the other hand enjoyed a cold beer on a hot day—or maybe any day—he smoked, and "I swore some to be part of the crowd."[13]

A serious young man, Simon kept his own evening company while other legislators inhabited Springfield bars and nightclubs. Some nights he met with fellow progressives, plotting tactics and studying policy proposals. Before Simon married in 1960, he and three other colleagues shared two apartments. Scariano explained: "Paul Simon, Bob Mann, Ab Mikva and I shared two apartments, small ones, two-bedroom apartments, and we had breakfast regularly together at the apartment. We had a woman come in and clean for us and prepare breakfast."[14]

Dixon, gregarious and conversational, became one of the regulars at places like the bar at the St. Nicholas Hotel, a Democratic hangout. Dixon said, "Legislators tend to be political animals, and want to be liked. I liked social settings with politicians, but Paul never bummed around at night. I don't know what he did at night. He wasn't at the St. Nick having a beer, that's for sure."[15] These differences prompted Durbin to call them "truly the odd couple."[16]

Their days together as seatmates inevitably led to stories they told many times. One developed from House debate on a bill sponsored by Senator Paul Broyles of Mount Vernon, who wanted every government employee to sign an oath of loyalty and declare opposition to communism. Dixon led opposition on the House floor, and Simon joined the fight. At a moment when Dixon was not speaking, a page brought him a note that read, "You're a communist and I'm going to shoot you from the balcony." Shaken by the threat, Dixon handed the note to Simon who read it slowly. Then Simon turned to his friend, saying, "I sure hope he's a very good shot." Dixon said, "Paul told that story 10,000 times."[17]

Dixon had his own experiences with official corruption at the local level, and he shared those with Simon. Growing up in Belleville, Dixon recalled all taverns had slot machines, but most were gone by 1949.[18] He had heard the stories of gambling and criminal elements but had no personal experiences. He recalled a bookie and gambling operation in a store at the Belleville city square, which was within walking distance of city hall, the police station, and the county courthouse. "Officials were in there from noon on drinking and gambling," Dixon said.[19]

In Dixon's memory, East St. Louis was a more wide-open town than Belleville. There were a variety of dice games in the Arcade Building across from city hall, for example. There was a "sense of tolerance" about crime in East St. Louis and "looser law enforcement policies."[20] The Paddock Tavern, which Buster Wortman and associates used as headquarters, catered to the city's most important people who went there for lunch and drinks. Dixon's rejection of official acceptance of gambling made him a welcome seatmate for Simon.[21]

Simon's experiences with official corruption in Madison County made him anything but naïve about the temptations of graft offered by people seeking special favors. The punchboard discovery erased any illusions of purity among those elected to office. It did not take Simon long in the state legislature to discover that state officials took corrupt practices to new levels. He later wrote, "The blatant corruption in the legislature startled me."[22] Simon heard members talking about "money bills," and "fetchers," a bill designed to "fetch" a payoff for killing it. These often involved businesses and industries that carefully watched for bills that could upset the status quo.

On one occasion, Simon introduced a bill for competitive bidding on bond issues by cities and a fellow legislator challenged him for introducing "his" bill. He informed Simon that he had done well financially introducing a similar bill and then making sure it did not go further, after contact by industry lobbyists. He suggested Simon kill the bill and split the proceeds. Simon refused, but the committee killed the bill 20–0, making several members happy.[23]

Those and similar encounters might have made Simon angry and disillusioned, but the subject that bothered him most was horse racing, more specifically, the questionable ethics of Representative Paul Powell, racing's high priest in the legislature. Simon butted heads with legislators including Powell who made huge profits as a result of favorable legislation for investors in horse racing ventures in southern Illinois and the Chicago area. Hardly had the freshman legislator taken a seat in the House when a bill that sweetened the pot for horse racing caught his attention. He vowed to stop the open favoritism for the racetrack lobby.

Long before 1955, the legislature had passed laws favorable to investors and backers of pari-mutuel betting. The first in 1927 regulated pari-mutuel wagering for thoroughbred racing, and in 1945 a law allowed betting on harness racing.[24] Rumors circulated in both instances of shenanigans and payoffs, but no eyewitnesses came forward. Once pari-mutuel betting was allowed on a limited basis, horse racing of all kinds in Illinois exploded. Crowds grew, tracks opened, betting increased dramatically, and the tax money involved became a powerful economic engine for the state. Inevitably, certain members of the legislature could see an opportunity for personal riches.

In the session of 1949, the first bonanza bill surfaced, produced by Speaker of the House Powell, a Democrat from Vienna.[25] At that time, Simon was in his first year as editor and publisher in Troy. Powell, serving the first of three terms as speaker, was no newcomer to horse racing or those involved in it, and he rallied interested parties in both houses of the legislature for a bill that allowed pari-mutuel harness racing at night in July and August. This constituted a huge expansion of horse racing across the state, especially in the East St. Louis and Chicago regions, and provided legislators with an opportunity to share in the spoils. A skillful legislator and Democratic party leader, Powell used his advantage as speaker to time the process and generate unanimous votes in favor of passage.

Governor Stevenson, serving in his first year and working with his initial state budget, encouraged support for the legislation by including the racing bill in the budget report. It stated, "An increase in the rate of tax on harness racing to bring it into conformance with that on running races is estimated to produce an additional $2.4 million."[26] The harmless-sounding note did not mention the expansion of harness racing.

The bill moved through the House and Senate quickly toward the end of the session, passing without a dissenting vote.[27] On July 1, Stevenson signed the bill, opening the door to more than a decade of laws expanding horse racing, promoted primarily by Powell and his pals. Although Simon never publicly denounced one of his favorite governors for playing Powell's game, as matters developed he must have wondered about Stevenson's motives. Those who recognized what Stevenson had done attributed it to the presumption that the governor would seek reelection in 1952 and could use the support of all those associated with county fairs.

Before Stevenson signed the bill, friends of Powell and his legislative band incorporated the Chicago Downs harness racing track. Organizers of the track offered forty people stock at ten cents a share, a ridiculously low price even for that time. Daisy Powell, the speaker's wife, became the single largest stockholder with 16,900 shares, purchased for $1,690.[28] Other legislators were offered substantially smaller amounts of stock, including Representative Clyde Lee, who bought 1,000 shares in his wife's name. Republican senator Everett Peters of St. Joseph, a political benefactor of the University of Illinois, purchased 1,000. The Chicago Downs board declared a $1 per share dividend in July 1949 shortly after Stevenson signed the bill.

The stock scandal, which Chicago newspapers divulged in August 1951, reached to the highest levels of the Stevenson administration. James Mulroy, a distinguished journalist who won a Pulitzer Prize while at the *Chicago Daily News*, had joined Stevenson's team during the 1948 campaign. A hard-drinking Irishman, he became a close aide and trusted adviser to Stevenson after the election. Mulroy bought 1,000 shares of Chicago Downs stock.[29] When revealed by newspapers, Stevenson and Mulroy came under heavy fire from editorial pages that had supported Stevenson's two-fisted approach to commercialized gambling. Mulroy refused to sell the stock, and Stevenson accepted his resignation in November. Simon must have recalled with sadness the exchange of letters with Mulroy from 1949 and 1950 in which Simon urged the governor to take direct action on gambling.

Feisty as always, Powell responded on several occasions when the scandal hit the papers. In a lengthy defense of his actions that he wrote for newspapers in southern Illinois, he said, "I do not propose to have any metropolitan newspaper influence my vote in the legislature against the best interests of the citizens of the 51st district who have bestowed upon me the honor of electing me as one of the representatives."[30] Calls for investigations went nowhere. Stevenson said, "I heard no objection to the bill when it was passed and none since. The stock was sold at a very low price, but whether it was sold as an inducement to pass the bill, I don't know."[31] No laws were broken before, during, or after passage of the law.

Nothing slowed Powell's commitment to enhancing horse racing opportunities or taking money for it. From the mid-1950s until his death in 1970, he received consulting fees from Illinois racetrack operations. Powell said about the consulting pay, "I decided I should get something for my time. I suggested they pay me direct."[32] From 1945 until his last year as a legislator in 1964, hardly a session occurred without major racetrack legislation passed—or opposing bills stopped—by the strong hand of Powell.

For years leading up to 1953, certain individuals with strong political ties to St. Clair and Madison counties and southern Illinois wanted to begin a thoroughbred racing operation in the East St. Louis region that would draw betting customers from St. Louis. Key individuals in the development of what became Cahokia Downs racetrack were former governor John Stelle, who since leaving office in 1940 had maintained close connections with Powell and racetrack interests; Dan McGlynn, an East St. Louis attorney and longtime downstate Republican operative; and Schaefer O'Neill, an Alton attorney and state representative dating back to the 1930s.[33] They found available land in Centreville Township between East St. Louis and Belleville and began putting together an investment group. Although organizational documents discovered later cleverly avoided using Powell's name, no racetrack in southern Illinois could operate without his approval. Powell bought his first shares of stock in 1954 when Cahokia Downs opened for business.[34]

Not everyone qualified for investing in Cahokia Downs, however. Knowing that political connections in Springfield would be important for Cahokia Downs and future racetrack legislation, only those with strong political connections locally and in the state capital joined the investor group. When the original investors were revealed in 1971, the names were familiar: Representative Clyde Choate, a longtime associate of Powell, from Anna; William "Smokey" Downey, an aide to Governor William Stratton; Dan Foley, East St. Louis city finance commissioner; East St. Louis mayor Alvin Fields; Senator Everett Peters; Dan McGlynn; U.S. Representative Melvin Price; Francis Touchette, the supervisor of Centreville Township near East St. Louis; Peter Rossiter, downstate Democratic patronage chief;

Representative Clyde Lee; and Edward Barrett, of Chicago, a Stelle and Powell associate dating to the early 1930s.[35]

When Simon got drawn into legislative affairs involving Powell and horse racing interests, none of the Cahokia Downs ownership arrangements were known. Because of laws that allowed land trust investors to remain anonymous, it was not until seventeen years later that newspapers published complete ownership lists. Newspaper editors and reporters in the vicinity of Cahokia Downs had their suspicions about the founders and investors, Powell among them, but they could not obtain the names. Again, none of the investors had broken any laws. However, their conflicts of interest were numerous.

During the 1955 legislative session, Simon's first, Powell had been pushed aside for leadership of House Democrats by Chicago mayor Richard J. Daley.[36] But even without official power, Powell commanded respect, attention, and the votes of almost all downstate Democrats. Most of all, Governor Stratton needed Powell's support and downstate Democrat votes to increase the state sales tax from 2 to 3 cents.[37] Powell never gave away anything; the tradeoff for him to assure the downstate Democratic votes was to help the two downstate racetracks, Cahokia Downs and Fairmount, which operated in Simon's district.

Powell's legislation amended the racing law to provide that on days when the betting failed to reach $300,000, the state tax on the daily handle—money waged on races—would be 4 percent instead of 6 percent.[38] This particularly benefited the two downstate tracks where the daily handle was usually less than $300,000. Simon did not think much of the sales tax increase, but he definitely opposed the racetrack tax reduction. He often said, "When the race track tax reduction came up the same day as the increase in the tax on a loaf of bread and a pound of butter from two cents to three cents, I attacked it." This was his first House floor quarrel with Powell—but not the last. Joining Simon in vocal dissent was Democratic representative Richard Stengel, who called it the biggest steal since he'd been in the legislature. Reacting to the two opponents, Powell said, "You're just mad because you're not in on it."[39]

Although the racetrack bill passed overwhelmingly, Stengel and Simon discovered a little-used legislative maneuver that allowed members to file a formal protest. They requested that Stratton veto the bill, although they knew he would not. In order to take the spotlight off Stratton, a close ally of Powell, Representative Carl Preihs, Pana Democrat, also a strong backer of racetrack legislation, introduced a resolution condemning Stengel and Simon as "men who lack integrity." That gave Stratton enough shelter to sign the racetrack tax reduction bill, and Preihs dropped the resolution.[40]

In a short time, Simon grew suspicious of almost any legislation that Powell backed. Another clash between the two occurred in the 1957 session over a bill requiring all trucks in Illinois to have specific hard plastic contour mud guards. Powell pushed the bill through the House in spite of opposition from truckers, who believed the guards accumulated dirt and caused a traffic hazard. The bill passed the House 133 to 20, with Simon in the minority. The bill passed the Senate 54 to 0.[41]

Rumors circulated that Powell had an interest in the mud guard business, but the Vienna Democrat denied the charge and said his friends were not involved financially. During House debate on mud guards, Simon read the names of the company officers: Schaeffer O'Neill, John Stelle, and George Edward Day, all of whom were associates of Powell in the Cahokia Downs racetrack and other business deals.[42] In an unpublished letter to the editor of the *Illinois State Register* in Springfield, Simon said the issue was not whether the mud guards made sense but that "John Stelle and the same race track crowd who had benefited by a bonanza the 1955 session passed, just by coincidence happened to be in the business of manufacturing mud guards."[43] Regarding accusations that Simon had signed up with the trucker lobby, he replied in the letter, "I have opposed the big truckers more often than I have been with them, as they could tell you. As a matter of fact, when a representative of a trucker offered me a campaign contribution a few years ago, I declined to accept it."

Simon had a bead on issues involving racetracks, and he pursued them without hesitation even if they involved Madison County businesses. One example, tied directly to his quarrels with gambling and corruption, occurred in 1958 involving the Fairmount track in Madison County. Simon complained to the Illinois Racing Board that the Rite Way Cigarette Company, which had connections to the Buster Wortman rackets gang, had installed machines at the Fairmount track in Madison County.

In a lengthy letter to the board, he set out to prove the connection between Rite Way and Wortman.[44] Citing numerous examples from files of the *East St. Louis Journal* and *St. Louis Post-Dispatch,* Simon showed that Edward "Ted" Wortman, Buster Wortman's brother, was president of Rite Way. The racing board replied that "Edward Wortman is at present a licensee of the Illinois Racing Board as a trainer . . . and is in good standing." Simon quoted articles that connected the Wortmans to similar businesses, especially Plaza Amusement Company, with offices in St. Louis. Plaza had been the subject of investigations by Missouri state officials and investigators for the Kefauver Committee. Kefauver established a direct connection between Plaza and

Pioneer News Service, the horse racing information service used by bookies and controlled by the Capone syndicate. Simon wrote, "It is clear you cannot separate Rite Way from Plaza and there is no question but that 'Buster' is a dominant figure in Plaza even though Ted is the president."

Simon quoted statements from Jerome Munie, mayor of Belleville, and Al Delbartes, mayor of Collinsville, that they would prevent any establishments from having dealings with Rite Way. Munie, a law enforcement reformer who threw the Shelton gang out of St. Clair County in the 1930s, said, "We don't intend to tolerate that kind of people in Belleville."[45] Delbartes said, "We intend to stick by our guns concerning the threatened infiltration by hoodlums in the coin vending machine business here."[46]

Simon's letter to the board continued, "From all of the above I think it should be clear that the cigarette machines now at the Fairmount track from the firm which Edward 'Ted' Wortman heads should be removed at once . . . I am taking the liberty of sending a carbon copy of this letter to Governor Stratton." In regard to the "good standing" statement about Ted Wortman, Simon stated, "This brings up the whole question of what standards you follow in licensing, if any, and the whole question of connections between the underworld and racing in Illinois." Simon also requested documents from the board about its policy toward racing by the hoodlum element.

Writing in a "P.S." column—written for *Tribune* readers only—two months later, Simon said, "You should be pleased to learn that the cigarette machines have been ordered out. The chairman of the racing board called me and told me they had ordered the machines out and that the investigation of the hoodlum tie-up with Illinois racing which I requested is continuing. We'll wait and see what develops on that."[47] Eight months later in "Sidelights from Springfield," Simon said the board had not answered his question about how the gangsters managed to get in at Fairmount in the first place.[48]

Simon had multiple experiences with Powell's strengths and weaknesses, not all of them in public. Of the legislative skirmishes Simon won few, but the state's newspaper reporters and editorial writers took note when he launched verbal assaults from the legislative column that was in the hands of more than 200 editors. Simon needed little provocation to throw barbs at the racetrack crowd. In a "Sidelights from Springfield" column on February 21, 1957, Simon wrote, "Who really has power in the Illinois legislature?"[49] He answered, "The biggest power in Springfield is obvious: . . . Governor Stratton can pass virtually anything he wants if he has the help of one other man." The second most powerful position belonged to Chicago mayor Richard J. Daley. Simon listed several candidates for No. 3 most powerful: educational interests, manufacturing and business, labor, trucking, and horse racing. Some, he said, operated on "a very high plane. Others do not and can hardly be considered working for the best interests of Illinois."

Simon ranked horse racing as not working in the best interest of Illinois. "Men who are powerful in both parties have financial interests in this area and when the racetrack group wants something, the public had better take cover." Regardless of favors already received, he promised the racetrack group would return, if not in the 1957 session. "If they do come back, some of us are planning to give them a vigorous battle," he wrote.

The depth of bad feelings between Powell and Simon can be seen in correspondence that never made public print. One incident occurred in 1956 after the presidential election in which Adlai Stevenson lost to Dwight D. Eisenhower a second time. Before the Democratic national convention, downstate Illinois Democrats with a record of animosity toward Stevenson called for a new candidate to challenge the president. Pro-racetrack promoters John Stelle and Paul Powell announced they preferred Senator Stuart Symington of Missouri. Joining them was former U.S. senator Scott Lucas, who apparently was unhappy that Stevenson had not backed his effort to be nominated to run against Senator Everett Dirksen. Stevenson had instead backed Richard Stengel, a favorite of Paul Simon.

Given the cast of characters in this election dust-up and the record of Powell in state politics, it was no surprise that Simon wanted to round up newspaper support for an alternative to Powell's leadership in advance of the 1957 legislative session. He directed attention to Milburn P. (Pete) Akers, executive editor of the *Chicago Sun-Times*, a paper whose editorial approach was more akin to Simon than to Powell. Prior to the election, the *Sun-Times* criticized the trio that opposed Stevenson. Simon's intent to find a way to undermine Powell's leadership was obvious in this letter to Akers after the election:

> Representative Alan J. Dixon from St. Clair county called me and suggested that since we are going to be in Chicago for a meeting Monday afternoon that we try to see you to discuss the downstate House leadership during the coming session. Both of us feel the Stelle-Powell influence on our party and the Republican party has been most unwholesome and we would like to discuss with you the ways and means of reducing their power in Illinois.[50]

Another case involved activities of the Democratic Federation of Illinois, which Simon helped organize and Powell opposed. The federation, organized in the mid-1950s, consisted of independent Democrats unaligned with

Chicago machine interests and opposed by the downstate Democrats led by Powell. It appealed to Democrats who wanted a more open party, including remnants of Governor Adlai Stevenson's administration and those alarmed at the strength of Chicago influence in the legislature.

Mainstream Democratic party people viewed the federation as a group of malcontents that lacked political power in the state and were no threat to party leadership. Those in the party hierarchy who made decisions about candidates for state office spoke with disgust of people calling for reforms. Simon was among those considered a troublemaker. In the legislature barely long enough to find the restrooms and take a seat in the House, Simon nonetheless had earned a reputation among organizers of the Federation as a potential leader. They asked him to be the first president of the new organization, and the young legislator agreed.[51] He held the position one year.

Action by the federation and Simon in 1958 to challenge Powell's authority in his legislative district became the subject in an exchange of correspondence involving Simon, Powell, and V. Y. Dallman, editor of the *Illinois State Register* in Springfield. The paper had a long history of supporting Democrats for office, including Powell and Simon. In advance of the primary election, Simon encouraged opposition to Powell, hoping to find a candidate who could unseat the Vienna Democrat. Powell, no fool, knew what was going on and could see the fingerprints of the Federation and Simon. In a letter to Dallman after the editor had criticized Powell's legislative record, the Vienna Democrat claimed a long faithful association with the party, defended his support of the mud guard bill, and took a swipe at Simon.

After taking Dallman to task for criticisms, Powell commented on the federation. "When the Federation was first organized, I made some statements at a Democratic County chairman's organization (which was several months ago) to the effect that any political organization should operate through and with the regular organization, which is constituted by the laws of our state. The Jeffersonian and Jackson Democratic Clubs have always done this."[52] He believed the federation to be an outlaw group. "During my campaign for the nomination for representative I have not made any speech against the federation, nor against either of my opponents, but am running upon the legislative record I have made and about which you have written several editorials—and, as you know, they have been in favor of this record."

Powell, referring to Simon as "your friend," ridiculed the attempt to stop the mud guard bill, saying he could answer any attack by Simon. He returned to a mention of the Federation, stating, "I have been a precinct committeeman for 35 years, and a county chairman for 12 years. In my county I welcome any club or group that wants to organize in the interest of the

Democratic Party, but I am still old-fashioned enough to believe that they should work with the Democratic organization instead of trying to divide, and have one working against the other." He added that if Simon "or anyone else cares to come into my district, they certainly have that privilege. I will be willing to compare my record of service to the Democratic Party and my legislative record with any of them."

Dallman sent the letter to Simon with a note, "Dear Friend Simon: Please call me COLLECT after you have read this letter. Help me to reply." Simon started his written response with a tongue-in-cheek comment about Powell and the Federation: "First of all you might commend Powell for apparently softening his attitude toward the Democratic Federation. His letter indicates an entirely different attitude than that expressed to many people."[53] Simon referred to a newsletter published in Powell's district about a Federation meeting in Harrisburg that stated Powell "will not pull any political punches when he says we have no room in Southern Illinois for Democratic crusaders trying to step in and start any funny Democratic business that is not regular politics." Simon called that an obvious reference to the Federation. Simon added if "funny Democratic business means getting more Democratic votes and getting more honest, independent citizens interested in our party, then we plead guilty." At the Harrisburg meeting, Simon noted, Powell did not say a word.

As might be expected in light of Powell's letter, Simon defended the objectives of the federation in a closing statement: "The final implication of his letter is that the Democratic Federation is somehow opposed to the regular organization. Wherever a regular organization tries to 'play footsie' with the Republicans and arrange deals with them, he is right, we will oppose that. But any organization of the Democratic party which is sincerely trying to stand for the right thing and to garner victories for the Democratic party, will find an ally in the Democratic Federation of Illinois." The Federation experience for Simon had far-reaching implications, although there was no way to know then what they might be. Daniel Walker, a Chicago attorney, succeeded him as president of the Federation.

The next public eruption involving Powell, his racetrack cronies, and Simon occurred in the 1959 session over a bill to add fifteen days to the harness racing season. By then, Powell and other legislators had investments in Chicago area harness racetracks. Simon warmed to the fight in a "Sidelights from Springfield" column of April 30. He called the bill in question "one of the worst bills so far this session." He also predicted it would pass.[54]

Simon said the bill extending operation dates gave added power and authority to the racetrack lobby. It would, he argued, add to an already long list of legislation to line the pockets of investors and racetrack owners. He mentioned the 1955 tax reduction bill and a bill that authorized subsidies of up to $1 million for the breeding of racehorses. "At the same time our mentally retarded are being given inadequate attention and some of our schools are not receiving sufficient funds . . . The racetrack legislation which has passed is a credit to neither party," he stated.

The column brought the issue home to the Fairmount track in Madison County "in an area where our county law enforcement officials have had a great deal of trouble with prostitution, professional gambling, and almost every crime in the book. Extend the racing season and you increase the problems of law enforcement in my county." He also spoke of tracks that attracted an unsavory part of the population. "Some of the people who are interested in racing in Illinois are people with connections which are not good." Finally, Simon said, "House Bill 884 will help those who least deserve our help."

Powell and friends took Simon's challenge seriously, in large part because the column went to hundreds of state newspapers. To defend the proposal and answer Simon's charges in the House, Powell chose his chum Clyde Lee, who never concealed his admiration and respect for the Vienna politician. Lee said he worked for weeks on a lengthy speech for his legislative colleagues.[55] He began the oration after Simon addressed the group, stating, "In addition to what he has said here today, he [Simon] recently wrote an article for his newspaper column that is published throughout Illinois and charges that this bill is the session's worst. In my twenty years of service in the Illinois legislature, this is the first time I have ever had a member make a charge of this kind against a bill of mine. I do not have a newspaper column to reply to him, so I must impose on your time today for his entirely wrong [statement] in his article as well as on some of his statements that he has just made here on the floor of this house."

Lee worked to build a case for horse racing as a huge economic engine for the state. He recalled the bill in 1949 that Governor Stevenson signed, declaring, "This bill increased the revenue to the state from about a half million dollars a year to about two million eight hundred thousand dollars a year. It is estimated that this bill has brought in an additional twenty million dollars into the state treasury in the past ten years. I think this bill is a credit to me, as well as a credit to the whole membership of the House."

Lee listed buildings at the University of Illinois and Southern Illinois University in Carbondale constructed in the previous fifteen years from horse racing money. He added, "We are now using approximately ten millions dollars a year to retire the veterans of World War II bonus bonds. If we didn't have this money available these bonds would have to be paid by personal taxes levied on every taxpayer in the state." He mentioned that horse racing funded about one hundred county fairs and buildings at the state fair.

Attempting to shame Simon for criticizing an economic advantage for Madison County, he recalled that the Fairmount track paid about $28,000 in real estate and personal taxes for 1958, and that the track employed 325 people with a payroll of $354,000. He added, "They paid out $600,000 in purses and much of this money was spent in Madison County. In addition to all of this, they paid $542,422 mutuel tax to the state. I am wondering if the gentleman from Madison would like to see this business driven out of his county and see the loss of taxes and loss of this payroll."

Lee concluded, "I'm sorry I've talked so long but there are many things that can be said on behalf of horse racing in Illinois and the many good benefits that we have received and are still receiving from it. I love horses and I enjoy seeing them race. And I just can't understand why the gentleman from Madison is so set against horses unless he was kicked or bitten by a horse when he was a boy." The last statement drew applause in the House and was widely quoted.[56]

The House vote on Bill 884 was 116–18, with Simon voting against. The minority votes included Mikva, Scariano, Jeanne Hurley (later Mrs. Paul Simon), and Dixon.[57] Lee referred to them as part of the independent group "that stuck together."

Simon had no illusions about the strength of the horse racing faction, and it allowed him occasional humor. Lee remembered in an oral history years later, "It was a long standing joke. I mean we kidded each other about it and still do whenever I see him." Lee added an anecdote about the ribbing Simon took. "When Simon and Jeannie [Hurley] got married . . . Powell was in the speaker's chair, and they welcomed Jeannie and Paul back from their honeymoon. They had each given a little talk, and then Paul let anybody else get up and make a talk. And finally I got up and I—oh, they were inviting everybody to come to their home and to come and see them. So I got up and I said, 'I'd just like to inquire if Mr. and Mrs. Simon would let me bring my horse when I come to see them.'"[58]

Lee, known in the legislature as a great storyteller, had one other anecdote about Simon and racetracks. Each night at the Washington Park racetrack in Chicago, someone from the audience was asked to present a special award to the winner of the feature race. The gift might have been a trophy, gold cup, blanket, or plaque. Lee remembered he invited Simon to the track on one occasion, and Simon made the presentation. "We were glad to have him come to Washington Park and see our operation and present the trophy," Lee said. "I knew of his background, his father was a Lutheran minister and I am sure he was brought up in an environment that was against racing, so I never had any ill feeling toward him." Lee acknowledged that Simon did not bet on the horses that night.[59]

Simon said of Lee, "He was always more of a gentleman. Always very good to me. I remember one time in debate he said I must have been kicked by a horse. I always felt he was a classy guy."[60]

Simon truly believed, however, that Powell represented evil. That led him to encourage an opponent for Powell in the 1958 election. While it did not materialize, Simon worked at other angles. In an exchange of letters early that year with Bill Boyne, managing editor of the *Southern Illinoisan* in Carbondale, Simon provided a list of questions for the editor to ask Powell when he came in for a candidate interview.[61] The subject matter indicates that Simon had a list of grievances he wanted Boyne to adopt, and Boyne seemed sympathetic. Some of the issues:

- Mud guard bill. "You might ask him if it isn't a bit strange to sponsor a measure requiring trucks to use something your close friends manufacture."
- The chiropractic bill of 1955. "That was the one where a huge sum was raised by the chiropractors and Powell was called before the Peoria Grand Jury. You might ask him where he got his great interest in chiropractors."
- He was the sole sponsor in the 1955 session of the "false teeth bill." "This is for a Chicago concern that makes 'mail order' false teeth. How did he happen to get interested in this?"
- "Powell is reported to have majority stock in two county fairs and stock in others as well. How much does he make from these? Financial support for the county fairs comes from the racetrack tax, which he has shown more than passing interest in. Does he regard this as a conflict of interest?"
- "Have him explain in detail the Chicago Downs deal. The legislature approved it and then he showed up with more stock than anyone else."
- "Does he have stock in Cahokia Downs?"
- "What is his relationship with John Stelle? Is he on Stelle's payroll?"
- "When Orville Hodge was state auditor whenever he came on the House floor he almost always went first to Powell's desk. Why? What was their relationship?"

Boyne thanked Simon for the questions and added, "I note that more than twice as much goes for the thoroughbreds and colts as goes for veterans' rehabilitation. Flag waving stops at the paddock gate."[62]

The war between Simon and Powell did not cool until Simon's election to the state senate in 1962 and Powell's election as secretary of state in 1964. No longer at each other's throats during legislative sessions, they actually developed a measure of mutual respect for each other. Simon acknowledged Powell's devotion to his constituents, to social issues, and education. He never backed away from other criticisms, however, and when racetrack finances and investors were disclosed, Simon felt redeemed. He said, "Powell always worked hard campaigning. We started a friendship in 1968 when we were on the state ticket together. . . . There was no question he was powerful, he was gutsy, he had courage, he was corrupt, and he had some areas where he did good things: Southern Illinois University, minimum wage, a philosophy of helping people."[63] An encounter that Simon liked to mention occurred when he opposed a bill strongly supported by Powell. "Powell clearly was getting paid off. He came up to me and said, 'Why are you opposing me on that bill.' I said, Paul, you know why I am opposing you. He said, 'You are wrong. If I stole a pig on this bill I would tell you.'"[64] Simon knew better.

Before the election of 1962, Simon wrote a letter to Powell stating, "It was a happy surprise to receive the $200 contribution from the Democratic Legislative Campaign Fund signed by you. Needless to say, I can put this to good use."[65] Simon always said Powell sent the money hoping Simon would win the Senate seat and no longer be in the House.

Bureaucratic quarrels among members of the legislature occur routinely and many of them are not worth study. What makes the jousting between Powell and Simon more important than other confrontations? In terms of immediate results, Powell was the winner hands down, usually getting what he wanted. Simon mustered few victories in the years 1955–1964 when both were in the General Assembly. However, the cumulative effect of Simon's frequent challenge to Powell's authority burnished the Troy legislator's image as a fighter of conflicts of interest and corruption, a public position he had established to a great degree as a journalist. When viewed over the span of Simon's lengthy public career, his fight for more open government, disclosure of finances, and ethical standards reached out to many people across Illinois. Without a direct personal stake in issues before the legislature, many citizens listened to those officials who had experience and spoke words of common sense. Simon scored on all those points, reminding the public of his positions in columns, speeches, newsletters, and introduction of legislation. Notably, he rarely resorted to written personal attacks on Powell, preferring instead to paint him as among those who chiseled away at the legislature's reputation and thwarted opportunities for a more responsible legislature.

While Powell never was officially charged with a law violation, indicted, or convicted of any crime, other public officials crossed the line into felony territory. Two of the most notable during the careers of Powell and Simon were Orville Hodge and Otto Kerner. While Kerner's offense occurred during his tenure as governor, he was not tried and convicted until after his elective service ended. Hodge's offense occurred while he held office, as did his conviction and sentence to prison.

Routine consideration of an appropriation for the department of state auditor Orville Hodge during the 1955 session put Simon at the edges of a scandal that still draws attention although others have outdistanced it in terms of the amounts at stake. An "emergency" appropriation bill for the department appeared before the legislature, asking $525,000. The appropriation for the next fiscal year requested $7 million, an increase year over year of 40 percent. Few questioned it. The only explanation given for such an increase was the need for new bookkeeping equipment. As expected, the House passed the emergency bill 129 to 2 and the annual appropriation 127 to 2. The two "no" votes were cast by Representative Ralph Stephenson of Moline, a Republican, and Simon, who later said he didn't accept the reasons given for the increase.[66]

A week after the votes, Hodge, a Republican from Granite City in Madison County who had been widely rumored as a candidate for governor, approached Simon on the House floor with Paul Powell in tow. Hodge said the vote raised questions about Simon's intentions and was hurting the freshman representative. Hodge said, "Say, Paul, everybody in Madison County is talking about how you voted against me. Even the maid in my house—who voted for you—wanted to know why you had voted against me. If I were you I'd ask for unanimous consent to have your vote changed." Powell said he could quietly arrange to have Simon's vote moved to "yea" on the official record. Simon declined the offer.[67] He surmised later that the appropriation had not cleared the Senate at that time and Hodge wanted to say he had unanimous support in the House.

In a "P.S." column for the *Tribune* a year later, Simon said, "I felt that there had not been adequate explanation of the need for such an increase so I voted against it . . . In fairness to the other legislators I should say that appropriation bills come to us with such limited information that a vote either for or against isn't really an informed vote. I voted against it not because I knew it was wrong, but because I hadn't been persuaded it was right."[68]

What happened by the time Simon wrote that column was that Auditor Hodge admitted embezzling more than $2.5 million. The *Chicago Daily News* first exposed discrepancies in state checks processed by the auditor.

As other newspapers joined the hunt, Hodge made no comment, but Stratton wanted his resignation so that the scandal would pass. Under pressure, Hodge eventually relented and resigned as auditor, candidate for reelection, and delegate to the Republican National Convention. He told Stratton, "I just don't know why I did it. I didn't need the money." Indictments followed, and after a plea of guilty, Hodge went to prison, all in a period of weeks.[69]

Simon expressed personal disappointment in Hodge's fate in that "P.S." column. "I would have to admit that while I did not—and do not—approve of Hodge's actions, I can't help having some real regrets. Orville Hodge is a friendly fellow anyone would like just meeting him the first time . . . If Orville Hodge had used his personality and talents for good purposes, rather than robbing the people, he could have made a real contribution to better government in Illinois."

Early in the 1957 session, Simon added these details to his earlier comment about the vote:

> I would have to admit I've received more praise and publicity for that vote than I deserve. I didn't have the vaguest idea of the extent of the operations in Hodge's office. The reason I happened to vote against it was really rather simple. At the beginning of the session the Illinois Taxpayers Federation handed out some little booklets pointing out the expenditures made by the various offices over a period of years. I kept the booklet and when Hodge's requests came up I saw that they represented an increase of almost two million dollars with hardly any explanation. I had practically no information—yet enough to be able to vote correctly.[70]

Simon cosponsored a resolution that passed the House, calling for more adequate budgetary information before voting on appropriations.

In his autobiography, Simon added further to the story of his near-involvement. Mike Howlett, the Democratic candidate challenging Hodge for auditor in 1956, approached Simon after his vote against the appropriations. He had information about peculiarities in payrolls of Hodge's office. Howlett knew of Simon's journalism background and asked him to pass along the information to a newspaper. But Simon had no luck getting attention: "I contacted two people at the *St. Louis Post-Dispatch* and to my amazement they showed no interest . . . When they failed to do anything, I suggested that Howlett go to Basil 'Snuffy' Walters, editor of the *Chicago Daily News*."[71] George Thiem, the reporter assigned to the story by Walters, won a Pulitzer Prize for his Hodge stories and wrote a successful book about the scandal.

Corruption in Springfield

Although many public officials withered and retreated in silence when confronted with misdeeds in the Illinois legislature, a handful did not, and they kept up a valiant if frustrating fight. That group included Simon, who never seemed to let disappointments and rebuffs cool his enthusiasm to do all he could to expose the practices. While he fought often in the lead position, he also joined forces with others who wrestled with special interests. Chief among those were Mikva and Scariano, who returned Simon's respect and remained friends for decades.

By 1963, during his first term as state senator, Simon and his friends had made enough of a ruckus that the state's newspapers watched the action and reported the clashes. One observer was Alfred W. Balk, a former reporter for the *Chicago Sun-Times* who had turned to freelance magazine writing. He contacted Simon about joining forces on a magazine article that would expose corruption in the General Assembly. Simon liked the idea, and he had plenty of ammunition, if not specifics. He provided information from his experiences, and Balk added to it and wrote the article.[1] The collaboration caused an eruption rarely seen in the state.

Harper's magazine expressed interest in the article. By its nature—accusations against government officials—the article raised legal questions of libel. That and other editing issues delayed publication beyond December 1963 when Simon hoped it would appear. His preferred date played into an attempt to find someone to run against Paul Powell for secretary of state. Simon addressed these matters in a letter to Balk.[2] He wrote:

> If the *Harper's* legal department has trouble with it [the article], perhaps they can send it to me and I can tone it just a little differently, to keep the point but sound a little less filled with malice. If this can be done to make clear "malicious intent" is not present, this solves the legal problem, at least helps. In addition, it would help in the practical situation I will be facing—working with the man I wrote about. Originally we were thinking about this thing coming out in December of last year, which would have given any hot heads thirteen months to cool off. Now that time will be almost nonexistent and this could present a few practical problems for

me in the Senate. We might work this out to solve their legal problems and my practical problems at the same time. The Powell thing which you mention in your letter I would have to treat carefully also. We were hoping to bring it out before the slate-making, certainly before the primary. I phoned, wired, cajoled to try to get someone to run against him, but could not. Now the man he is running against is of the same breed, Elmer Hoffman. I feel there is in essence no choice and no reason for me to bolt the party. I would not want the article to indicate I was.

Supreme Court interpretations of libel law and the Constitution state that libel of a public official requires the plaintiff to prove "malicious intent."

Simon's concern about how the article would go down with members of the legislature, and especially the Senate, indicates his understanding of the unwritten rule that members did not divulge unpleasant news about each other. Also, having tried to interest two Chicago newspaper editors in investigating legislative corruption without success, Simon knew the subject matter presented problems. "We did not have something that could be easily proven," Simon admitted.[3] Regardless of the risks and realities, Simon indicated no thoughts of backing down or stopping publication.

The article appeared in the September 1964 issue of *Harper's* under the headline "The Illinois Legislature: A Study in Corruption."[4] That got the attention of many people. In the article, Simon dealt mostly in information for a magazine audience outside Illinois with a number of anecdotes about suspicious behavior previously published in the state. These were the article's essential parts: horse racing influences, featuring Paul Powell, who Simon never mentioned by name; the so-called West Side Bloc of Republicans whose ties to the Chicago underworld were well-known and documented; conflicts of interest, featuring complicity by both political parties; and a review of the Orville Hodge scandal with questions about its handling by officials. Much has been revealed since that time about shenanigans among legislators.

Perhaps the most provocative quote in the article was made by Noble W. Lee, a Republican representative and dean of the John Marshall Law School in Chicago. Lee, who had served eleven terms in the House, estimated that one-third of the members received payoffs, disguised as legal fees, public relations services, and campaign contributions. Neither Simon nor Lee provided any proof of the statement.[5]

Simon told a dozen or so anecdotes designed to demonstrate how payoffs worked without providing any corroborating evidence or names. A number of the citations were well-known incidents previously mentioned in newspaper articles and discussed in Simon's columns that appeared statewide.

Some stories obviously referred to tales about Powell, vague but providing enough information that many Illinoisans knew the central player. Readers unfamiliar with Illinois politics might have wondered about the veracity of the stories, especially when the culprit was not identified.

In one story that could only have been about Powell, Simon acknowledged, "There are rumors—which obviously I cannot verify," that a "prominent Representative" received $100,000 a session when his party was in power. In a discussion of legislative support for racetrack interests, Simon described the Chicago Downs stock deal that enriched Powell and his wife. The 1955 session tax reduction bill that favored the Cahokia Downs and Fairmount tracks received a lengthy review, with emphasis on the shortage of revenues in the state to meet other needs. Simon said, "We [Simon and Richard Stengel] were so ostracized that Stengel, in phoning me, quipped, 'Hello, Measles, this is Smallpox.'"[6]

The point of describing the West Side Bloc was to show the legislative connection with racketeers and describe how the bloc conspired with other legislators to quash bills that might lead to disclosure of special interests or provide improved law enforcement. The article described the bloc's members as "a few syndicate-backed Chicago aldermen, one state senator, and several representatives." A footnote mentioned that Charles H. Percy, Republican candidate for governor, had attempted to purge bloc members from public office, calling them "dry rot." Percy and sympathetic Republicans prevented bloc legislators from appearing on the 1964 ballot.[7] The bloc called Percy's action "dictatorship," and "un-American." One bloc member said, "You may be dynamite, Mr. Percy, but you better learn how to aim the dynamite."

Simon described efforts to establish an Illinois Crime Investigating Commission to look into illegal activities and suspicious behavior of public officials. Simon said, "In session after session, proposals to create a [commission] were defeated. Few legislators opposed the Commission publicly, though there were some who expressed sincere concern that it might be used for political purposes or would waste money." Finally, during the 1963 session, supporters tried again and succeeded. Simon credited "pressure from the press and civic organizations."[8]

Simon noted the legislature cut the commission's proposed budget in half and the new law prescribed that eight of the twelve members of the group would be legislators. He took offense at the refusal of House officers to appoint Representative Scariano, who sponsored the House bill, to the commission. Simon said the action broke "a long-standing tradition," and praised his friend from the Chicago area as "a courageous, honest suburban legislator who has aggressively fought organized crime."[9]

Simon cited egregious patronage abuses by both parties. He mentioned that one unnamed senator privately represented the state's largest highway contractor association. Among his clients was an engineering firm "organized just in time to win a $600,000 state contract for a toll road survey. Such conflicts of interest are common in both parties." Only a few legislators from downstate and a handful of independent legislators from Cook County argued against patronage deals. Simon said, "I am one."[10]

The article brought up the Hodge scandal, mentioning that Simon voted against the auditor's appropriation requests a session before the embezzlement surfaced. He added, "A thorough investigation and major reforms seemed imminent. Hodge was quickly tried, and convicted of misappropriating a portion of the total funds. Then he was hurried off to prison without extensive public questioning. Only minor fiscal reforms were enacted, and proposals for a full-scale legislative probe were defeated. In 1963, Hodge was paroled without ever having told his full story." Simon mentioned how Hodge was bribed with $35,000 by a utility company representative to get favorable treatment of a tax bill. The story underscored the cynicism of those dealing with legislators with a quote from the utility man: "We didn't think the fee was excessive. We got what we wanted. The fee was in line with what we were used to paying."[11]

At the conclusion of the article, Simon criticized the Illinois press for not paying enough attention to legislative affairs. "Only a handful of papers—most of them in Chicago—even attempt full-scale legislative coverage. All too rarely is even a roll call published statewide showing how legislators vote. Nor is there a complete daily journal of proceedings beyond the mere disposition of bills. Clearly, this lack of public scrutiny is an open invitation to mischief which, I fear, is equally present in many states."

The magazine was in great demand when it hit the newsstands in Illinois. Simon said, "*Harper's* had been on the stand only a few hours when it became a scarce item in the state. I tried to get a few extra copies and when I requested *Harper's* at one small newsstand in Springfield the vendor said, 'I could have sold 600 more copies of that magazine if I had them.'"[12] Simon's survey indicated that readers included "lobbyists, precinct captains, and some of our least articulate political leaders, many of whom perhaps had never even heard of *Harper's*."

Every legislative correspondent and major newspaper editorial page weighed in immediately. With few exceptions, they applauded the article. John Dreiske, political editor of the *Chicago Sun-Times*, expressed the cynical response: "Simon's 'expose' exposed nothing any correspondent assigned to cover the legislature has not already known. But this information really is quite useless because of the libel law protection given to those who pay money for votes in the state legislature. Any reporter at Springfield or here [Chicago], for that matter, 'knows' that this sort of thing goes on and he knows all of at least some of the persons who take money. But he cannot prove it legally and so he just periodically mumbles about it in print without names. And the bribery goes on apace."[13]

Dreiske characterized the reaction of legislators as "I've been in Springfield 20 years and I've never heard of any corruption there. If Simon knows of any, he should report it to the state's attorney or the Illinois Crime Investigating Commission." Simon said the reason he did not report it to a state's attorney was that he did not have the kind of evidence that a prosecutor could take to the grand jury. He did not tell the commission because eight of the twelve members were legislators.

Simon's irate Senate colleagues sent a loud message to their colleague at the annual dinner for members, attended by 800 people including most of the lobbyists in Springfield.[14] Simon chose not make an appearance. Party officials charged $10 per plate, with the profits going to Democratic and Republican leaders. During the festivities, Simon was presented the "Benedict Arnold Award." The presenter said previous winners were Aaron Burr and Judas Iscariot. Simon had violated the unwritten rule that legislators should remain silent about any subject that might reflect poorly on colleagues.

Simon may have been fortunate that the article appeared in September when the legislature was not in session. However, rumors proliferated in the months before the end of the year. Apparently some colleagues, including members of the crime commission, wanted a resolution of censure. On a radio program, Scariano blistered one member for talking about censure instead of having the commission start an investigation.[15] With newspapers joining in, the commission said it would investigate if the legislature did not. As the 1965 session opened, Speaker John Touhy, a Democrat, and Senate Majority Leader W. Russell Arrington, a Republican, issued a joint statement that there would be no legislative investigation and the commission should take on the challenge.[16]

Simon could see how matters were shaping up. The legislature did not want the chore of investigating its own members and kicked it over to the commission to relieve political pressure. With eight legislators on the commission, odds were that an investigation would be inconclusive, with the result that Simon's claims would evaporate in a bureaucratic haze.

The Illinois Crime Investigating Commission was created by statute in 1963, with twelve commissioners. The House appointed four members, the Senate four, and four others served at large. The Senators named at the time of the corruption investigation were Robert R. Canfield, John P. Meyer, Thomas A. McGloon, and Paul A. Ziegler. Representatives were George S. Brydia, Edgar Lehman, Leo Pfeffer, and Raymond J. Welsh Jr. Public members were David E. Bradshaw, Lawrence Morell Gross, Harlington Wood Jr., and Prentice H. Marshall. Senator Canfield and Marshall were co-chairs. Serving the commission as executive director was Charles Siragusa, former deputy director of the state Bureau of Narcotics, often credited with talking more about stopping crime than doing much about it.[17]

By law the commission had authority to investigate the "practices of public officials and employees which are inconsistent with any laws of the State." The commission staff interviewed 134 persons, including those charged with misconduct, those who had years of experience working with or observing the General Assembly such as writers and reporters, and Simon and Scariano. Relevant documents also were reviewed.[18]

The commission asked Simon to submit details of incidents involving legislator bribery or attempted bribery. He complied in a letter to Siragusa on January 22, 1965.[19] Simon quoted political reporters for the *Chicago Sun-Times* who said most reporters covering the state capital knew the charges to be true. Simon added, "The charges, then, are true and those who deny the charges do it either to protect themselves or because they are moral vacuums with political ambition." He asked the commission to send a letter to all legislators declaring:

1. That the commission recognizes that there has been abuse and that you intend to do what you can to stop it in the future.
2. Support for disclosure laws, both by the legislators and lobbyists.
3. Support of salary increases for legislators, to reduce the financial dependence of legislators on outside sources of income.
4. Support of Rep. Scariano's proposal for no legislators on the commission.

Simon's appendix to the letter mentioned thirteen incidents or reports of incidents, without disclosing any names. Some of the items were in the *Harper's* article. He mentioned two newspaper reports. "The *South End Reporter* disclosed that on the floor of the Senate an envelope containing money was handed to a member and returned." The other account, from an unnamed newspaper, reported that a legislator received a public relations fee, reportedly $20,000 for a year "when the legislature was in session and a bill greatly affecting that particular industry was under consideration." This report implicated Powell and his connections to the horse racing business. Subsequently, disclosures from Powell's tax returns revealed $92,200 in "finder's fees" from a horse racing insider in the period 1956 to 1966. Additionally, the $20,000 annual fee was paid directly from Chicago Downs to Powell for three years.[20] But little in the appendix could have helped the commission in its investigations.

The commission issued a six-page report essentially dismissing the charges made by Simon. It began by declaring the statement that one-third of the General Assembly was corrupt "while easily made, is virtually impossible to prove or disprove." The report rejected the charge that legislative members influenced the investigation outcome. It stated,

> Many of the allegations were vague, based upon hearsay or rumor and date back in some instances more than 15 years . . . The allegations are by their very nature extremely difficult to prove or disprove . . . Public hearings are unwarranted and would be grossly unfair in view of the nature of the allegations and results of the investigation . . . The facts adduced in these proceedings do not show any clear violation of existing Illinois conflict of interest law . . . The Commission concludes that none of the allegations of specific acts of wrongdoing are supported by substantial, admissible, credible evidence. Accordingly, the identity of those accused of these acts has been withheld.[21]

Regarding the Hodge affair, the report said, "Those who were guilty in the Hodge case have been punished. No good is served by a constant rehash of the charges made against them. Indeed, it is unjust to do so. The Hodge case should be laid to rest."[22]

In its discussion of conflicts of interest charges, the report stated investigations disclosed "situations in which persons having substantial direct pecuniary interests in particular business activities have assumed positions in state government in which they have been called upon to judge the nature and extent of governmental regulation of those business activities," and "situations in which members of the General Assembly have substantial indirect pecuniary interests in contracts paid for in whole or in part with state funds."

The commission called attention to conflict of interest legislation before the 1965 legislature and urged "serious consideration to regulating situations of the type described. They are not conducive to, and in fact tend to impair, the people's confidence in their government." This statement was the only concession to Simon's complaints.

In his "Sidelights from Springfield" column at the end of the 1965 session, Simon complained that a commission composed of three members of the House and three members of the Senate voted to postpone action to strengthen conflict of interest laws.[23] "The commission decision to avoid taking proper action is perhaps the great tragedy of this session," he wrote. The commission waited until two weeks before the end of the session to issue its report calling for a two-year study. Simon noted that the crime investigating commission had urged consideration of a change in existing law on conflicts, and he praised Canfield for saying the public trust was being abused and calling for changes in the law. The House overwhelmingly approved a conflict of interest bill, but it stalled in the Senate.

Simon believed the debate of his article and its accusations of misconduct generated discussion for positive changes in state laws on disclosure, criminal syndicate operations, and conflicts of interest. "For the first time in my eleven years in the legislature, we have something of a spirit of reform here in Springfield," he wrote in "Sidelights" while complaining the commission report was "worse than no report at all. It has given those who look for excuses, good cause to avoid slowing down abuses of a public trust."

All but two members of the crime investigating commission—Prentice H. Marshall and Harlington Wood Jr.—signed the majority report. Those two men, both of whom later became distinguished federal judges, wrote a twelve-page response that attacked each of the majority points, concluding the "report disposes of nothing. It is unfair to the people, the General Assembly, those who precipitated the investigation and the Commission. An entire branch of Illinois government has been accused of venality. The people are entitled to know if the accusation is true or false."[24] The minority report scrupulously followed rules of commission procedure that no testimony taken in executive session could be used without approval of the majority. This prevented release of evidence and factual material gathered by the staff and commission.

Marshall and Wood said four of seventy allegations of misconduct deserved a full explanation, with names of the parties and the witnesses. They said, "These factual reports should also include any explanation given by the person charged . . . At no time have we advocated publication of the identity of the accused in the remaining sixty-six allegations and the disclosure of the identity of all 134 witnesses who were questioned, and we do not advocate such a wholesale disclosure."[25]

The members said two additional cases regarding conflicts of interest came to the attention of the commission that deserved public scrutiny. "They are situations which should be frankly discussed to the end that an intelligent conclusion can be reached as to whether conduct of like character should be prohibited or regulated in the future. The majority refusal to engage in this meaningful discussion renders impossible a valid appraisal of the problems confronting our government."[26] The majority ignored the recommendations of the minority report.

Simon reported on one confrontation with Powell, then secretary of state, over the article's reference to an influential legislator getting $100,000 a session in bribes. In his autobiography, Simon called it "a none-too-veiled reference to Paul Powell." Powell testified before the commission, and afterward he asked Simon where he got the $100,000 figure. "I told him it was a widely circulated rumor. 'You can't prove that,' he told me. I assured him I could not. 'You shouldn't say it if you can't prove it,' he responded angrily. At no time in our fifteen-minute conversation did he deny the truth of the report but he obviously felt I had violated the unspoken rule of silence that legislators should follow to protect each other."[27]

Nine months after the *Harper's* article appeared, the legislature had done little to improve the government environment. The crime investigating commission dodged virtually all issues raised by Simon and Balk. The episode damaged Simon's standing with many in the legislature, although some offered him quiet encouragement. Mikva later observed, "It was a tough, tough year for Paul. He became known as the skunk in the church. I think he learned a lot from the experience. It was very brutalizing."[28]

Among his enemies in the Democratic party, few were willing to forgive and forget. When Simon came before the state Democratic slating committee a few years later seeking endorsement for statewide office, members confronted him about the accusations of corruption. He reminded the politicians that Balk did the writing and came up with some of the examples.[29] Election opponents cited reports that Simon told one Chicago official he was "misquoted" in the article, but Simon later denied he said that.

The boost to Simon's reputation came from the citizens of Illinois who were inclined to take him at his word, with or without evidence and named culprits. The charges sounded plausible given the low opinion people had of the General Assembly. Simon's ongoing call for more open government and increased vigilance for corruption rang clear, and elevated his star with many. What at times seemed a huge blunder on Simon's part had a silver lining.

6

Newspaper Mogul

Simon and his partners in the *Troy Tribune*, Johnsen and Fedder, had their eyes on the purchase of additional weekly papers. The three partners assumed that Fedder would move from Troy to manage the next paper purchased. While Fedder gave the *Tribune* additional strength in management, having all three partners associated with one weekly paper constituted a payroll burden.

The search for additional properties reflected confidence by Simon and the others of their ability to manage more than one newspaper.[1] None of the individuals had extraordinary financial resources. In 1955, Simon had total income of $7,180, a modest savings account, and a mortgage on a newly purchased home in Troy. Of his total income, $5,000 was from the state of Illinois for service as a representative and $1,413 from the *Tribune*. With confidence in their ability to operate a weekly paper successfully and a willingness to live with debt, Simon and his partners began to build a newspaper group in 1958 with purchase of the *Carterville Herald*. When the group was completed with ownership of fourteen papers including the one in Troy, the net result aside from cash profits was a major extension of Simon's name from his home base of Madison County to central regions of the state.

Carterville is a small southern Illinois town between Marion on the east and Carbondale on the west. In 1958, Carterville had a clear identity of its own and a weekly newspaper under the same ownership for just short of thirty-five years when Simon, Fedder, and Johnsen made the purchase in April. The paper had less than 900 subscribers at the time.[2] The newspaper announcement stated, "A town has one mouthpiece—its hometown paper and a town without a paper dies a slow and gradual death—just like a town without a bank dies."[3] The article highlighted Simon as "a newspaper man who fought successfully the rackets in his area." The article also mentioned his role in government: "Simon, who is a state representative, is most widely and very favorably known for his ability and his high standards of statesmanship." Typical of sale announcements, it praised the new owners, saying the paper "is falling into excellent hands and the town should rally to its support."

For their first acquisition in the group, the owners hired an editor—the title meant the person was the manager as well—with little newspaper experience. William Epperheimer had a southern Illinois background and was finishing his degree in journalism at Southern Illinois University in Carbondale.[4] Epperheimer remained editor about three years.

The saga of the successor to Epperheimer, one of the more intriguing episodes of Simon's acquisition of weekly papers and human relations experiences, began with the announcement of a new member of the *Troy Tribune* staff in July 1961: "The *Tribune* is fortunate to have an experienced newspaperman, Dave Saunders, join the staff. Dave has expressed himself as being very happy and appreciative of the fine treatment he has received already and that he knows he will enjoy his work here. Dave would be an asset to any newspaper staff and we are happy to have him with us."[5]

Shortly after the announcement, the *St. Louis Globe-Democrat* published an article under the headline "Murderer to Work for Troy Newspaper." It revealed that Saunders, who was twenty-nine years old, had been convicted and sent to Menard State Penitentiary in 1950 for killing a liquor store proprietor during a holdup in Paris, Illinois. At the time of the killing Saunders was seventeen.[6] A judge sentenced him to forty years in prison, but Governor William G. Stratton commuted the sentence to thirty-three years, which made Saunders eligible for parole. Simon said the St. Louis article shocked people in Troy, including the woman in whose home he had arranged as housing for Saunders.

Simon heard of Saunders from the chaplain at Menard who said Saunders had a clean record in prison and edited the prison newspaper, *The Menard Time,* a prize-winning publication. Simon and the chaplain had worked together on a plan to change the state parole system. Simon introduced a bill, which became law, calling for release of prisoners on good behavior ninety days early and giving them supervision on parole. To get an early parole, the inmate needed a job. Simon said, "I checked with the prison warden who spoke highly of Dave. I offered him a job, thinking we could handle things quietly in the community." Simon should have known better.

Just ahead of a parole hearing in 1961, Saunders wrote his parents, John D. and Orena Saunders of Garden Grove, California.[7] He mentioned their planned visit to Illinois a few weeks later and spoke of his upcoming hearing. "Don't worry about the hearing, now—everything is in fine shape. As far as newspaper jobs are concerned, we have my application in at the *Southern Illinoisan,* and Jack Mabley [of the *Chicago American*] and Paul Simon have written letters. Had a letter from Paul this week about writing the [parole] board—he added a very casual p.s. that two of the new members are friends of his and that he 'played a small part' in getting one of them his job, which he didn't think would hurt my chances."

Saunders wrote his parents that Simon "made me a good proposition for Troy . . . I'm taking it instead of something down here . . . Am writing Paul tonight to make arrangements for him to prod the release machinery a little and to authorize Ray Johnsen, his Troy editor, to sign my papers in [Simon's] absence . . . I think the surest way of being out is to make the arrangements with Paul. This is the job setup I'm going to present to the board."

Members of his family attended the hearing. Also present were the widow of the man he killed, her two daughters, and a son-in-law, who testified against parole. Saunders hoped for some indication of a decision from the board, but "I just don't know what to think."[8] He expected to hear from the board in about three weeks. A few days later his parents wrote Simon and his wife, Jeanne, thanking them for actively supporting the parole request. They started for Illinois to meet their son.

Paul and Jeanne, learning of the upcoming visit of Saunders' parents, said they would be out of town during that time but offered their home in Troy for the California visitors to use. The Saunders couple wrote, "When we first read David's letter [about the offer] our first reaction to accepting your generous hospitality was just unthinkable, as we'd never done anything like that. The more we thought about it, we felt we should accept your generosity, and we do humbly and gratefully if it works out that we will be in Troy before you return. Out of this terrible experience we have met some wonderful people and made some deep friendships."[9]

The board approved the application for parole, paving the way for Saunders' release and employment in Troy. In a few months, the editor's position at Carterville opened and Simon appointed Saunders to the job.[10] Although none of the three partners in the Carterville operation mentioned any difficulties during Saunders' tenure at the *Herald*, adjustments were necessary by all. Saunders said later in an almost perfect description of the editor's duties on a weekly paper, "Inside [prison], there was always someone else to make the decisions—and there was no economic problem. Now, I must make the editorial decisions as well as take care of advertising, circulation, and other purely business matters, as well as hire help, write news items and take care of mechanical work."[11]

Saunders took his role as editor seriously. In September 1962 he published "A Statement of Principle" on the paper's editorial page.[12] He reprinted a journalist's creed written by a former dean of the University of Missouri School of Journalism. The words might have been written by Simon, who surely agreed with the principles as stated. Saunders added to the creed,

"Any newspaper which lives by this creed cannot help but serve the public interest—and most newspapers do. The *Herald* has done, and will continue to do, its best to serve the interests of its readers and the people in this area." It was an appropriate statement in advance of Saunders' columns before the upcoming general election.

Simon encouraged all his editors to write a local column, as he had done successfully for many years. Saunders, who never lacked for opinions, called his column "Scrapbook." In an October 1962 column, he laced into a network television special on integration issues in Mississippi. Saunders said, "I was sickened as I watched nearly four hours of what was presented as factual news coverage."[13] He added the show "could hardly have been more distorted if it had been skillfully slanted to propagandize the public with the 'image' of the national administration." He called the presentation pleasing to President John F. Kennedy.

Saunders said the program was slanted to make Governor Ross Barnett look bad, an "attempt to make him appear a demagogue." He claimed most of the program placed Attorney General Robert Kennedy in a good light, while it stated Barnett had caused rioting by withdrawing state police from the University of Mississippi campus. "The program offered a brief statement from Barnett," Saunders said. "Personally, I am more inclined to believe the governor's version . . . I'll look for my factual news in the papers, where you can get every side of the picture." While he expressed concern over the program's balance, Saunders did not indicate sympathy for Barnett's views on integration.

This must have caused Simon's blood pressure to escalate. A week after Saunders' column, Simon provided an editorial page rebuttal that laid out a defense of the television program and Robert Kennedy.[14] He stated the reason for his column in the opening sentence: "Dave Saunders wrote a column last week with which those of us involved in the ownership of the newspaper strongly disagree." Simon then turned his cheek slightly, adding, "That's the way we want it. We want the editor to have the freedom to write what he wants, whether we agree or not. At the same time we want to make clear there is another side."

Calling on memories of his trip to Alabama and Mississippi in 1957 when southern governors and other officials resisted efforts at integration, Simon said he disagreed with Saunders' statement about the bias of television reporters.[15] He said if the report made Barnett look like a demagogue, "it was an accurate portrayal." Simon, a strong supporter of President Kennedy, said it was the president's duty to back up rulings of the courts, and Barnett had failed to do his duty. Much of the column discussed the importance of extending freedom and rights to all people. "'With liberty and justice for all' have to be words that we live, not just words written on paper," he added.

The episode and exchange of columns underscored Simon's leniency toward his editors for opinions with which he disagreed. It also revealed that Simon would exercise the rights of an owner to provide a second opinion. That attitude got an additional test in the days ahead.

Saunders had definite opinions about who should prevail in the fall elections across Illinois, and they did not match with Simon's ideas. The Carterville editor indicated to Simon that he intended to endorse incumbent U.S. Senator Everett Dirksen in the contest with U.S. Representative Sidney Yates of Chicago. Perhaps Saunders knew of Simon's disagreement with virtually everything Dirksen said and did, and his boss's earlier hope of running against Dirksen in 1962. Simon's response to Saunders in a letter repeated the editor's rights and the owner's, too. "In your column, feel free to do what you want, but I want to have the freedom to disagree with you, too. If you endorse Dirksen . . . I want to put in a word for Yates."[16]

Three days later on the *Herald* editorial page, columns by Saunders and Simon faced each other. After attacking President Kennedy for his handling of the attempt to overthrow Castro in Cuba, Saunders said the president was also wrong for recommending Yates to succeed Dirksen.[17] Simon devoted his entire column to praise for Yates, with biting criticism of Dirksen's approach to public policy and his positions. Of the senator, he said, "I recognize that he is a spell-binding speaker; but the record makes the words sound empty."[18]

The following week, Saunders mounted a further defense of Dirksen's record. He wrote, "Our country needs Senator Dirksen because his conservative voice raised in opposition helps to hold in check the drive toward one-party rule and to protect the rights of the minority."[19] This time there was no column by Simon on the other side of the page.

Although decidedly Republican in 1962 candidate endorsements, Saunders touted Democratic representative Kenneth Gray for Congress and Representative Paul Powell of Vienna for the state legislature. Speaking of Powell, who had clashed with Simon on dozens of policy issues through the years, Saunders said, "He has done so much for southern Illinois, and in fact, for the whole of the downstate area." He endorsed two Democrats in local races, but supported many more Republicans.

A day before the election, Saunders wrote Simon wrapping up the political subject with the owner. He asked for understanding by Simon of the approach taken with endorsements. He believed it helped the paper's reputation among readers. "I hope the way I handled it [politics] with my column was satisfactory with you. I am sure it has helped the paper here . . . because we've had so much comment—both from Democrats and Republicans—that they are glad to see the Herald taking a position of any kind again." He added bluntly, "Let's be honest, being so far away your columns aren't local enough to stir the Democrats here on the county level and besides this is a Republican town."[20]

Saunders offered some local gossip to support his point. "I learned Friday that after your column on Yates, the Herald was written off by the Republicans in a county meeting because they expected that you would make me endorse a straight Democrat ticket. After last week's paper they concluded that either you're a fine fellow or I'll be fired before this week's paper."

Later Saunders added a footnote to the political discussion. "I learned Sunday that during the campaign after I had endorsed Republicans, they had calls at Menard from county Democratic officials, and the Parole Board was also contacted, in regard to getting my parole taken and getting me back in Menard. We have nice Democrats down in this neck of the woods."

All things considered, matters in Carterville looked good in terms of his acceptance in the community, although Saunders admitted some concerns. "At first, I worried about what I would do or say when I had it [prison] thrown up to me. It has happened just twice and I did and said nothing. The people of Carterville have accepted me as a human being and as a newspaperman and judged me on what I am doing now rather than what I once did."[21] As far as relationships with Simon, their differences of opinion apparently did not have a lasting impact. Simon never said or wrote anything but praise for his Carterville editor.

Saunders continued as editor in Carterville until 1965 when the Simon group sold the *Herald*. He went to work at Southern Illinois University in Carbondale, retiring in 1993 as director of enrollment services for the College of Technical Careers. In 1999, the Southern Illinois Editors Association presented Saunders its Golden Em award as a master editor. He died in 2001 at age sixty-nine.

After beginning the search for additional weekly newspaper properties, Simon and his close associates anticipated installing Fedder as editor. That occurred when a deal was signed to purchase the *Metamora Herald* in June 1958.[22] Metamora provided a major step up in newspaper size from Troy and Carterville. When purchased, about 1,400 copies of the *Herald* went to subscribers each week.[23] The investor group was joined this time by Alan Dixon.[24]

The purchase ended the paper's long history of one-family ownership. The eighty-year-old proprietor, William C. Ryan, had invested fifty-three and a half years as editor and publisher. Simon, Fedder, Johnsen, and Dixon, all Democrats or in sympathy, found the editorial policy of the *Herald* compatible. Ryan never had wavered from editorial loyalty to the Democrats.[25]

Until Fedder got established, the public face of the ownership group belonged to a smiling and cordial Paul Simon. Soon after the purchase, Simon spent a week in Metamora, ushered from meeting to meeting by Bill Ryan. At the end of the week, Simon's column in the *Herald*, "P.S. by Paul Simon," sang Ryan's praises and waded through a list of thirty names of individuals he had met, including "two very friendly waitresses at Goldie's."[26] This was Simon at his handshaking, name-remembering best. While it was good business, Simon always left the impression that he enjoyed meeting new people.

Simon's characterization of Ryan for people who had known him as long as they had lived in Metamora included these observations: "It was interesting to see Bill Ryan greet people by their first names, know about the troubles they face and the vacations they've taken. When someone came in for a piece of information, Bill could almost unbelievably go right to the spot where it was and bring it out. On Thursday when the paper came out it was a hot day, and Bill was perspiring as he fed the sheets into the press. I was doing a little cleaning on the opposite side of the shop. It was good to see him working there: Bill Ryan of Metamora, a living legend."

Simon had stories to tell, too. He mentioned meeting Bill Ryan at a newspaper meeting about a decade earlier. "I had no idea that some day I might be connected with Metamora and the Metamora *Herald*." Simon knew Ryan's son "young" Bill, who worked as a reporter for the *Alton Telegraph*. In passing, Simon spoke warmly of his friendship with Fedder and said he enjoyed spending a week in Metamora. He promised to return "from time to time."

Two and a half years later in 1961, the Simon group had an opportunity to add a companion newspaper in the Metamora vicinity. The *Washburn Leader*, published in the *Herald*'s shadow about ten miles northeast of Metamora, had a paid circulation of just under 800.[27] The same four investors made the purchase. Fedder became editor of both papers, with the *Leader* printed in Metamora.

With the addition of papers in Metamora and Washburn, Simon extended his political voice beyond southern Illinois to north central Illinois, a stronghold of Republican votes where the Troy legislator had less visibility. While many of the papers in this region published his legislative "Sidelights" column during each biennial legislative session, his appearance as a newspaper owner and columnist created broader recognition with the public. Simon was no longer just a distant political voice; he had a stake in the prosperity of the region.

The weekly newspaper grapevine always seemed full of juicy opportunities, although only a small percentage panned out. In early January 1961, Ray Johnsen heard of papers for sale in west central Illinois, between Galesburg and Peoria.[28] Walter I. Shockey owned three properties, the largest being the *Abingdon Argus*. The other two papers were the *London Times* and *Avon Sentinel*. The investor group for the Abingdon papers included Simon, Johnsen, Fedder, Dixon, and two new names. The first was Carl Soderstrom, an attorney from Streator and a Republican member of the Illinois House of Representatives. The second was Robert Edmiston, who signed on as editor.

In the issue of April 20, 1962, Simon spoke for the first time as head of the ownership group, announcing Edmiston as the new editor and stressing his background in community newspaper work. Simon added, "Politically this paper will be independent. Bob Edmiston will call the shots as he sees them and will be free to write what he wants . . . I am involved in publishing newspapers in four other communities. In the process of thirteen years of publishing I think I've learned a little about the newspaper field. I frankly feel that this area offers some real opportunities. But all of us involved in the purchase of the newspaper are aware that this paper will grow only as your community grows."[29]

Again, Simon appeared as the public face of the purchase, although Edmiston would be the resident representative. This was not just a step up in purchase price and debt, but in size, coverage area, income potential, and staff resources. The *Argus* had a circulation of about 1,600 paid subscribers, the *Sentinel* 375, and the *Times* about 200.[30]

As the group acquired more papers, requests for appearances by Simon in the communities and pleas for time to discuss decisions increased. In the case of Abingdon, Edmiston frequently asked Simon when he would be able to visit. On one occasion in the first year of ownership, Edmiston wanted Simon to address the local Rotary Club. Simon's reply gave a glimpse of the pressures on his time and finances: "I think I had better take a rain check on your Rotary program . . . Right now I am trying to get my head above water financially after an expensive [1962] primary campaign."[31] Edmiston followed with a letter that opened, "Are you planning to come up anytime soon?" A few weeks later he asked, "Will you be coming up our way one of the days now, Paul?"

Not far from the Abingdon papers, Daniel E. Maher owned weekly papers published in Elmwood, Williamsfield, and Yates City, all hugging the border of Knox and Peoria counties. Maher wanted to sell in 1964, and published a "for sale" article stating the combined circulation of the three as 1,400 weekly, published in towns with a total population of 3,000. The Simon group purchased the papers on September 1.[32] About the same time as the Elmwood purchase, the Simon group added the *Farmington Bugle*, published not far from the other six papers. The paper had a weekly circulation of about 1,000.[33]

Virtually on the eve of the 1962 election in which Paul Simon sought a seat in the Illinois state senate, his ownership group announced purchase of the *Roodhouse Record*.[34] Roodhouse was in Simon's senate district. He had an opportunity for headlines that cast him in a positive light at a politically advantageous time.

The Simon group became only the third owner of the *Record*. Grover Shipton and his wife had bought the *Record* in 1955 from Frank Merritt Jr. In his last column before turning the paper over to Simon's group, Shipton wrote, "Paul Simon is, by the way, a long time friend. As a newspaperman of vast practical experience, he's a 'roll up your sleeves' worker. The same philosophy applies to his political life. He's state representative now, and will become, I'm sure, your state senator for this district come the November election."[35] Simon could not have written a better statement of the connection between journalism and politics in his life. Simon group investors for this venture looked slightly different from their other newspaper purchases. Joining the familiar names of Simon, Fedder, Dixon, and Soderstrom was Martin Simon, Paul's father and author of religious magazines and articles.[36]

Simon's visibility in the purchase matched or exceeded public exposure in Carterville and Metamora. On the day of Shipton's last column, a story introducing the new owners appeared on page 1, along with Simon's photograph. Simon stated familiar first words after a purchase: "We like Roodhouse and this community and we want the *Record* to continue to be a community asset. The *Record* can only grow and prosper as the community prospers. We hope to help the community to do that."[37]

Following a pattern established in other communities, Simon took to the streets of Roodhouse, with Shipton in tow, to meet the town's merchants. He stayed a week to meet with subscribers. Until a new editor was named, Simon said he would serve as interim editor, spending several days a week in Roodhouse. The first of Simon's column "Sidelights from Springfield" after purchase appeared in the *Record* in early 1963.

Hardly any time passed before another opportunity occurred in the vicinity of Roodhouse. In the spring of 1963 Simon began negotiations with Malinda Jennings, an owner of the *Winchester Times*. The other owner was

Richard Y. Rowe Sr. In the *Times* of July 12, Jennings, who had operated the paper by herself for nine years, informed subscribers of the new ownership headed by Simon.[38] In a separate announcement, Simon said all employees would be retained. A week later the paper ran a notice signed by Simon, under the heading "Proud to Be Part of Your Area."[39]

Simon had a way of communicating in a friendly manner designed to reassure advertisers and subscribers that he and other investors were pleased to be part of the community. He wrote, "I well remember the first time I came to Winchester. Because of my interest in history, my wife and I came here to see the Stephen A. Douglas statue. Living in a large, old home, we were also impressed by the many beautiful large old homes you have in your community." He added, "The business district looks good. Businesses appear to be progressive. Like every small community, people are friendly. But there is unquestionably some added 'something' that Winchester has. And that something is good."

As Simon had done in other purchases, he addressed the issue of partisanship and expectations of subscribers. "Associated with the purchase are both Democrats and Republicans. The Winchester Times will be a politically independent newspaper, calling the shots as we see them, and not hesitating to criticize wrong if it occurs by those in either party. The aim is to publish a good community newspaper, not a party organ." Fedder left Metamora to manage operations in Winchester and Roodhouse.[40]

The final piece of the picture fell into place in April 1965 with purchase of the nearby *White Hall Register-Republican* by the Simon group.[41] It completed an efficient cluster of papers, all of which could be printed in a single plant. Fedder assumed management control of White Hall as well. The weekly White Hall circulation of nearly 1,500, was added to 1,500 in Winchester and 1,200 for Roodhouse.[42]

With the White Hall purchase, Simon and his group of investors owned fourteen weekly newspapers spread across the lower half of the state. Simon personally engineered the purchases, maintained the role of principal, and with Fedder and Johnsen guided the properties to a position of profitability that allowed the owners to pay off debt. The political benefit to Simon was obvious, providing business ownership and public awareness across a major portion of the state. The accumulated papers had a weekly circulation of more than 13,000. The group did not remain the same for long, however. Almost simultaneously with the addition of White Hall in 1965, Simon, Fedder, Dixon, and Johnsen sold the papers in Metamora and Washburn. That left Simon and investors with the *Troy Tribune,* Abingdon newspapers, and the Winchester cluster.

A series of events in 1965 or earlier, convinced Simon that his ownership and involvement with the weekly papers should come to an end. Simon said he had to make a major equipment decision while he was busy with state business during the legislative session. He wrote that episode "moved me to decide on something I had contemplated earlier: to divest myself of my newspaper holdings."[43] He denied that the papers caused a conflict of interest with ambitions for higher office, saying they were "too small." He recalled efforts through the years not to use the papers in self-promotion. No matter how hard he tried to play it down, they did provide name recognition and political reach.

While those reasons cited by Simon may have been in play, another concern was his health. Gene Callahan, who later became a trusted staff member and political adviser, said in an interview that a doctor told Simon he could not continue to run newspapers, work in the legislature, and write books with a bleeding ulcer. Callahan said, "Simon decided to get out of newspapers and stay in politics."[44]

On January 6, 1966, Simon announced his decision to sell the *Troy Tribune*.[45] He wrote, "It has become increasingly clear that I cannot continue to do justice to my legislative duties, requests for writing books and magazine stories, and to my newspaper responsibilities. Reluctantly, I have determined to gradually dispose of the newspaper properties which I own. In the case of the Troy Tribune, the decision was made easier by the fact that Ray Johnsen and Elmer Fedder know the community and will continue to give this area a fine newspaper." The *Tribune* did not stay in the Fedder-Johnsen fold long. A few years later they sold it, and Johnsen ended up serving as an aide in Simon's political offices in Illinois and Washington. In 1969 Johnsen was elected from Simon's old senate district as a delegate to the 1970 Illinois Constitutional Convention.

Simon, Fedder, and Johnsen sold their interests in the Abingdon papers to Edmiston, and Simon sold his holdings in the Winchester papers to Fedder, Johnsen, and his father, Martin. By late 1966 when Simon ran for reelection to the state senate, he had sold his entire interest in a business he started in 1948 at the age of nineteen. He received payments for his stock and interest on the unpaid balances for a number of years.

Aside from the income, interest, and sale of stock, what did Simon have to show for eighteen years in the newspaper business? Throughout the remainder of his political career and the writing of books and magazine articles, Simon called attention to his experiences as a newspaper owner and journalist. In Troy, he built a reputation as a crime fighter that those who wrote about him seldom failed to mention. The involvement with weeklies gave Simon a strong feeling for living and working at the grassroots of America and for the needs of people committed to life outside urban centers.

The keys to Paul Simon's ability to create and perpetuate a political identity were communication, consistency, and visibility. He mastered all first as publisher of the *Troy Tribune*. As an anticrime journalist, he used the newspaper voice to identify culprits, to call for action by elected officials, and to point out how corruption affected the lives of everyday people. He took risks that others were unable or unwilling to take to get attention and to lift himself and his issues to an expanded audience. He paid a personal call on houses of prostitution, sued the sheriff and pleaded his case before a grand jury, attempted to get the state's attorney censured, and appeared before a nationally televised anticrime hearing in St. Louis. Consistency and visibility moved him to the forefront of an anticrime crusade.

In the legislature, Simon needed a voice. To get that he generated a newspaper column during legislative sessions that circulated among as many as 300 newspapers statewide. He commented on issues that fit his agenda of open government and pleaded for care of the state's needy citizens. He became an activist in the legislature by contesting the status quo and those he believed were taking the state down the wrong road. He angered the leadership and colleagues, but he did not stop. In a national magazine, Simon called these people corrupt, something few other officials would have done.

From his first days in the legislature, he declared personal positions that he followed as long as he served in office. He made a public statement of his income every year, he disclosed details of his expenses for reelection, and he pressured others to do the same. He called for open meetings and open documents laws where there were none. Simon claimed as his own any issue that was about "good and open government." Simon owed a great deal to the *Troy Tribune* where he first learned that what succeeded and sold papers in Troy could build a larger audience and pay big political dividends.

Spreading His Words

Among Simon's many opportunities for public attention, none served as consistently well, and as long, as the columns he wrote for papers across the state during seven legislative sessions. People knew more about where he stood than almost any other lawmaker. He provided the column, called "Sidelights from Springfield," during sessions of the General Assembly at no cost to the newspapers. Many papers using the columns had no correspondent in Springfield or access to journalistic efforts in legislative matters.

While Simon was a legislator and a dedicated Democrat, he maintained the aura of an independent voice. Sid Landfield, editor of the Mt. Sterling *Democrat-Messenger,* offered this testimonial about the column: "Just this note to let you know that your current column, having to do with schools, is a dandy and voices many of my sentiments, so I decided to run it this week on our front page. This is a first for any political column."[1]

Chuck Hayes, editor of Paddock Publications in Arlington Heights, eventually became a strong supporter of Simon's political ambitions. His organization published papers in twelve suburban Chicago communities. Hayes used Simon's legislative column in his papers before becoming a political backer. In a letter to Simon in late 1958, Hayes asked a series of questions about prospects for the column in the 1959 legislative session. He also offered a supportive comment. "It's that time of year when we appraise the year past, savor our accomplishments, rationalize our failures, and anticipate the year ahead and all it promises. I know it's been a good year for you, and I am confident that 1959 holds much in store for our progressive young legislator. It will be a particularly meaningful year for Paddock Publications if we may count on once again publishing your thoughtful commentaries on the general assembly."[2]

Simon's journalistic experiences frequently worked to his advantage among newspaper editors, no matter their partisan leanings. His background in newspapers broke down the routine skepticism of editors about politicians selling their wares. A good example occurred at the end of the 1961 legislative session, in an editor's note appended to Simon's final "Sidelights" column for the term. Joseph J. Cullen, editor of the *Flanagan Home Times,* wrote:

It has been a pleasure to bring Representative Simon's "Sidelights" to our readers. His column differs from most columns of this nature, in that they are personally written. So often a legislator offers a column to a paper, and if accepted, the first few are interesting, but soon it is common knowledge to the readers that it is written by a secretary, or a press agent and its interest vanishes. Being a publisher in private life, Mr. Simon is aware of this, and it is the editor's opinion that he goes to great lengths to present his views in his own manner, and in a way that holds the interest of readers.[3]

Simon's legislative columns touched on many of the hot-button issues facing the state and the elected decision makers. For the breadth of issues, and for their civil tone, the columns are notable. Rarely did Simon take a personal swipe at any other legislators, friend or foe, and he handed out compliments sparingly. When he took a position, he stated it precisely and explained his reasons. He often presented the opposition arguments as part of his discussion. In many ways, it was a conversation about the workings of the legislature as well as a position paper on the issues. He took readers inside to educate them about their public servants. Other legislators might have drawn an entirely different list of significant issues, for Simon did have his points of view. Nonetheless, he avoided concentrating on the same issues time and again unless to update progress or lack of it. Given the arguments he had with Paul Powell and the racetrack crowd, for example, he might have commented endlessly on that subject. Rather, he said just enough to remind readers of his position that betting on horses should be taxed at a higher rate.

Among the subjects before the legislature, he wrote most frequently about crime, education, and taxes, all mainstream subjects before the House and Senate. Following are some of the statements he made about those subjects over the years.

Crime. With his background of fighting crime in his home district, Simon supported direct involvement by state law enforcement, although local officials in most counties preferred for the state to stick to traffic citations. In a 1957 column, he faced the issue of whether the state police should participate in gambling raids. "If the state police close down the gambling operations, you would think that law enforcement officials would be pleased at the assistance they are receiving. If they're not happy because the state police are making raids, sometimes it may be because these 'law enforcement officials' are interested in seeing to it that the gambling continues."[4]

Simon noted that governors Stevenson and Stratton used state police to raid gambling operations "when in their opinions, law enforcement has not taken care of the job. That seems to me to be a wise policy. The influence of the professional gambling element has not been a healthy one for our government. If we can use the state police to lessen that influence, they will be performing a rightful and necessary function."

In the 1959 session, a movement began for a referendum to legalize bingo for nonprofit organizations. In his legislative district, Simon reported that 6,000 persons had signed petitions in support of the measure, but he said, "I am personally opposed to the proposal and will vote against it if it comes up for a vote."[5] He cited three reasons for his opposition:

1. Our experience in Illinois with legalized gambling has not been a happy one. At the present time horse racing offers our only legalized gambling. Some of the elements interested in horse racing in Illinois are not the best. In addition, the racetrack lobby is probably the most powerful in Springfield.
2. Studies indicate clearly that many of those who lose money at bingo are those least able to afford it.
3. It will be difficult to establish legalized gambling without having criminal elements moving in before long.

A bill to establish an Illinois crime commission came before the legislature during Simon's first term as a senator. The bill had appeared before only to be defeated. Simon's column on the subject recited a litany of crime influence in Illinois before calling the proposal "one important weapon in this constant war against the underworld."[6] He pointed a finger at the legislative interests that had defeated similar proposals in the past. "The same votes which are ready to go out of their way to do favors for the race tracks are opposed to a crime commission." The legislature created a crime commission during the 1963 session.

Education. On a number of occasions, Simon spoke in favor of a board of higher education to eliminate duplication of degrees and programs and reduce building costs. He said, "Competition is good, but when state universities fight each other, and the legislature has to guess who should be the winner, two sure losers are the taxpayers and the cause of education."[7] As evidence of the need, Simon described the argument between Southern Illinois University and the University of Illinois over creation of an engineering program at SIU. "Speaking frankly and practically, the winner will not be determined by which school has the better cause, but by which school can exert greater pressure on members of the legislature." When another state university asked for creation of its own board, Simon objected, saying, "Instead of another board spending time, postage and printed matter coming to the legislature for the special interests of one school, we need an over-all board to take a

thorough look at our universities' needs and present a balanced program."
On another occasion, Simon called for coordination of community colleges
to improve academic standards.[8] The Board of Higher Education was created
in 1961 with authority over all public colleges and universities.

Simon also wrote about the need for a state board of education with jurisdiction over elementary and high schools. He cited the need for long-range
planning instead of the session-to-session approach that had prevailed. "For
our high schools and elementary schools we tend to live from legislative
session to legislative session, from emergency to emergency, not sure of the
direction in which we are heading." He recommended a state board of education "not to replace any local school boards or assume their authority, but
to take the long range look at our problems."[9] As part of the plan, he recommended making the state superintendent of public instruction an appointed
officer rather than elected. He added, "These two suggestions can easily be
combined in a board of education whose duty it would be to appoint the state's
top school man. If we take it out of politics, I think we'll find some answers to
our educational problems that may not be politically popular but are sound."
A state school board was created that now appoints the superintendent.

Taxes. In his first legislative session, Simon argued numerous times
against raising the sales tax to cover state programs, no matter how needy.
His remedy, years before it happened, was to have a state income tax. Until
then, he suggested finding revenue sources in the nooks and crannies of
state government or broadening the application of current levels of the sales
and property taxes.

In a titanic battle over Governor Stratton's proposed half-cent increase
in the sales tax in 1959, Simon expressed his opposition by voting with
House Democrats led by Chicago interests. But Powell, who had become
speaker of the House by defeating Mayor Daley's choice for the job, held
onto thirteen downstate Democratic votes. Those, combined with all but
six Republican votes, provided the margin for passage, 92 to 79. Powell's
plea for the tax increase was to provide increased funding for schools. Simon was joined on the losing side by the "Young Turks," Mikva, Scariano,
Dixon, and Hurley.

In a 1959 column, Simon stated his opposition to the sales tax increase. He
wrote, "Illinois has the questionable distinction of having one of the most
'regressive' tax structures of any state in the United States. Economists who
have studied our tax structure have been very critical, stating that we have
great inequities."[10] He called for a state income tax, joining labor unions and
the Farm Bureau in the request, but noted that both party platforms in 1958
opposed such an answer. An income tax was approved in 1969.

A sales tax increase returned to the legislative agenda in 1961, this time proposed by Democratic governor Otto Kerner. Instead of an increase in the sales tax rates, Kerner recommended broadening the tax to cover items not taxed. Simon noted that an individual building his own home paid sales tax on the lumber, plumbing, nails, and other materials, but "if you can afford to have a contractor build the home, not a penny is paid in taxes on the same material that goes into that home."[11] Kerner also proposed increasing the corporate tax, which concerned Simon. "What needs to be done is to increase this tax without creating an unfavorable tax climate for business in the state," said the man who owned a number of newspapers in Illinois. A one-cent sales tax increase was approved.

Throughout most sessions Simon addressed various social issues. He asked for more funds for mental health. He became an outspoken opponent of capital punishment, and if the legislature took up any matters that infringed on the activities of labor unions, he jumped to the defense. He argued against discrimination in housing, a hot topic in the legislature. Simon picked some unusual issues, too, such as the proposed bonus for Korean War veterans. An Army veteran of that time, Simon stood to receive $240 under the proposed bill. He believed the state could find a better place to spend the money, such as funding schools, providing for disabled people, assistance for the aging, and a handful of other social services. He commented, "I believe that men in uniform serve our country in the belief that our government stands for the very finest. I am true to their trust when I help our government stand for the finest."[12] He expected to be in the minority on the proposal, and was one of just four House votes against putting it on the ballot. The proposal failed in a statewide vote.

Simon continued his fight for a more open and accountable state government with columns on campaign expenses and contributions. In a 1959 column, he spoke from personal experience with disclosure of campaign costs. He said, "In my district I make a public statement of my campaign contributions and expenses and my personal income. This is something which the voters in my district are entitled to know—and it's a healthy thing for me personally. If a contribution is offered about which I have any question, perhaps the fact that I'm going to make it public will help me say 'no.'"[13] In his three previous campaigns, he spent from $1,900 to $3,800, the bulk of which came out of his own pocket. "During these three campaigns I have received few voluntary campaign contributions and five times I have declined sizable campaign contributions which were offered 'with no strings attached.'" He called for a state law on disclosure but added, "Frankly, I don't think this will happen." The idea was adopted years later.

In the course of his many columns published statewide, Simon took an occasional unpopular position—such as opposing the Korean bonus—or argued against the conventional wisdom. An off-beat position he promoted was outlawing professional boxing. He argued, "Professional boxing is a 'sport' only in the sense that Nero's throwing Christians to the lions was a sport. It is the only 'sport' in which the goal is physical injury to the opponent."[14]

Living in downstate Illinois, he understood the animosity that prevailed against Chicago political interests. While hardly an ally of the Chicago legislative agenda, Simon argued against knee-jerk opposition to reapportionment of the legislature to meet a court decree in the mid-1960s. Simon acknowledged a fear on the part of citizens that with reapportionment, Chicago would control both houses of the legislature. He explained how that fear connected with the patronage system in Cook County: "Illinois has a patronage base for its politics and through control of patronage the head of the party in Cook County has considerable control of the vote by Cook County legislators, whether the party leader is a Democrat or a Republican. There is always fear when a large group of votes is controlled."[15] He asked, "How real is the Cook County vs. Downstate fight?" He answered, "Not as real as most people imagine. In more than 10 years in the legislature I have never seen a vote which was divided exactly Cook County vs. Downstate. In those 10 years, I have heard more than 30,000 roll calls." He believed that with reapportionment came the potential for more independent legislators. "In my opinion this is all for the good." He also noted that suburban legislators often voted with downstate interests. "All of this means that those who fear the worst out of the reapportionment of this session may be in for a pleasant surprise."

Changes in the legislative process, and what Simon believed were improvements, drew his support. He spoke for annual sessions instead of the biennial meetings and supported expenses for personal staffs, neither of which occurred until the late 1960s. On annual sessions he argued, "The legislature is the board of directors of the state. It would be ridiculous for a one million dollar business not to have a board of directors meeting except every two years—and the state of Illinois is a three billion dollar business."[16] He mentioned the increased load of legislative business in recommending a two-month session in May and June in the off year. "This would give us time to handle emergency measures and other items of a pressing nature," he said, acknowledging there was little sentiment for annual sessions and the additional cost.

Simon's column also provided an occasional lesson in state government. He made no excuses for a legislative system that at times appeared broken, or not up to the demands of a growing population and increased social needs. He complained when sentiments expressed in his mail leaned toward issues of lesser importance, such as the state bird.

Simon rarely lapsed into a completely negative column. However, at the end of the 1961 session he figuratively threw up his hands in disgust. "In many ways it has been a depressing meeting of the legislature—depressing because things that should have happened did not happen, and many bills which should not have passed, did pass."[17] He cited an increase in the sales tax, no increased tax on racetracks, and defeat of a proposed crime commission. In conclusion he stated, "I have served four terms but this was my most discouraging session."

At the end of a legislative session, Simon never forgot to urge greater public involvement in the affairs of state, and he always thanked the host newspaper for providing his column. He was at their mercy, and he knew it. At different times his wife, Jeanne, and mother, Ruth, received his thanks for helping distribute the columns.

The "Sidelights" columns served essential purposes: to provide Simon's thoughts about business in Springfield for people across the state and push his idea agenda. During his legislative years, his readers were potential constituents in addition to those who lived in Troy and his district. Simon also needed to maintain contact with readers of the *Tribune* at other times, the off years when the legislature did not meet and the rest of the year after the six-month session. He called the local column "P.S. by Paul Simon."

A survey of his "P.S. by Paul Simon" columns from 1956 through 1962, when he was elected to a four-year term as state senator, indicates a more folksy, local touch, similar to what appeared in his "Trojan Thoughts" columns before he became a legislator. Occasionally he touched on a legislative issue, such as the Korean bonus that he opposed and capital punishment that he wanted outlawed. Elections also were held in the even-numbered years, and he was on the ballot. Keeping in touch and reminding people that he had not left town was important, although he spent less and less time on *Tribune* business.

Simon made his mark with Troy readers beginning in 1948 by conversing with them every week. While he did not hit every week after his 1954 election to the legislature, he chose subjects that kept locals reading. He commented on a popular Troy citizen who had died, pitched hard for a library, talked about the *Tribune* moving to a new office, and addressed the need for a four-year college in the region while jumping on the bandwagon for the Southern Illinois University campus at Edwardsville.

Before the statewide and federal elections, Simon let everyone know of his choices and why. In 1956 when Adlai E. Stevenson faced off a second time against President Dwight Eisenhower, Simon remained loyal to his Democratic friend. He cited two reasons for supporting Stevenson: he could provide world leadership and he had the courage to be unpopular when demanded. Simon acknowledged the popularity of President Eisenhower, but he hoped voters could distinguish between popularity and world leadership.[18]

Simon rarely expressed support for candidates other than Democrats. He lined up solidly for John F. Kennedy for president, Paul Douglas for Illinois senator, and anyone against Senator Everett Dirksen. Simon's faithfulness to Douglas was expressed in a letter to the senator dated September 13, 1950. Simon included this confession: "Somehow you manage to kindle a flame in my heart as so very few do."[19] In 1956, his legislative colleague Richard Stengel sought Dirksen's seat, unsuccessfully. Hoping to change the habit of party leaders, mainly the mayor of Chicago, in choosing nominees for state offices, Simon backed former Democratic national party chairman Stephen A. Mitchell for governor in 1960. The organization-backed candidate, Kerner, won easily. Simon walked a careful line when it came to being a party maverick, and when his candidate failed, he joined in backing the party's nominee.

Simon's support of Mitchell—a moderate Democrat who had never held public office in Illinois—brought him in open conflict again with Paul Powell. In 1958, well before the 1960 Democratic primary, Mitchell's name surfaced as a possible nominee. Powell, with whom Mitchell had quarreled over party issues, went on the attack. At a party gathering in July, Powell berated Mitchell, calling him a "phony" and a "cry baby." In an open threat to Mitchell and his followers, Powell said if no one else ran for governor as a Democrat he would run just to deprive Mitchell of the nomination. Powell said, "There's nothing I'd rather do than debate issues all over the state against that cry-baby who is trying to be a candidate for governor." A year later, before the Democratic hierarchy in the state named Kerner as its favorite for governor, Powell said he wouldn't run unless it was to oppose Mitchell. Powell said he would win "because I think the people would prefer my kind of state government to his." Simon maintained his support of Mitchell through the primary. Kerner put an end to Mitchell's ambitions, and Powell never had to make good on his threat.

In "P.S." columns of 1958, Simon spoke against the death penalty, noting that it was a penalty reserved mostly for poor people. "If you have the money to hire the best attorneys, you won't get the death penalty," he wrote.[20] On the fall ballot, he addressed a proposed $248 million bond issue to finance buildings for state universities and welfare institutions. He preferred a "pay-as-you-go" approach to state capital expenditures rather than incurring large debts for future generations to pay. He feared passage of the bond issue would delay the state in recognizing the need for a state income tax. He said the issue was not whether the projects were necessary but how to pay for them.[21] The proposal failed on a statewide ballot.

The capital issues reappeared on a ballot in 1960. This time the legislature provided two separate requests for voters, one for higher education capital expenses and one for health and welfare institutions. Simon voted to put the measures on the ballot but did not support them for the same reasons as in 1958. The measure passed, with $25 million set aside for beginning work on the SIU-Edwardsville campus. Voters of Madison County overwhelmingly approved the bond issues. His opposition to large bond issues and support of pay-as-you-go financing continued through his years in state and federal governments.

When not at work on legislative matters, Simon wrote magazine articles and book reviews and began a routine of foreign travel that took him to the Middle East, Asia, and Europe. He wrote articles about the travels for the *Tribune* and any other papers that would take them. With the off-session columns for the *Tribune,* there hardly seemed a moment when Simon wasn't pounding on what he called his "old clunker" typewriter.

The range of subject matter established the Troy editor as something of a Renaissance man. Beginning in the 1950s and continuing in the 1960s, he submitted articles to publications such as the *Christian Science Monitor, Christian Century, Saturday Evening Post, Progressive, Commonweal, Journal of Social Philosophy, Quill, Atlantic Monthly,* the magazine of the Lutheran Church–Missouri Synod, and the *American Salesman.* He wrote letters to the editors of newspapers and did book reviews for the *St. Louis Post-Dispatch* and the *Christian Century* on religious and specifically Lutheran subjects. Some were published, others rejected.

Simon wrote on a multitude of subjects, many having to do with religion, such as "Your Post-Election Responsibilities," "Montgomery Looks Forward" (about civil rights in Alabama), "Responsible Citizenship," "Let's Integrate Our Teachers More Rapidly," "The Christian and Politics" (based on talks at Lutheran gatherings), "Answering Your Questions about Christians and Politics," "Anti-Communism Loses Its Punch," "Catholicism and the Elections," "Dirksen's Opponent in Illinois" (about Richard Stengel),

"Church-Related Colleges Face Some Years of Struggle," and "What Do Your Legislators Think of You?"

Simon was a throwback to earlier times when he reported from travels to foreign countries. Before average citizens had the money and inclination to travel abroad, or there were commercial organizations devoted to providing trips, newpaper editors and publishers felt an obligation to inform citizens of issues, people, and places in other countries. The articles also provided tax deductions for travelers. Simon's accounts offered a meaty slant on foreign affairs and rarely lapsed into a travelogue of beautiful places.

On his foreign trips, Simon occasionally traveled with other legislators and sometimes with his wife Jeanne. In October 1957, after his second Illinois legislative session, he went to Europe, the Mideast, and Russia with a dozen legislators from seven states. Simon talked with a travel agency about pulling together a group of legislators for the journey and sent a letter to every state legislator in the United States.[22] For his work assembling the group, Simon traveled free. He also made some money on the journey by selling articles to Illinois newspapers.

As expected, the legislators were treated to sites and introduced to people that tourists would not encounter. They toured Tunisia and talked to leaders trying to establish a democratic society. "In this Arab country there is as much excitement, intrigue, and world politics as we experienced in 1776. And talking to their leaders . . . it is not difficult to imagine yourself talking to our early fathers," he wrote.[23] In his article exploring the problems and opportunities facing Tunisia, the eye of a reporter was evident.

One highlight of the trip was an audience with Pope Pius XII at his summer residence away from Rome. Simon, a devout Lutheran, reported through the eyes of a Protestant in a Catholic setting. During the audience, the pope greeted each politician individually. He apparently thought the twelve were senators. Simon reported, "When he was told that I was only a representative he wanted to know where I was from. When Illinois was mentioned he asked, 'Chicago?' I hate to disappoint the 1,500 proud residents of my hometown but 'Troy, Illinois' didn't seem to click . . . All of us—Catholic and Protestant alike—felt a bit moved by this 82-year-old gentleman who shoulders one of the world's most difficult positions."[24]

In Tel Aviv, Israel, and later in nearby Jordan, Simon discovered countries and people living without peace and experiencing the hatred that influenced daily lives. In Russia, Simon found reasons to appreciate "the freedom we are so fortunate to have."[25] After a visit to Poland, Simon wrote a summary column in which he reviewed the international tensions he had witnessed.

He concluded, "If I were to add one final word it would be that we must increasingly view our current world struggle in terms of human beings . . . If we have the finest [weapons] the world has ever seen, and do too little to meet the needs of the hungry, the dirty, and the illiterate, we shall lose."[26]

In writing of foreign trips, Simon occasionally touched on a subject that he would revisit over the years on his political path in Illinois and in Washington, D.C. In a series of columns for *Tribune* readers in the fall of 1959, Simon reflected on his travels to foreign lands and visits with U.S. diplomats and families. He wrote, "The most serious weakness is that of language. Too few of our personnel are able to speak the language of the country in which they serve." Simon mentioned another newspaper editor who asked a diplomat how many of the embassy personnel spoke the country's language. "The approximate reply was: 'We have only a few who speak the language here, but it's not too important since most of the educated people speak English. It's true this prevents us from reaching the poorer people, but the few we would speak to are only a drop in the bucket in this large country.' I thought it was a weak answer."[27]

Sounding a note that he repeated later in a book about the importance of learning foreign languages, Simon added, "This weakness in our program abroad is largely a reflection of a general American indifference toward foreign languages. You cannot expect a nation which spends little time in studying foreign languages to produce embassies staffed with linguists. The recent emphasis on foreign languages in U.S. schools eventually will be felt on the diplomatic level."

In the early 1960s, Simon started writing books for publication. Before his death in 2003 he would have twenty-three to his credit, including those written with coauthors. He wrote most of the books during his years as a U.S. representative and senator. By all accounts—his and his associates—he wrote them on a standard typewriter at odd hours of the day and night. He devoted most of his books to issues facing government, political parties, and citizens of the United States. They included an autobiography published in 1999 and a reminiscence of his 1988 run for the presidency. Taken as a body, they opened Simon's thinking process and public policy approaches to an audience well beyond the state of Illinois, or colleagues and friends in Washington.

Simon said he had not thought of writing a book until an episode during his early years in the legislature. Wanting to read an account of Abraham Lincoln's years as a state legislator—among Simon's heroes, Lincoln had no peer—he went to the Illinois state library and asked for a book on the subject. He was told that no such book existed. Still not thinking of it as a personal project, he wrote Lincoln historians Carl Sandburg and Allen Nevins, urging them to take up the project. According to Simon, they tossed it back in his lap.[28] He accepted the challenge and wrote a scholarly tome on Lincoln's legislative years, titled *Lincoln's Preparation for Greatness*. It was published in 1965 during Simon's first term as a state senator.

That was his first major book project, but his first published book appeared in 1964, titled *Lovejoy, Martyr to Freedom*. Written for a youth audience, the book explored the tragic life and times of Elijah P. Lovejoy, an abolitionist newspaper editor and publisher killed by a mob in Alton, Illinois, on November 7, 1837, for his antislavery beliefs.[29] Simon expanded on the topic for an adult audience in *Freedom's Champion: Elijah Lovejoy*, published in 1994.

It was more than a coincidence that Simon's first two books were about a political idol and a journalism idol. It cannot be overlooked that Lovejoy was the son of a minister or that he and Lincoln were murdered after striking blows against slavery and taking courageous stands in the face of countless threats. Simon stated that his favorite book of all those he wrote, and the one that sold the fewest copies, was the story of Lovejoy. Simon defined Lovejoy's story as a fight for human dignity and the oppressed.

As a journalist and politician, Simon had opportunities to meet presidents and past presidents, attend national political conventions, and write about them for hometown readers. *Tribune* readers got a taste of Simon's growing celebrity on two occasions after he began his political climb: a visit to Troy by former President Harry S. Truman and the assassination of President John F. Kennedy.

In August 1962, almost a decade after leaving the presidency, Truman, still a spry seventy-eight years old, took a memory-filled tour through parts of Illinois and Missouri. During his successful run for the presidency in 1948, Truman had made three whistle-stop campaign trips in Illinois that helped him win the state's electoral votes and the presidency. When Simon heard that Truman planned a speech near St. Louis, he called the former president and invited him to extend the trip and to help celebrate the community homecoming in Troy.[30] Truman agreed, and plans were made. He appeared first at the county fair in Highland and then traveled to Troy.

Accompanying Truman in the presidential car were Governor Kerner, candidate for the U.S. Senate Sidney Yates of Chicago, and Simon. Public officials gathered for the event included state senators, congressmen, county officers, judges, mayors, the state treasurer, and the state superintendent of public instruction. A crowd Simon estimated at "several times the population of the city" lined the streets to see the former president.[31] One town official estimated the gathering at 8,000 to 10,000. On the parade route, the car stopped in front of Simon's home for Truman to have his picture taken with Jeanne and their one-year-old daughter, Sheila.

Simon took a place of honor in Truman's convertible, sitting in the front seat where Truman could grasp his shoulders and lean forward to make comments. Not only did Simon enjoy the moment, it was a credit to him that the president made a stop in Troy. The publisher wrote glowingly of the event in page 1 stories. Later he remembered, "The warmth of the crowd greeting him [Truman] was overwhelming."

Simon's article about President Kennedy had a different tone as he reminisced about a man the publisher admired and supported. "I met John F. Kennedy perhaps a dozen times, and a dozen other times I was near him or heard him speak. In no sense did I know him well, and yet like all Americans I felt I knew him well," Simon wrote shortly after the assassination.[32] Simon recounted his first brief meeting with Kennedy at the 1956 national convention in Chicago when Kennedy nearly was nominated to run as vice president with Adlai E. Stevenson.

Simon was asked during the 1960 presidential campaign to work nationally to reduce the impact of Kennedy's Catholic affiliation. Simon declined the national role but volunteered on many occasions to speak throughout Illinois and nearby states on the subject. He wrote of those events, "As it turned out Illinois was enough of a problem. Religious prejudices—like any other kind of prejudices—do not die easily. I was in debates as far north as Wheaton and far south as Steeleville on whether democracy could survive if we had a Roman Catholic president. It is one of the tributes that can be paid to John F. Kennedy that to a great extent he buried that prejudice."

Commenting later about the Wheaton appearance, Simon said, "At Wheaton College's jammed auditorium I sensed that the only two people in the audience on my side in the debate were my wife and my mother."[33] He was roundly booed at the appearance. At these events, Simon discovered how deep the feelings were across Illinois against having a Catholic president. Simon, a Lutheran, and Jeanne, a Catholic, later wrote a book about their "mixed marriage."[34]

During the campaign, Simon attended a Kennedy appearance at the Orlando Hotel in Decatur. Kennedy sent word that he wanted to see Simon in his hotel room. After asking about the downstate political picture, Kennedy mentioned former Illinois governor John Stelle and Paul Powell, both of whom had supported Missouri senator Stuart Symington during the primaries. Kennedy said to Simon, "They're both crooks, aren't they?" Simon could do no less than confirm what Kennedy had heard. Simon later said of Powell's work for Kennedy, "Powell, to his credit, campaigned as hard for Kennedy as anyone did after the Massachusetts senator became the nominee . . . Powell played a role in securing the bare majority Kennedy received in Illinois."[35]

The Truman visit in August 1962 was one of many high points on the Simon list of moments when his star advanced toward statewide recognition. The saga began in 1961.

Simon made it clear to Chicago mayor Daley in advance of the 1962 election that he wanted to be on the Democratic ticket for U.S. senator against incumbent Everett Dirksen. In order to impress the mayor with Simon's credentials, friends and acquaintances began building support across the state. A poll of newspaper editors conducted for Paddock Publications in suburban Cook County revealed that 44 percent favored the candidacy of Simon, while Paul Powell ran second with 27 percent.[36]

Simon concentrated on public appearances and on contacts with newspaper people across the state in order to gain recognition. While he made few public references to the contest, Simon worked hard to maintain connections, and most associates knew of Simon's hopes. In a letter to Simon after a talk in Sterling, John Manion of the *Daily Gazette* wrote, "As for your future ambitions let me assure you that you have a good many local persons that are for you. Count me in your corner 100%."[37] He received a similar letter from Sid Landfield of the *Democrat-Messenger* in Mt. Sterling.

Chuck Hayes of Paddock Publications, a strong supporter of Simon's run for the senate, pulled together a group of influential citizens in the suburbs of Chicago for what he called "our little Summit Conference." The purpose was to get an idea of Simon's views on national and international issues. He anticipated the group would be interested in helping further Simon's candidacy. In a May 22 letter, Hayes said, "As far as how extensive the organizational aspect of this becomes, that will be up to you. What are your plans, what can we do, what do you expect of us, where do we go from here?"[38]

The two sponsoring groups for the Simon gathering were the Bensenville council of the League of United Latin Americans and the Opportunity Council, a group of suburbanites alarmed at living conditions for Mexican Americans, particularly transients and migratory farm workers. Hayes explained, "Generally, we are concerned with minority group rights and problems, with expanding opportunities for education-health-housing-employment and in tackling the overwhelming problems of migrant farm workers, all of whom in this area are Mexican-Americans."

Hayes continued his activities for Simon by forwarding articles and columns from other papers. Simon usually wrote a note to the writer. On one occasion, Hayes sent an editorial from the *Independent-Register* in Libertyville, titled "The Criminal Hand on Springfield." Simon complimented editor James McCulla, saying, "I am sure that if this is typical of your editorials that there are many who like them—and many who do not. Keep up the good work."[39]

Other newspaper friends of Simon expressed interest in a potential contest with Senator Dirksen. In a July 1 letter, Irving Dilliard, living in Collinsville, had this to say about the prospect, stopping short of an outright endorsement:

> Let me say that I am very glad you know Paul Simon and admire him for that puts us together in an area which I hope will include ever and ever more Illinoisans. I have tried to help Paul ever since he took over the paper in Troy only seven miles from Collinsville. This letter easily could become my testimonial to Paul and now to his wife Jeanne. An ecstatic testimonial, I might add. As for the senatorship matter, the one most important thing is that a plan be worked out which will give the Democratic party a nominee with the best chance of beating Dirksen and seating along with Paul Douglas someone who will not cancel out Douglas's vote on almost every roll call. We will work all this out as carefully as we can.[40]

Godfrey Sperling Jr., political writer for the *Christian Science Monitor*, often wrote of prospects for Congress, and he mentioned Simon's name in a column early in August. Simon responded, "Many thanks for your generous inclusion of my name in your article. Within a couple of weeks I will have a story of some substance for you."[41]

That story appeared in papers across the state the last week of August 1961. Two men familiar with Illinois politics announced they had formed a Paul-Simon-for-Senator committee.[42] They were Walter Johnson, chairman of the history department of the University of Chicago and head of the "Draft Stevenson" movement of 1952, and Senator Robert McCarthy of Decatur. The article contained a lengthy biography of Simon, beginning with his days as editor and publisher in Troy. The announcement stated, "Every sounding we have taken shows wide support for Paul Simon throughout the state. The recent poll of newspaper editors, showing that Paul Simon is their first choice by a wide margin is just one of the many indications. We believe that we can offer the Democratic organization a winner in the candidacy of Paul Simon, and more important, we believe that we can offer the state and nation the kind of U.S. senator who should join Paul Douglas in Washington."

Another downstate politician had his eye on the Democratic nomination for the senate: Paul Powell. The Vienna representative encouraged speculation about his candidacy, primarily because he wanted Mayor Daley to know of his interest in a statewide campaign and office. On May 9, Powell held his biennial legislative dinner in Springfield, a tradition for all the state's Democrats. Mayor Daley appeared and uttered pleasantries, saying Powell "earned the right to represent the state on a national level—on the floor of the United States Senate."[43] Powell knew that did not mean much and told reporters he did not consider it an endorsement. He also did not take himself out of the running.

In August, about the time of the Simon announcement, Powell and his friend John Stelle paid a call on Kennedy in Washington, urging the president to campaign vigorously in Illinois for the Democratic nominee. The callers may not have known that Kennedy questioned their honesty. They spoke with presidential aides about chances for a victory over Dirksen. Following the meeting, Powell said, "I'm happy where I am," but he would be available if chosen by the mayor. He added, "I'm a politician. I take orders. But we have plenty of good men to run against Dirksen."[44]

As time drew near for Daley and the state Democratic organization to choose their candidate to run against Dirksen, the mayor had two well-known downstate politicians who wanted to do battle with the incumbent. Neither of the two would have been Daley's choice if the pick was a reward for loyalty to the mayor. Powell had made a career of pushing Chicago Democrats out of the way to protect his position in House leadership. He could be the mayor's ally if there was something in it for downstate interests and his friends. Simon, who held no position of authority or power in the House, fought with interests in his own party that were often aligned with Daley and Chicago.

Considering the realities, neither of the two had much chance for Daley's patronage. He chose Sidney Yates, a congressman from Chicago who was loyal to a fault to the city and the mayor's agenda. Simon's supporters always believed Daley feared a split in downstate Democratic votes if he chose either Simon or Powell, so he picked a friendly face from Chicago.[45] Simon recognized that Daley could choose whomever he wanted whether the young Democrat liked it or not. Simon's effort to get Daley's attention had failed. Simon had known his chances were miniscule, but he encouraged friends to use their energy and resources in spite of the odds. The exposure was worth the trouble.

With the decision made, Simon announced his intention to seek the state senate seat from his district left open by the retirement of James O. Monroe of Collinsville, owner of that town's weekly newspaper. After cheering for the selection of Yates, Simon said, "I hope I have compiled a record in the House of Representatives which merits consideration for the state senate race. My only pledge is to work hard at the job and to vote the issues as I see them, regardless of pressure. I have done this in my terms in the House and I shall do it in the Senate."[46]

The announcement mentioned Simon receiving a "best legislator" award after each session since 1955 from the Independent Voters of Illinois. It also listed him as part of the "economy bloc" that spoke out on tax and budget issues. Simon's sponsorship of the "right to know" law making it a public policy that government meetings should be open to the public also made the announcement list.

Simon expected the toughest campaign of his short political career. Democratic party officials in Madison, Jersey, and Greene counties saw an opportunity to pay Simon back for what they believed were his abusive comments and rejection of party discipline by endorsing his opponent. They had tried to put him away in 1954 and failed. They had another chance in the 1962 April primary. Taking the challenge of defeating Simon was Probate Judge Patrick O'Neill, the son of Schaeffer O'Neill, who had worked with downstate politicians to build Cahokia Downs racetrack near East St. Louis. Judge O'Neill decided to step down from the judiciary for this get-even contest.[47]

Simon believed that Paul Powell and his associates worked behind the scenes to raise money for Judge O'Neill and provide volunteer workers in the district. He wrote, "I am reasonably sure that Powell's not-so-delicate hand played a principal role in this, Powell hoping to get rid of me from the legislative scene." Such an effort by Powell was not beyond belief given the feelings that existed and Powell's relationship with the O'Neill family.

While O'Neill had name familiarity in the district, other circumstances also made Simon's election questionable. In the four House races before 1962, Simon benefited from cumulative voting, which allowed a voter to cast as many as three votes for a candidate. In his first race against an organization candidate, cumulative voting clearly provided the advantage Simon needed to win. In the state senate election, however, one vote counted as one vote. There was no cumulative voting.

The battle was between O'Neill's "family man" ads and accusations about Simon's record, and Simon's issue-oriented campaign and defense of his record. Articles in the *Troy Tribune* tried to stay neutral in characterizing the contest, although references to the party "slate" appeared frequently and at least one article pointed to heavy financial backing for O'Neill from the party organization. As election day neared, the contest became a battle of newspaper advertising. Simon answered O'Neill with an ad titled "The Charges and the Facts!"[48] The ad included these arguments:

The charge: Simon is an independent, not a Democrat. He frequently does not support the programs of Governor Kerner and other Democratic leaders.

The facts: It is true that I do not always follow the party line 100 percent. If the people want a puppet who jumps when someone pulls a string, then I'm not their man. I am a Democrat—and proud of it . . . My party happens to oppose a Crime Commission to investigate the alliance between crime and politics. I am for it. Am I wrong? . . . When the 50 percent increase in the sales tax was passed the same day the tax on Cahokia Downs and Fairmount was reduced by one-third, I opposed the sales tax increase and also opposed the give-away to the race tracks. In both of these matters, I went against the strong party pressures. Did I do wrong?

The charge: Simon has done nothing for the Democratic organization in his eight years in office.

The facts: I have not conceived of my job as primarily being a gear in the Democratic machine, but I have cooperated with the Democratic organization as fully as I could in good conscience. I have not hesitated to speak of worthy Democratic candidates. When John Kennedy was seeking the presidency, the talk I made against religious bigotry to a group of Lutheran ministers in Wisconsin became the most widely published piece on the religious issue during the campaign, reprinted in several Protestant and Catholic magazines . . . This is but one of many examples I could cite. At the same time I confess I am not a puppet for the county Democratic organization, whose leaders have not always stood for better government.

The charge: By voting against the sales tax increase, Simon opposed adequate financing for our schools.

The facts: I have always opposed the sales tax increases. They impose an unfair burden on low income groups and on businessmen in border areas, such as ours. While we are tied with two other states for the highest sales tax in the nation, we have the lowest taxes in some other areas. These I felt should be raised before we raise the tax on a loaf of bread and the necessities of life.

On the eve of the primary, Simon ran an advertisement titled "Look at the Record and vote for Paul Simon for State Senator."[49] The introduction to the ad read, "You should judge Paul Simon—or any other candidate not by what they say about themselves, but by what others say about them. Take time to read this ad and see what others say about the man you can nominate on Tuesday for state senator." The ad listed praise about Simon's service in the legislature that had appeared in the *Moline Daily Dispatch, East St. Louis Journal, Bloomington Pantagraph, Sparta News-Plaindealer, Staunton Star-Times, Armington Helper, Arlington Heights Herald, Vandalia Leader, Chicago Daily News, Alton Telegraph,* and *Edwardsville Intelligencer.* The *Moline Dispatch,* in a part of the state where Simon had little exposure, made this generous comment: "One of the most capable legislators in the House, and without a doubt, is one of the most honest men to serve in any legislature anywhere . . . His vote has never been bought because his principles—especially those concerning honesty in government—won't permit it. This alone makes him a man among men, politically speaking."

A handbill Simon supporters spread across the district announced "An Urgent Appeal" and carried Simon's fight directly to the county political machine and the forces he had fought for years. It read: "This is an urgent appeal to you. Tomorrow the machine and the big money are combining to put one of their men in the office of State Senator. They want to beat Paul Simon. Paul has served you faithfully for eight years as your State Representative—but his only chance is for you to go to the polls and show your independent judgment. Fight the machine and the race track crowd."[50]

In a corner of an inside page of the *Tribune* published the Thursday before the election was a one column statement under the headline "IF. . . ." It was an appeal for Republicans and independents to ask for a Democratic ballot, and carried no signature or indication it was a paid ad.

> If you want to have a voice in who your next State Senator is, then you must go to the polls on April 10 and ask for a Democratic ballot. There is no Republican candidate. The choice is between Paul Simon and his opponent. The power and money of the few who try to dominate Madison county politics is behind Paul Simon's opponent. Paul Simon has dared to step on powerful toes. If it is a small vote—if the people fail to take an interest—then Paul Simon will be defeated. The controlled vote will dominate in an election where only a few vote. A large vote will mean the people winning, not the bosses. Make sure you go to the polls on Tuesday, ask for a Democratic ballot, and vote for Paul Simon for State Senator.[51]

Simon received 26,788 votes and O'Neill 13,876. Jarvis Township, which included Troy, voted for Simon 317 to 40. He carried every township in Madison County, while barely winning in Jersey and Greene counties.[52] By winning the primary election in a heavily Democratic district, Simon had all but won election as state senator. In a quieter general election that fall, Simon ran more subdued ads, including one that simply quoted the *East St. Louis Journal*: "Rep. Simon has had an outstanding record in the state legislature. He has established himself as an outspoken member and never has been subservient to party interests. There are few men in public life, at any level of public office, who merit support as Paul Simon. We recommend his election as State Senator." Simon won over his Republican opponent Harold O. Gwillim 43,204 to 16,754.[53] Next door to Madison County, in St. Clair County, Simon's friend and political ally Alan Dixon won his first contest for the state senate. They would remain seatmates in the senate.

In terms of Simon's image, the 1962 primary contest served another purpose. While Simon had for years worn a bow tie when dressed for work, it became an official characteristic when a reporter for the *Alton Telegraph* referred to him as "the candidate in the bow tie." Simon said, "I figured, by golly, that's as good an identifying label as any. Why not?"[54] Four years later, Simon had no opponent in the primary, and the Democratic party endorsed him en route to an easy reelection in the fall.

Simon always had plenty to talk about when running for reelection. In comments about his service, he mostly left an impression that regardless of frustrations, he enjoyed politics. After his first legislative session, he wrote, "To the legislator who tries to do a conscientious job, there's a great deal of work and a great deal of heartache and disappointment, and a great deal of satisfaction. Apparently the satisfaction of trying to do a good job outweighs the heartache and disappointment. Because I'm running for re-election."[55] During the 1956 general election, his newspaper advertisements made these points under the headline "Look at this Record":

- Selected by the Independent Voters of Illinois as one of the five outstanding members of the Illinois General Assembly.
- Picked by Springfield newspaper correspondents as one of the two outstanding new members of the House of Representatives.
- Perfect attendance record.
- Endorsed by the AFL-CIO and Railroad Brotherhoods.
- Praised by business leaders for his fair and honest approach to their problems.
- Recommended by the Better Government Association and the Legislative Voters League.
- Praised by newspapers throughout the state.[56]

Two years later, his campaign advertising contained twenty-one positive comments and endorsements by Illinois newspapers, organizations including the Taxpayers' Federation of Illinois, and stalwart Democratic officeholders such as former governor Adlai Stevenson and U.S. senator Paul Douglas. As his star rose, so did the numbers of those who wanted to be in the cheering section.

When it came to personal responsibilities as a state legislator, or an elected official at any level, Simon felt a need to give more information than required by law or common practice, putting him in stark contrast to virtually every public official throughout Illinois in a way that resonated with citizens. The disclosures created a sense of openness that played well with a statewide constituency. A prime example was disclosure of his campaign finances, long before states and the federal government required this information for public consumption. During the forty years in which he held public office, Simon always provided more information about his personal finances than demanded by law.

Simon began income disclosure with information about his 1955 finances, which he published in the *Tribune* and sent to newspapers throughout Madison County. He itemized income amounting to $7,180.83, including $5,000 in salary from the state of Illinois.[57] The next largest amount was $1,413.74 from the *Tribune*. The remaining $767.09 came from speeches and stock dividends and for writing a booklet titled "The Christian and Politics."

Simon's lengthy explanation for the 1955 numbers required the bulk of a "Trojan Thoughts" column. He noted that the $7,180.83 total was not net income. "Out of that comes hotel expense, travel expense, secretarial help, stationery, postage and other items." According to the 1870 state constitution, the state gave him $50 expense money for all incidental legislative expenses, and there was no provision for paid staff. He wrote, "Obviously things have changed considerably since 1870, both in price and demands on the state legislators. My expense for postage alone for the year ran many times the amount allotted by the constitution to cover many items for both years."

He offered a reason for his modest income. "I could have improved my personal financial picture by spending more time at my business. This past year I have spent very little time working for my newspaper. I feel I was able to do a better job for my district and for the State of Illinois as a result, but if I were married and had a family I would not have been able to devote as much time to state work as I did." That statement held up until 1960 when he and state representative Jeanne Hurley married.

Simon drew practical conclusions from the disclosure. "My experience confirms the common knowledge that other fields are more profitable financially than the political arena. However, I have no regrets . . . happen to enjoy politics . . . What it may lack in financial reward is made up by the hope that you are doing something for people. As long as I can serve with a good conscience, I hope to enjoy the field of politics."

Simon's statement also showed assets and liabilities.[58] Under assets, he listed $7,700 par value of Troy Publishing Company stock, about $397 in a savings account, a 1951 Chevrolet with no loan, and a house and lot purchased in Troy for $4,500. His liabilities included a house mortgage of $3,591 and a personal note for $250 to "the fellow from whom I bought my house."

Simon's disclosure for 1962 indicated the changes that had occurred in his life, politics, and businesses.[59] He showed total income of $17,120 for the year, with $6,067.40 coming from the State of Illinois as legislative salary. Significantly, he reported income of $8,555.81 from newspaper properties: *Troy Tribune,* $5,935.33; *Roodhouse Record,* $2,027.63; *Abingdon Argus,* $258.85; *Metamora Herald,* $314; and *Carterville Herald,* $20. Other amounts came from property rental ($603.14), sale of property ($475), and profit on sale of stock ($200). Stock dividends amounted to $70.86, and he received $889 for sixteen talks to groups of all sizes. Two published articles contributed $170 and Simon included $67.50 for his wife's legal work.

A cover letter to editors addressed a number of subjects related to campaign income and expenses for his contested primary and general election to the state senate in 1962. Until that election, Simon had paid for most expenses out of his pocket and accepted only a few small campaign contributions. That picture changed in 1962, and he explained a "new" method of raising campaign funds: tickets to a campaign dinner at $7.50 each. He did not include details of the dinner cost and net revenue, but said those could be obtained at the *Troy Tribune.* He mentioned individuals who helped with the dinner and thanked labor unions and local businessmen. He explained, "The campaign was by far the most expensive I have engaged in. Yet compared to many in the state the cost was not great."

Three years later, Simon's disclosure showed total income of $17,312.53, almost the same total as in 1962. The total included $7,644.60 from the State of Illinois, $1,770 from the Troy Publishing Company, and $1,150 from gross income on the sale of the Metamora newspapers. The report listed thirty-four speaking engagements, stock dividends, and payments for newspaper and magazine articles.[60]

More meaningful than the minutiae of income details, the annual disclosure became a part of what Simon stood for in public service. He wanted the public to believe that he operated ethically and openly, and had no secret deals up his sleeve or covert alliances. It gave him standing when he criticized colleagues for taking suspicious payments or payoffs for services and favors rendered. In a more personal way, it revealed the modest income he had from sources other than a state salary. Unlike lawyers and owners of businesses who spent just a fraction of their time on state business for a minor percentage of their total income, Simon relied more heavily on his salary as an elected official. The numbers also showed dramatically how he built a newspaper ownership group on a shoestring and the thin profitability of those ventures. While his income during the formative years of his political career did not put him on poverty row, he always had to watch his pennies. He wanted the public to think that was how he viewed the state budget.

On July 14, 1965, one of Simon's favorite people, Adlai E. Stevenson II, died. Within a year a book was published that contained personal reminiscences of Stevenson, including one by Simon titled "Young People Loved Him." Simon recalled his first invitation to meet with Governor Stevenson in Springfield. "I was among those who sided with him and soon I had an invitation to have lunch with the Governor. I was not yet twenty-one, and it impresses me more now than it did then that he should have taken time out to have lunch with someone not even old enough to vote."[61] Simon recalled receiving letters from Stevenson that surprised the young editor. One arrived as Simon's call to the Army approached. Stevenson's note said, "I hear today from Carl McGowan that you are shortly to be inducted into the Army. I find myself of two minds: I am delighted on the one hand that you are going to be serving in the armed forces, and disappointed on the other hand that your emphatic and clear voice is going to be stilled here-abouts for a while."[62]

During Army service in 1952, Simon showed his support of Stevenson for president by sending a check for $50 to the campaign. Simon received a thank you letter from the candidate, reading, "I am touched more than I can say by your letter—and your contribution. I can well imagine that the salary of a private first class is not such as to give him much room for leeway, and that a political contribution comes at the very bottom of the priority list. I can only say that I shall value this contribution much more than many larger ones I will receive . . . I know that it has been hard to have your journalistic career interrupted by military service. I can only voice the hope that you are finding your stay in Germany interesting and full of material for future reflection. It is apparent from your letter that you know, better than most, what the real issues are in this campaign."[63]

In the book Simon said, "As I look back on it now, Stevenson appealed to youth and had an interest in them because he was always young himself, always growing, always eager to explore and probe untried paths."

Upon reelection to the state senate in 1966 without significant opposition, Simon could look ahead at least four years, although the picture may have appeared somewhat out of focus. He had sold all his interests in fourteen weekly newspapers but still had a cash flow of principal and interest from the contracts that would reach well beyond the next four years. With two books and their royalties to his credit and ideas for more books and a demand for articles, Simon had an opportunity to add political reach and cash flow. He was assured of demand for his "Sidelights" column during the legislative sessions every two years, and he could count newspaper reporters and editors across the state as friends and admirers. The 1962 flirtation with a statewide campaign for U.S. senate sent a clear message that he wanted something more than the title "state senator." The table was set for something big.

Part Three

Rapid Rise, Sudden Fall, 1966–72

The Big Bounce

Paul Simon, newly elected to a second term in the Illinois state senate and buoyed by media attention, began thinking about 1968 and the prospect of a statewide campaign for the seat of Senator Dirksen. As he talked with media friends and made public appearances across the state, Simon encouraged quiet talk and speculation about his ambition. Nothing had dimmed his long-held desire for a head-to-head run against the incumbent senator.

While Simon showed determination to serve as a U.S. senator, his long-time legislative seatmate, Alan Dixon, recalls from their many discussions about each other's ambitions that the governor's job was a priority. "Both of us were ambitious," Dixon said. "During the long day and night legislative sessions we talked about our ambitions. Paul wanted to be governor. There were things he wanted to do. I had thoughts about making it to the U.S. Senate. We were hopeful for a full future, but there were times when we didn't see it clearly."[1] Early in their relationship, Simon may have indicated a preference for governor, but his ambition for a senate seat took form not long after he entered the legislature. From 1961 to 1969, Democrats held the governorship, and it looked as if Simon's chances for that office were minimal on the short term.

From a purely practical point of view, Simon's quest for the nomination as the party's U.S. senate candidate did not make sense. Why would Democratic party officials choose someone who had never run a statewide campaign? How would it look to slate a state senator from Troy and one who had never held a leadership position in the legislature, against one of the nation's most powerful U.S. senators? Finally, what did the party owe Simon, who had spent a fair amount of time disapproving of Democrats and the candidate selection process? The sum of answers to those questions was that Simon did not have a chance of taking on Dirksen.

Simon's pursuit of Dirksen had an emotional side that might have influenced his judgment. The senator defeated Simon's friend Richard Stengel in 1956 and carried on a philosophical war in Washington with his hero, Senator Paul Douglas. After Douglas's defeat in 1966 by Republican Charles H. Percy, Simon saw an opportunity to complement the record Douglas established on causes such as civil rights. On the practical side, in spite of his record of winning three elections for the Senate, Dirksen posted relatively small margins of victory. In 1950 against Senator Scott Lucas, Dirksen won with 53.88 percent of the vote; against Stengel in 1956 he had 54.1 percent; and in 1962 against Representative Yates, who rarely took the fight to Dirksen downstate, the senator received 52.9 percent.[2] Combined with advancing age, a history of poor health, and sluggish campaigns in Illinois, Dirksen looked vulnerable.

Simon's political future was on the line in the years leading to the 1968 elections, and that provides one of the reasons for an energetic exposure effort. Simon took greater risks with his choices from 1966 to 1968 than any time since 1948. By selling his interest in the weekly newspapers, he abandoned the safety net that would provide work challenges and income if political fortunes dimmed. Unlike most members of the legislature who had a business or professional career when not in Springfield, Simon for the first time faced an all-or-nothing situation with politics. If he failed to gain a place on the 1968 state ballot, Simon faced completing his second state senate term, which ended in 1970, with little chance of meaningful party responsibilities. What then? Running for state treasurer or auditor did not satisfy his leaning toward public policy issues. His outspoken manner and fights with legislative leadership made him a pariah in many party circles.

Simon's run for the Senate nomination was only part of a plan to remain visible so party leaders could not ignore him. As 1966 began, an immediate concern was finding ways to keep his name before the media, especially political columnists and editorialists across the state. He knew that a politician, especially a Democrat from downstate, was only as good as his most recent clippings. The state senate, controlled by Republicans, did not provide a particularly good platform for attention. Democratic competitors lining up for the 1968 elections included three men who had run statewide campaigns, had proved their ability to win, and had pulpits that gave them easy assess to media. They were Michael J. Howlett, state auditor, Paul Powell, the incumbent secretary of state, and William Clark, attorney general.

In 1966 he needed a voice beyond his senate district. That led in part to Simon entering an agreement with Howard Long, head of the SIU Department of Journalism and a Simon advocate, to circulate the senator's columns in a nonlegislative year. Long headed the International Conference of Weekly Newspaper Editors, which provided a number of services and programs to editors and publishers. He convinced Simon to have the conference distribute columns for subscribing weekly papers during 1966 for $3 per week. The conference order form for the column cited Simon as

"Author of books. Member, Illinois State Senate, Weekly Newspaper editor," and replayed the story of Simon resurrecting the *Troy Tribune*.[3] It also mentioned the *Harper's* magazine article from 1964 and Simon's campaigns for good government at local and state levels.

Solicitations went to editors in February 1966, and Long reported the first sale late in March, with the initial column to be provided in mid-April. For the balance of the year, Simon wrote thirty-seven columns. By September the customer list included the *Auburn Citizen, Galesburg Post, Collinsville Herald, Red Bud North County News, Columbia Star and Monroe County Clarion*, Chicago North Side Newspapers, *Highland News Leader, Vandalia Leader, Sparta News-Plaindealer, Greenville Advocate, Hancock County Journal* (Carthage), and the Troy-Roodhouse Publishing Company in which Simon owned an interest until 1966.[4] The total was a far cry from the 300-plus papers that received the free legislative columns.

If subscribers thought they would receive columns similar to his "Sidelights from Springfield," they were surprised. A review of the columns sold to those and other newspapers in 1966 shows subject matter that ranged far and wide, mostly beyond the boundaries of Illinois. Editors may have wondered what inspired some subjects and why they warranted attention from an Illinois state senator. Simon wanted to demonstrate a national viewpoint as part of his challenge to Dirksen.

For example, Simon's first column, titled "Draft Revision Desirable," proposed dramatic changes in the military draft then in place. He pleaded for a form of universal military training, stating, "Even a man with one arm could work in a supply room." He excluded extreme mental and physical handicaps, and "where a farmer with a heart condition needs his son to operate the farm," but not much else. His idea of the draft would make it as much a social program as military. "Those who are rejected for service because they cannot read or write should be drafted and made to spend the first six months or year of their service acquiring these very basic skills," he said. The social side of his draft plan had an urban redevelopment aspect. "Helping to rehabilitate some of our urban centers could count as service; serving as a teacher to the unskilled or semi-skilled could count as service; a two-year stint with the Peace Corps could count as service."[5]

Simon wrote often about race relations and civil rights. One column featured an election in Alabama; others were titled "Race Relations Can Be Good News," "Signs of Progress in Race Relations," "Anti-Semitism Is Still With Us," and "The Strange Case of Julian Bond." Urban centers throughout the nation faced protests and violence in 1966 and 1967 in which people died and were injured and serious property damage occurred. Seizing on that national issue, Simon wrote "A New Look at Crime," "Riots in the Streets," and "Television Spotlights Crime Problem." He drew on his foreign travels for a column on the nation of Guyana and one titled "Elections Easily Misunderstood Abroad."

In a column about an Illinois subject, Simon paid tribute after the death of Howe Morgan, publisher of the weekly paper in Sparta, a town of 3,500 people. Simon described his friend, a leader among the state's weekly publishers: "In a very personal way he gave his community something to cry about, to shout about, and he taught them to laugh at themselves on occasion as he gently deflated some local balloon."[6] Simon also wrote about a few favorite subjects, such as campaign costs, the right of privacy, and open meetings, but beyond those, few of the columns directly addressed regional or state issues.

The list of subscribers reached Simon's goal of twenty papers by November. Simon had difficulty maintaining a steady flow of columns due to a full schedule of commitments during his reelection campaign in the fall. Assuming the program would continue into 1967, Long promised more aggressive promotions. Simon had a different take. Late in the year he wrote, "When the legislature begins I will resume my free column—dropping this one temporarily—until the first of July."[7] He anticipated resuming the subscription program during the summer and wanted to try a sample mailing to other states.

Simon's plan disappointed Long. He wrote, "I suppose it is more important to your career to supply free columns to all the papers in Illinois than it is to sell these columns to as many as we can. However, I hate to see us interrupt our project after we are off to such a good start. If you really feel that you must give your column away during a legislative session, we will put a note to that effect, stating it a little more diplomatically of course."[8]

Simon resumed "Sidelights from Springfield," by far the most lasting and popular part of his outreach program, in 1967. As Illinois struggled to find a source of new revenue, Simon reiterated his support of an income tax. "Within 10 years the answer will have to be a state income tax, and a reduction in the real property tax and personal property tax to go with it."[9] With both parties opposed to an income tax, Simon realized that would not happen in 1967. He could see the broadening of the base of the sales tax, an increase in the gasoline tax, and probably a hike in the sales tax. Simon again opposed the sales tax. Late in the session, he saw support building for options to avoid a tax increase, including more bonding for highway construction and university buildings and a trend toward toll roads. He was one of four senators to vote against the toll road idea, and his argument against more bonding had not changed.[10]

On the crime front, Simon supported bills that would compensate victims and provide backing for a modest gun control law. He opposed a stop and frisk bill as too risky, saying, "I confess to some amazement at seeing people who regularly denounce excessive centralized government by a national administration vote for measures which give police sweeping powers. Generally, we can be proud of our policemen, although we ought to gradually improve their required training and we should pay them more adequately. But to give to the police, no matter how highly trained, the authority to stop and search someone simply because they think he might commit a crime at some time in the future, is unwise."[11]

Simon had his fingers crossed for passage of an ethics law, although the General Assembly had killed the idea in the 1965 session. He believed it might pass because Senate Majority Leader W. Russell Arrington was the principal sponsor. Although Arrington gave the plan top priority, by February nothing had happened. That made Simon nervous. He wrote, "In a state with a long history of scandal in government, the current session hopefully can do something constructive to improve the picture—and make citizens a little more proud of our state government."[12] An ethics bill did pass and was implemented in 1968.

The legislature faced one of its toughest challenges with a housing rights bill. Advocates in and out of government argued the subject endlessly and with passion. A compromise seemed unlikely. Simon, however, fought to expand housing opportunities, especially for African Americans. He stated, "So long as we preserve the myth that segregation can bring with it equality of opportunity, as well as justice and order—to that extent we fool ourselves."[13] A strength of his legislative columns continued to be a willingness to confront the most divisive issues facing Illinois.

Simon did not return to the paid column plan favored by Howard Long at SIU. As soon as the session ended, he and Jeanne headed to Europe, the Middle East, and Asia. As on previous foreign travels, Simon wrote articles at each stop along the way. On stationery of the *Chicago Daily News*, for whom he was writing about his travels, Simon sent three questions to the North Vietnamese embassy in Poland, hoping for answers.[14] He asked:

- Would North Vietnam accept an invitation from a neutral country—such as Norway or Pakistan—to a meeting to discuss possible negotiations for peace?

- Would their government accept such an invitation from the secretary-general of the United Nations?
- If there was a cessation of the bombing of North Vietnam would they be willing to enter into immediate, direct negotiations for peace?

Not surprisingly, Simon received no communication from the Vietnamese government. He stated at the end of his column, "My experience over the years has been that virtually all governments, friendly and unfriendly, are eager to get their viewpoints across to American journalists. Hanoi apparently feels its message is being heard on the field of battle."

With the word out that Simon wanted to take on Dirksen in the 1968 election, he needed to remain visible and hope for the best. No one dared beg for a spot on the Democratic ticket or talk directly with Mayor Daley. But there were good signs for Simon, including a strong endorsement by the *Post-Dispatch* prior to his reelection in 1966.

Simon got other encouragement before the election from a political writer for the *Illinois State Register* in Springfield. Gene Callahan, who eventually would become a Simon staff member and close friend, wrote Simon with this praise: "You have made definite strides within the framework of the Democratic Party, and still you have not prostituted yourself on any level. You have a quality which I also admire very much in my father. My Dad and I strongly disagree on some issues (not too many really), but we still come away from our 'arguments' respecting each other's points of view. My Dad would never agree with me on anything merely for the sake of agreement. You wouldn't either. And this I like."[15] Such reassurances meant Simon's connections to the media remained strong; Simon's standing in a poll of editors across the state showed him the choice for the Democratic nomination by 60.1 percent to 15.8 percent for Adlai E. Stevenson III.[16]

Other friends and admiring journalists sent notes of encouragement as the time for staking out political ground opened in 1967. Adlai Stevenson III, a favorite of Mayor Daley because of his name recognition, disclaimed any interest in running for the Senate and then tossed bouquets to Simon. Whether that helped Simon with Chicago party slatemakers is an open question. Paul Douglas sent Simon a $200 check for campaign expenses, and Jack Mabley, political columnist for the *Chicago American,* wrote, "If I thought I could influence Daley, I'd ask him to pick State Senator Paul Simon of Troy to run against Dirksen."[17] They were whistling in the dark, for none of them had close ties to the mayor.

With Simon seeking consideration for a statewide Democratic ticket in 1968, his attitude and commentaries about Mayor Daley and Chicago politicians weighed heavily. For all that Simon wrote during his legislative years in favor of Democratic party reforms, he only occasionally wrote about Mayor Daley and the candidate selection process. In the columns he wrote for publication across the state, Simon kept a civil tongue about the mayor and the Chicago political operation with only an occasional slip. One occurred in a column written for Troy readers in 1960 just before the state primary.

Simon had announced his support of Stephen A. Mitchell for the nomination as governor on the Democratic ticket, knowing that Mitchell came to the political fight with few credentials among Illinois Democratic leaders. He had not held elective office in the state, but he had close ties to Adlai E. Stevenson II and his run for governor and president. As the April primary election neared, Simon made his pitch for Mitchell, taking a shot at the method by which the party selected its candidates. He wrote:

> Do you want to continue to have one man (the mayor of Chicago) picking the candidates for governor of the Democratic party? If you don't think this is healthy—and I find it hard to believe anyone does—then you should vote for Stephen A. Mitchell for Governor. Mayor Daley has inherited a system. I do not blame him. But the system is wrong. Selection of party nominees should not be in the hands of one man in a democracy. This belongs to the people . . . The bad effects of the present system are felt in both parties, because if one party does not do its best, the other party is not forced into doing its best either . . . Illinois needs some political fresh air. The nomination of Steve Mitchell will bring it.[18]

Mitchell did not have a chance. With the backing of Mayor Daley and the state central committee, Otto Kerner easily was nominated for governor, and he won in the general election. As usual after backing a primary loser, Simon pledged support to the Democratic nominee.

Viewed by party officials, Simon's column could only be recognized as head-on criticism of the mayor and the system. Did the column end up in the file of some Chicago aide to the mayor? Hardly anything escaped the eyes of those watching for the slightest denigration of the mayor and his time-tested display of political power. Further angering Daley aides, Simon polished a high approval rating with people who openly criticized the mayor's administration, including the Better Government Association and the Independent Voters of Illinois. Daley routinely ignored those organizations.

Simon walked a fine line in the legislature. His votes often clashed with Chicago interests and received little sympathy from the mayor's loyalists. It did not help that Simon kept company with legislators who undoubtedly made the mayor's blood boil. Because Simon promoted ideas for ethics laws, anti-corruption proposals, and a much more open approach to government than existed in Chicago and praised independent voting records among legislators of both parties, there were people close to the mayor who had their doubts about the voice from Troy. Nevertheless, the record is mild when compared to other critics of Daley—although Simon may have been less discrete in private conversation, correspondence, or even an occasional public appearance. However, by challenging the methods of Mayor Daley, Simon exposed himself to charges of hypocrisy later when slated by the organization.

During the last part of 1967 and first two months of 1968, Democratic party members, potential candidates for statewide office, and the media waited impatiently for meetings of the state central committee at which decisions would be made about the party ticket. For most of that period, columnists included Simon's name among possibilities to oppose Dirksen although they offered little hope for Simon. Nevertheless, he continued to set an optimistic tone in public comments. Early in January, he told a columnist for the *Illinois State Journal*, "I have reason to believe I'm being seriously considered, but I'm not asking for any commitments at this point."[19] Nor was he likely to get any.

In February, Governor Kerner dropped the bomb that he would not seek election to a third term. Later he accepted appointment as a federal circuit court of appeals judge and turned over the governorship to Lt. Gov. Samuel Shapiro. His announcement set off days of speculation about Daley's choice for the governor and senate races. Shapiro and Adlai E. Stevenson III, elected in 1966 as state treasurer, were names at the top of lists. Simon got no mention. When Dirksen announced in mid-February that he would seek a fourth term, the last paragraph of the Associated Press story mentioned Stevenson, Simon, and Sargent Shriver, head of the War on Poverty, as possible opponents.

On February 23, the state central committee met in Springfield—a prelude to a meeting two days later in Chicago—to hear presentations from prospective candidates for state offices.[20] All the top party people appeared: Mike Howlett, Adlai Stevenson, Paul Powell, Samuel Shapiro, and William Clark. Stevenson said he would "accept the call to duty" if nominated for governor or senator, but that he would prefer to run for governor. Powell said he was interested only in nomination for secretary of state. Some reporters mentioned Simon as a possibility for the U.S. senate or lieutenant governor.

Four days later, the central committee announced its selections. Simon was chosen to make the race for lieutenant governor.[21] Shapiro got the governor slot and Attorney General Clark was the senate race choice. Others

chosen were incumbents Powell and Howlett. Stevenson remained in office
as treasurer, causing no shortage of speculation that Daley did not want
Dirksen to face a strong opponent who questioned the war in Vietnam.
Newspaper editorial pages panned the choices, and columnists said Daley
had given fresh hope for Republicans to win in November. Ken Watson,
of the *Illinois State Journal*, voiced the sentiment of others that Simon,
whose ballot strength was in Madison County, would not add strength to
the campaign.[22]

Regarding the party decision for lieutenant governor, Simon had first-
hand experience of the central committee's deal making. Here is his "inside"
story:

> Then one day Joe Knight, a wealthy gentleman farmer from Dow phoned
> me. Knight, a bachelor, had his whole life wrapped up in politics . . . He
> served at one point as treasurer of the state party, but he had more influ-
> ence than that title indicates. Daley, State Democratic Chairman James
> Ronan and the small circle of people who really ran the Democratic party
> in Illinois liked him and trusted him. In his slow-talking deep voice Joe
> said to me, "I've been authorized to ask if you were slated as lieutenant
> governor, would you take it?" When he said "authorized" I knew that
> came from Daley.[23]

Simon did the obligatory "I'll get back to you," and promptly solicited his
wife's opinion. They agreed it provided a stepping stone to the governor's
office or U.S. senator if he could pull off a win. It also meant he would have
no primary opposition and could marshal campaign funds and staff for the
general campaign. He told Knight it was a deal. Of course, the party central
committee went through the motions of meeting, hearing the prospective
candidates, and discussing their merits and demerits. Regardless of the
show, there was only one vote that counted. The mayor made his list and
the party agreed: Simon for lieutenant governor.

There was more than a grumble or two from members of the central committee, especially legislators who considered Simon too independent and
unlikely to do the party's bidding. Representative Clyde Choate of Anna,
a close friend and acolyte of Paul Powell who never warmed to Simon, is
alleged to have said, "But Mayor, he might become governor." To which
Daley is supposed to have replied, "It's Simon."[24]

Simon's selection was the good news; other names on the ticket were the
not-so-good news. Although in those days the lieutenant governor candidates
ran their own campaigns and were chosen separately from the governor,
history had shown that voters selected governors and lieutenant governors

of the same party. Voters generally did not realize they cast separate ballots for each office.

Simon faced the reality that Shapiro did not stack up as a winner. Shapiro had served in the state legislature and had been elected lieutenant governor with Kerner in 1960 and reelected in 1964. Although a downstate politician from Kankakee, he had little name recognition outside his own part of the state and had not achieved much in the short time he had served as governor. Friendly enough, Shapiro did not leave an impression as a dynamic leader for Illinois. Republicans chose former Cook County sheriff Richard B. Ogilvie as their nominee for governor after a primary contest with John Henry Altorfer of Peoria, a moderate and favorite among downstate party people. For lieutenant governor, Republicans selected Robert Dwyer, an insurance executive from Winnetka who had never held elected office and had no familiarity to anyone other than party insiders.

Simon's acceptance of the lieutenant governor slot puzzled many supporters who held dark thoughts about associating with Daley. Some accused him of being a party stooge. While it appeared Simon had hopes of running for governor in 1972, that seemed a hard sell if Shapiro failed to win. To some, it appeared Democratic opponents had succeeded in setting Simon up for oblivion.

A further negative for Simon was the position itself. After John Nance Garner of Texas served two terms as vice president of the United States with Franklin D. Roosevelt, the press paraphrased his opinion of the position as not "worth a bucket of warm spit." Garner said the vice president is "just a waiting boy, waiting just in case something happens to the president." Substitute lieutenant governor and governor in Garner's statements for an idea of the position Simon sought in 1968.

The 1870 Illinois constitution provided two jobs for the lieutenant governor. The official acted as governor in the absence of the governor from the state and presided over sessions of the state senate. This hardly amounted to even a part-time job. The lieutenant governor had almost no staff because the governor's was available if needed, and there was no provision for accommodations while in Springfield. No wonder hardly any citizens of Illinois could name a single lieutenant governor who had served in their lifetimes.

Events beyond Simon's reach put a cloud over the campaign. Citizens might be forgiven for ignoring the lieutenant governor race during 1968 when so many cataclysmic events occurred to rock the nation. President Lyndon Johnson on March 31 said he would not run for reelection. On April 4, Martin Luther King Jr. was assassinated in Memphis. In the national primary campaign, Robert Kennedy was shot and killed in Los Angeles after winning the

California primary. By the time of the Democratic National Convention in Chicago, selection of Vice President Hubert Humphrey was assured, but that was about all that could be predicted. Fearing negative outcomes from the convention, Simon lamented to staff that party leaders had chosen Chicago.[25]

As the world remembers so well, the streets of Chicago erupted in violence with policemen and National Guard soldiers battling Vietnam war protestors every night of the convention. Meanwhile, inside the convention hall, a party split over the war and the seating of minority delegations paraded its divisions before a national television audience. At the center of the convention melee was the Illinois delegation headed by Mayor Daley. Images of an angry Daley on his feet shaking his fist at words and people he disliked became the poster boy for anti-Chicago and anti-Daley sentiments.

Delegate Simon, chosen because of his presence on the statewide ticket, wrestled with his conscience. How far down the line should he go with the Daley forces that dominated the delegation? He cast a vote for Humphrey, as did 112 of 118 delegates, but he made a separate stand on two high-tension issues. He voted for the minority "peace plank" on the Vietnam War—which failed—while Daley fully backed the war and President Johnson's pursuit of it. Only thirteen Illinois delegates voted for the minority plank, including Dick Mudge of Madison County, Cameron Satterthwaite of Champaign, Attorney General Clark, Adlai Stevenson, and Simon.[26] On another emotional issue that threatened convention decorum, Simon voted to seat the minority delegation from Georgia in a dispute over credentials.

After the convention, Simon looked for an angle to express concern for convention proceedings and the quality of news coverage. In a column, Simon reviewed the issues and placed blame.[27] Mostly he pleaded for responsible actions on all sides and exonerated all but the fringes of the protestors and police. His words:

> 1. Many of the criticisms of the system are justified . . . Improvements are needed. For example, a bill I have sponsored in several sessions (which has always been defeated) calls for a candidate for delegate to a convention to indicate on the ballot whom he favors for the presidential nomination. Most people in Illinois haven't the foggiest notion which candidate for president they are supporting when they vote for a delegate.
>
> 2. Booing and name-calling cannot be stopped by regulation but various delegation chairmen ought to discourage that type of childish display.
>
> 3. Adequate security was essential at the convention. If Mayor Daley had not provided security and 20 people had been killed and the convention halted, criticisms of him would be much more severe than they are now.

4. The majority of police acted responsibly and the majority of demonstrators acted responsibly. In all of the fuss and furor I'm afraid most people have not learned that simple fact. A small minority of policemen and a small minority of demonstrators went too far.

5. Police policy in such a situation should be adequate manpower and great restraint. If people want to hold a meeting, let them. If they want a peaceful parade, let them.

6. Those who come to a convention city should understand clearly that they will be permitted to exercise their legal rights, but when they violate the law they will be promptly arrested.

7. Young people who became involved in the [Eugene] McCarthy and [George] McGovern races (or in the Rockefeller race in the GOP) should not become disheartened. A criticism frequently leveled at reformers is that they are "one-shot fighters." I hope the many outstanding young people who involved themselves this year will not fit that description.

He said those watching television on Wednesday night, when the violence escalated, "knew much more than those of us on the convention floor. The first I knew of the incidents in downtown Chicago was when Senator [Abraham] Ribicoff made his speech, and then a few minutes later a tearful young McCarthy supporter came and talked to me." Simon's calm and rational approach to what happened in Chicago, written so close to the event, stood in stark contrast to the uproar of the aftermath.

Simon did not stop with a column on the subject. Speaking at a journalism convocation at Northern Illinois University in DeKalb, he urged Sigma Delta Chi, the professional journalists' organization, to review convention media coverage and report to the nation. Addressing journalists, he said, "We are probably too close to the event to make a fair appraisal of that coverage, but the national journalism fraternity which has as one of its aims the improvement of quality news work, would be doing the nation and the profession a service with a thorough review."[28] He suggested choosing two or three journalism school deans to make the survey, with financing by a private foundation.

As the 1968 election campaign gained momentum after the convention and Labor Day, Simon faced many hurdles. He did not have sufficient money to counter a television advertising campaign by his wealthier opponent, Dwyer. Simon bought only minimal radio time. Operating on a shoestring, he made the campaign a family affair by enlisting the services of his brother Arthur, who took a leave of absence for most of 1968 from duties as pastor of Trinity Lutheran Church on Manhattan's Lower East Side. Arthur described his role: "I started at the bottom of the state in March and worked my way up the state visiting communities, walking the business districts and handing out materials, telling them I was Paul's brother."[29] Simon's father took time away from his religious work. His mother spent untold hours on the telephone going through the state's phone books to tell people she was Paul's mother. After noting she had made thousands of calls, one politician said, "How many mothers does Paul Simon have?" When school and family duties allowed, Simon's wife Jeanne and their children Sheila, age seven, and Martin, age four, joined the campaign, often traveling in a cramped station wagon.

Campaign frustrations annoyed Simon and staff. Hardly anyone paid attention to the Simon-Dwyer contest until near election day when endorsement editorials appeared, most favoring Simon. He recalled holding press conferences where no reporters showed up. Coordination with the Shapiro campaign was minimal, which in the long run cost the gubernatorial candidate. While some of the Democratic candidates made occasional appearances downstate, most preferred to campaign with billboards and paid media announcements. Simon recalled a meeting of party candidates in Chicago during the national convention. When they compared plans for the campaign, Simon, Howlett, and Powell all had long lists of commitments for appearances, the other candidates hardly any. Simon, Howlett, and Powell worked the whole state energetically. Simon admitted he developed a modicum of respect for the hard-working Powell on the campaign trail. "We started a friendship," Simon acknowledged, while making it clear that he did not excuse Powell's past transgressions.[30] Simon spent about 70 percent of his campaign time in Chicago and suburbs where he had less name recognition than downstate.

Simon was on his own, although he remained loyal to Shapiro and worked in the governor's behalf whenever appropriate. An example occurred late in the campaign. Gene Callahan, who worked for Shapiro, called on the editor of Lindsay-Schaub newspapers in Decatur to pitch for endorsement of Shapiro.[31] The organization owned newspapers in Carbondale, Edwardsville, Decatur, East St. Louis, and Champaign-Urbana, with a combined daily circulation of 170,000. They constituted the most important single endorsement downstate. In a meeting with the group editor, Callahan discovered that while the editor had no enthusiasm for Ogilvie, the papers would not endorse Shapiro without an opportunity to talk with the candidate. Callahan's conversation with Simon about the situation resulted in Shapiro's appearance in Decatur. Though it is unclear whether that conversation had any impact, the papers endorsed Shapiro and Simon.

Campaigning for a position that had no specific responsibility for public policy and in support of Shapiro, Simon had to be careful about presenting a detailed program of initiatives and change. Simon's staff confronted that situation with tactical questions. Should Simon be aggressive in discussion of issues? If Simon can't buy news, should he make it? How does Simon protect his future? Staff members' campaign suggestions included addresses at major forums, advertising frequency and message, use of task forces and citizen committees, and formal presentations in speeches.[32] Simon made his own decisions and in the end decided not to overplay his hand with Shapiro and the Democratic organization by aggressively going it alone.

Doing the rounds of newspaper editorial boards, Simon spoke in generalities about the possible relationship with Shapiro and how the two could work together. He hoped to influence the governor to adopt programs for urban areas and promised to ask Shapiro for permission to spend two or three days a month in the cities as an ombudsman to meet with citizens who had issues about state government, and report to the governor. Those appeared to be modest requests, but doubters could not imagine Daley allowing Simon to resolve government complaints in Chicago. Getting more specific seemed inappropriate and maybe even politically dangerous.

Newspapers across the state offered separate endorsements for lieutenant governor, with Simon receiving some alongside an endorsement of Ogilvie. An exception was the *Chicago Tribune*, which referred to the candidate as "talkative State Senator Paul Simon, an advocate of many ultra-liberal causes."[33] An editorial in the five Lindsay-Schaub newspapers complimented Simon for his votes at the Democratic national convention and stated, "His excellent House and Senate records would qualify him for an active position in determining party and state policy."[34] Maybe the most impassioned endorsement appeared in papers formerly owned by Simon. Elmer Fedder, editor of three weekly papers, praised his former business associate: "He is an honest man, he is a hard working man, he is a good Christian, he is a man who has the capabilities to serve his state well in high office . . . He is qualified by ability, integrity and desire to serve the people of Illinois."[35]

Debates over how Simon would conduct himself and the issues he would address changed dramatically on election day but not before some early anxiety. During the vote counting, Simon recalled concern and disappointment among family and friends as the state totals came in. Because most commentators believed the governor and lieutenant governor ran as a team, few gave separate returns for Simon. As the counting continued into the early hours of the next day, it became clear that Simon had scored a stunning victory. Anxious to get his own confirmation of the outcome, Simon talked with Daley about 3 A.M. The mayor assured him there were enough votes—as it turned out, about 100,000 more than the Republican candidate received.[36]

Simon became the first lieutenant governor in Illinois history elected with a governor of the opposing party. Ogilvie narrowly defeated Shapiro for governor, receiving 51.2 percent of the vote. It was also the last split vote of the offices. The 1970 Constitutional Convention put the governor and lieutenant governor candidates on the ticket together, with the first vote in 1972. Simon's 1968 victory may rank as one of the biggest upset victories in state elections and certainly led to the strangest arrangement between the governor and lieutenant governor. Two days after the election Simon met with a full room of media representatives. Remembering the campaign, he asked, "Where were you when I needed you?"[37]

The peculiarity of the arrangement with Ogilvie guaranteed high-profile attention from the media. With the governor out of the state, Simon would be in charge with full powers to act as governor. One Ogilvie staff member said, "It doesn't look as though we'll be making any extended foreign tours."[38] At his first press conference after the election, Simon said that his duty to the people "requires cooperation with the governor so that the machinery of government does not get stopped by partisan bickering."[39] In a column written after both men were in office, Simon commented:

> Shortly after I learned the election results, I phoned the governor-elect and told him I would not use the authority of the lieutenant governor to be an obstructionist. When he leaves the state and I am acting governor, no bills will be signed or vetoed, no vacancies filled, no cabinet members fired. All of these things I could legally do, but will not. I also assured him if tragedy should strike either of the United States Senators—when I am acting as governor—and I hope and pray it does not—I would not fill the vacancy by appointment, though I have the authority to do it. For his part, the governor-elect assured me of his cooperation saying he agreed the lieutenant governor must have an adequate and competent staff.[40]

Simon struck just the right chord. The press applauded and the people approved. The professional attitude of both lasted through the four years of the term, 1969–1973, although each was counseled to pull dirty tricks on the other. Simon wrote of Ogilvie, "While he and I had our occasional differences, he had courage and integrity, both qualities not found in abundance historically in Illinois politics."[41] For his part, Ogilvie said of Simon, "I think he is a high-class legislator. I think he is a high-class gentleman."

Ogilvie and Simon shared a common interest in battles before arriving in Springfield in 1969. Each had earned stars for fighting crime and corruption, Ogilvie as a federal prosecutor in Chicago, then as sheriff of Cook County. Simon did his anticrime work as a newspaper editor. In their own ways, they were thorns in the side of Mayor Daley. Ogilvie won the race for sheriff in 1962 in order to confront crime in Daley's backyard, followed in 1966 by winning the presidency of the county board of commissioners. Simon fought with Chicago interests in less direct fashion, speaking through his columns and in the legislature. Their differences over philosophies were well known. Ogilvie strongly supported the presidency of Richard M. Nixon while Simon shared common interest with memories of John F. Kennedy and the liberalism of Paul Douglas. As matters developed, they had major differences in the running of the state, but they agreed on many ideas and policy decisions.

Troy Call, Weekly Newspaper, Purchased By Paul Simon

Paul Simon's entry into the newspaper business was announced in Highland, Illinois, where his parents lived.
Special Collections Research Center, Morris Library, Southern Illinois University Carbondale

Published For 50 Years By Ben Jarvis

Paul Simon, son of Mr. and Mrs. M. P. Simon, and a student at the present time at Dana College in Dana, Nebraska, has purchased the Troy Call, a weekly newspaper in Troy, Ill., from Ben Jarvis, previous owner and publisher for the past 50 years.

Mr. Simon is a journalism major at Dana, and previously had taken courses in this line at the University of Oregon. His parents are publishers of the Christian Education Company of Highland. He will complete his schooling this semester, and will officially take over publication of the Call about June 1.

Mr. Jarvis has been associated with newspaper work for more than fifty years, but recently retired from business due to ill health. Since his retirement, there has been no newspaper in Troy, but several neighboring papers have been attempting to collect and publish the news and advertising from that community. Mr. Jarvis' sale includes the business and machinery.

In making the announcement of his son's purchase of the newspaper yesterday morning, M. P. Simon stated that the transaction had the approval of the Lion's Club of Troy, and further stated that business men there declared that sometime in the near future a bank would be reopened in Troy, and that plans were being made to install a waterworks system and a street-lighting whiteway.

THE TROY TRIBUNE

News of Troy, Marine and St. Jacob

Troy, Illinois

June 1948

Dear Friend:

In a few weeks THE TROY TRIBUNE will begin publication.
Each issue will contain a very complete coverage of Troy's
news and a great deal of news from Marine and St. Jacob. In
addition to this news of you and your neighbor, THE TRIBUNE
will carry advertisements which can serve as your shopping
guide. In this way THE TRIBUNE will be a big money saver for you.

We plan to give you all of this for two dollars a year.
Be a charter reader of THE TROY TRIBUNE by sending your money
now in the enclosed envelope together with your name and address.

There are many people who formerly lived in Troy, St.
Jacob, or Marine, or are very much interested in happenings there.
If you know of any we would appreciate it very much if you would
send us the names and addresses. You know how you have missed
your weekly Troy paper. They miss it too.

So far, plans for the paper are going very well. The main
trouble seems to be that paper will be quite scarce for a while.
We are aiming to have eight pages or more each week.

We'll be waiting for your envelope.

Cordially,

Paul Simon

Editor

P. S. Subscribe for your friends and neighbors. A subscription to THE TRIBUNE makes an excellent gift. We will be
happy to send a gift card from you if you subscribe for someone.

Shortly before the first issue of the *Troy Tribune*, Simon sent a letter to residents soliciting
support and promising eight pages or more each week. Special Collections Research Center,
Morris Library, Southern Illinois University Carbondale

PRINTING & PUBLISHING

TELEPHONE 4

THE TROY TRIBUNE

PAUL SIMON, EDITOR & PUBLISHER

Troy, Illinois

7-23-49

Governor Adlai Stevenson
Springfield, Illinois

Dear Governor Stevenson;

The situation in Madison county regarding gambling is becoming increasingly worse, so bad that I am taking the liberty of writing to you.

One of the things which was given much publicity in the recent elections was the fact that the Green administration
did nothing about the gambling in our county. Since that
time the situation has become increasingly worse. Some
action was taken a few months ago by your attorney general
and I sincerely appreciate this fact. However, the two
places which he closed are again open and as wide-open as
ever.

The entire situation does nothing to slacken criticism
which your opponents are shouting to those of us who supported your group for the reasons mentioned above.

I am not suggesting what action should be taken, only that
it should be taken.

While I am writing I should add that you are quietly making
a very impressive show for those of us who are sitting on
the sidelines. My best wishes for your very able administration.

Thanking you for whatever consideration you can give the Madison county situation, I remain,

                        Very cordially,

                        Paul Simon

A Progressive Newspaper In A Progressive Town

Simon wrote Gov. Adlai E. Stevenson about serious crime problems in Madison County.
Courtesy of the Abraham Lincoln Presidential Library

TROJAN THOUGHTS

BY PAUL SIMON

It seems the headlines in last week's Tribune about the prostitution which is being practiced in the county "shocked" a good many people.

According to many, I had no business publishing the article.

Before the last embers of talk have died, I would like to take a few minutes to explain my reasons for doing what I did.

◆ ◆ ◆

This article is being written long before this issue comes out and perhaps some news on the front page that the sheriff has again locked the doors of the joints will be more than proof enough for the publication of such an article.

And maybe there won't be any such news.

Regardless of whether the sheriff or state's attorney took action the readers of the Tribune now know what they have done and what they have not done. If they continue to do nothing, it's well that you know it so that when election time rolls around you can vote some good men into office.

Another thing is that the newspaperman has the responsibility to bring you the news—particularly when it concerns possible corruption on the part of public officials. If it shocks you I'm sorry but that's my business: to bring you the news.

Finally, if that helped in any way to close those places along Route 40, I will be very, very happy.

If some weak-kneed fellow was saved from the results of a disease, it was worth publication.

Of one thing you can be certain—however much you may have disliked our publication of the story, there were county officials and "business men" near Collinsville who disliked it much more than did you.

◆ ◆ ◆

Here and there . . . In last week's story on the Formosa school one gentleman told me he got the impression we were hitting at Les Bohnenstiehl for not investigating further last week when the toilet was reported dumped at the school . . . Poor Les Bohnenstiehl and the other members of the Formosa board . . . Alvin Loyet and Mike Bequette . . . They have had so much trouble there that it was getting to be routine . . . If we had more men like these three who are willing to take on public responsibility even when it means plenty of headaches, things would be much different in this old world . . . In the "Other Editors" column this week we have some good material . . . As there is every week . . . If we don't have it in this issue already, we shortly will have a column in German running each week . . . I'm afraid I won't be able to get much out of it but many of the people around here should enjoy it.

Simon explained in a column why he wrote articles about his visit to houses of prostitution near Troy.

A youthful Simon, right, and *Tribune* employees at work producing a paper in January
1951. *St. Louis Post-Dispatch*

Simon, seated at far left, attended an anticrime hearing in February 1951 conducted by Sen. Estes
Kefauver, center with back to camera. Courtesy of the Abraham Lincoln Presidential Library

Tribune Editor Takes Legal Steps Against Dallas Harrell, A. Lewis

Mr. Charles B. Stephens
Executive Secretary
Illinois State Bar Association
First National Bank Building
Springfield, Illinois
Dear Mr. Stephens:

You may consider this letter a request for the proper committees of the Illinois State Bar Association to institute disciplinary proceedings against Austin Lewis, a member of the Illinois Bar Association and at the present time State's Attorney of Madison County.

Austin Lewis served as assistant state's attorney for a number of years prior to his election in 1948. After his election he continued what he called "common sense law enforcement," but which I have termed dollars and cents law enforcement. Under this system Madison county was opened to big-time gambling, and the gambling kings became the big contributors to political campaigns of both parties, thereby wielding a political influence far and above the weight they would carry as citizens ordinarily.

Periodically the gamblers were brought to court and given a nominal fine, but they continued to operate with the full knowledge of the state's attorney. The procedure followed by Lewis brought the legal profession into ill repute and made a farce of legal procedure by his failure to mention that the defendants were guilty of more than one offense. There is no question but that his actions brought the courts of Madison county into disrepute.

As a result of his failure to take action he was approached by the governor of this state and the attorney general with a request to eliminate this flagrant state of the law in Madison county. The close cooperation of those who violate the law with the law enforcement officials was too binding a thing to allow Lewis to act. Finally the governor ordered state police into our county to do what Austin Lewis, with the cooperation of the sheriff, should have done months previously.

Since the governor's actions there has been a marked improvement of the situation in Madison county — but there has been no repudiation of those who cooperated in making such an unfortunate situation arise. If there is a change in state administration, or if the courts should rule the governor has no legal authority to clamp down in Madison county, I have every reason to believe the former situation would prevail again.

I therefore am requesting that you refer this complaint to the Committee on Inquiry, the Committee of Grievances and the Board of Governors of the Illinois State Bar Association for appropriate action.

This is in no sense caused by personal animosity or political motive. Today I also am filing a complaint asking the next session of the grand jury to indict our former sheriff, Dallas Harrell, a Republican. Austin Lewis is a Democrat. I am on personally friendly terms with both men.

If I can be of help to you in any way, feel free to call on me. If your group can take some type of disciplinary action, it would be a healthy thing for the legal profession and the courts of our county and state, and it would be a real service to the people of Madison county.

Thanking you in advance for your efforts, I remain,

Very cordially,
PAUL SIMON

A complaint was filed Tuesday in the State's Attorney's office asking the next session of the grand jury to indict the former sheriff, Dallas Harrell, for "palpable omission of duty" in failure to prevent the wide-open gambling which was prevalent in Madison county before Gov. Stevenson acted.

In addition a request has been made to the executive secretary of the State Bar Association to institute "disciplinary procedure" against the present state's attorney, Austin Lewis.

Both actions were instituted by Paul Simon, editor and publisher of The Troy Tribune.

State's Attorney Austin Lewis has assured Simon of his cooperation in bringing the matter of Dallas Harrell to the attention of the grand jury when it meets in March.

The maximum fine against the sheriff is $10,000 according to law and the maximum penalty for the state's attorney would be disbarment.

Action against the sheriff would come in March or April while final action of the Illinois Bar Association cannot come for some months since they first must make an investigation and then make their recommendation to the state supreme court.

The complaint alleges that the sheriff was aware that there was wide-open gambling in Madison county but made no effort to stop it as he is required by law.

The letter to the Illinois Bar Association is printed elsewhere on this page.

In announcing his action Simon said, "If this can in any way help clear the air of political corruption which has hung around Madison county, then it's well worth the effort.

"One thing I hope will result from this action is that the corrupting menace to good government in Madison county called 'common sense law enforcement' will die a hard, permanent death."

The complaint against the sheriff reads:

Plaintiff, Paul Simon, complaining of the Defendant, Dallas Harrell, says:

Simon took direct action against Madison County officials in a fight against corruption.

Paul Simon, pictured at age twenty-seven in 1955, began his career in elective office as a member of the Illinois House of Representatives. Courtesy of the Abraham Lincoln Presidential Library

In 1958, Simon attended a banquet in Chicago featuring Eleanor Roosevelt and former governor Adlai E. Stevenson II. Special Collections Research Center, Morris Library, Southern Illinois University Carbondale

Simon rides with former president Harry S. Truman during a parade at Troy in 1962. Gov. Otto Kerner is seated at Truman's left. Special Collections Research Center, Morris Library, Southern Illinois University Carbondale

Simon, with a bust of Abraham Lincoln, enjoys a moment in 1965 during the announcement of his book about Lincoln's days in the Illinois General Assembly. Courtesy of the Abraham Lincoln Presidential Library

Simon and Anthony
Scariano, right, who
served in the legislature
together, shared strong
feelings about the need
for more openness in
government. Courtesy
of the Abraham Lincoln
Presidential Library

Simon, on one of his
many foreign trips,
visited South Vietnam
in 1967. Special Collections
Research Center, Morris
Library, Southern Illinois
University Carbondale

Democratic candidates
for state offices in 1968
included, from left,
Simon, Paul Powell,
William G. Clark,
Samuel Shapiro, Michael
Howlett, and Frank
Lorenz. Simon, Powell,
and Howlett won.
Courtesy of the Abraham
Lincoln Presidential Library

Simon, the new Illinois lieutenant governor, and his wife, Jeanne, attend the 1969 inaugural ball. Courtesy of the Abraham Lincoln Presidential Library

Jeanne and Paul Simon, in 1972, stroll on the grounds of their home in Troy. From the *St. Louis Globe-Democrat* archives of the St. Louis Mercantile Library at the University of Missouri–St. Louis

Sen. Edward Kennedy helped Simon campaign for Congress in southern Illinois.
Special Collections Research Center, Morris Library, Southern Illinois University Carbondale

Simon in 1985 takes the Senate oath of office with Vice President George H. W. Bush, attended by his family: Sheila, Jeanne, and Martin. Special Collections Research Center, Morris Library, Southern Illinois University Carbondale

Longtime friends Simon and Sen. Alan Dixon served together in Washington. Courtesy of Alan Dixon

Simon questions a witness at the 1990 hearing for Supreme Court candidate David Souter. U.S. Senate Historical Office

Patti and Paul Simon attend a public policy institute event for Walter Cronkite in 2003. Southern Illinois University Photocommunications

An Agent of Great Change

Selecting staff members was among the first duties for Simon as lieutenant governor. In the appointments of three, Simon began or continued close personal relationships that lasted the remainder of his life. The relationships were based on loyalty but even more on respect. The three he hired were Ray Johnsen, Richard Durbin, and Gene Callahan.

Ray Johnsen and Simon began their relationship at Dana College in the late 1940s. They became newspaper partners in the *Troy Tribune* and other weekly papers until 1966 when Simon divested himself of financial involvement. Johnsen continued as chief operator of the *Tribune* in partnership with Elmer Fedder for a few more years. After Simon won the 1968 election, he hired Johnsen to handle lieutenant governor office paperwork. Johnsen continued to run the U.S. representative and U.S. senate offices for Simon until 1994.[1]

Richard Durbin, a native of East St. Louis, did his first political work as a volunteer in the office of Senator Paul Douglas while attending law school at Georgetown University. That is where Simon met Durbin. After graduating with a law degree, Durbin joined the lieutenant governor's staff in 1969. He worked all but the last months of the four-year term and soon began his own climb in elective politics, including seven terms as a U.S. representative from central Illinois beginning in 1982 and election to the U.S. senate seat vacated by Simon in 1996.[2]

Gene Callahan and Simon met in 1958 while Callahan was a reporter on the *Illinois State Register* in Springfield.[3] He started covering police news and in 1960 was assigned to work the statehouse as a political reporter, writing two columns a week. That soon expanded to five columns a week. Callahan and Simon took an immediate liking to each other, which led to talks about politics during the legislative sessions. In 1967 Callahan left the newspaper to do freelance political work for the Democrats. He recognized Simon as a potential future star in the party.

Callahan started volunteer public relations work for Simon in downstate areas. Callahan recalls receiving monthly checks of $35 from Simon, but he did not cash any of them. In September 1967, Governor Shapiro hired

Callahan as assistant press secretary "at much more than I was paid in newspaper work." Callahan had known Shapiro since childhood. During the 1968 campaign, Callahan traveled full time with the governor and remained on his staff until the Ogilvie administration began. Callahan received job offers from Auditor Howlett and Neil Hartigan, a rising star in Chicago politics. He turned them down to work for Simon "for less money." During the lieutenant governor term, Callahan worked as press secretary and administrative assistant. He wrote press releases for Simon, but Simon wrote his own columns, continuing a practice begun in 1948.

Callahan became more than just a staff member. He served as consultant, press aide, recruiter, and political operator. He courted the statehouse press on behalf of Simon. Callahan said simply, "I really liked Simon." After Simon finished his lieutenant governor term in 1973, Callahan joined the staff of Treasurer Alan Dixon and continued as an aide until Dixon's defeat for reelection to the U.S. senate in 1992. Through all those years, Callahan remained a close adviser to Simon, often helping in election campaigns on loan from Dixon.

Callahan more than earned his keep with Simon from 1969 to 1973, helping his boss make news and working with the Springfield press corps and media people across the state. It seemed he knew all the players by their first names and shared mutual experiences that kept them connected. Like most good political press relations people, Callahan knew his role: helping Simon's star shine bright.

While some political pundits predicted four years of exile as lieutenant governor, Simon was more than equal to the challenge, demonstrating brilliant communications skills in defining the position and his unique role. On paper the objective looked simple: keep his name in play across the state and relate it as much as possible to issues. Genius may be too strong a word for Simon's creativity in achieving this goal, but during this period only the governor got more ink than Simon, and on some days not by much. It irked Ogilvie's staff and leaders of the legislature and gave Simon's enemies additional ammunition, but Simon managed to stay a step or two ahead of them all.

One of his first acts as lieutenant governor was to launch the ombudsman program. No matter how clever an idea, making it work required an energetic and articulate person. Simon had the knack, the stamina, and the help of a small but smart staff and hundreds of volunteer soldiers in the field. He made the lieutenant governor plan work with visibility and the aid of an attentive press corps. The nerve of this still young man to make a constitutional office in his image had the feel of history in the making. Reporters and editors pushed Simon's star higher than ever before.

Not every voice sang praise, an example being the *Cairo Evening Citizen* and its editor Martin Brown. An editorial questioned the new direction of the lieutenant governor's office, preferring, it appeared, the situation when Shapiro held the office and one aide and one secretary did the work. Lamenting Simon's plan to expand the office into new territory, the editorial said, "The office of lieutenant governor in Illinois apparently is about to be launched into orbit and forgotten forever. It started when Paul Simon made history by becoming the first man to get elected to that office when he belonged to a different party than the governor."[4] The editorial recited Simon's background, including his time as newspaper editor, adding, "We've no doubts about his capabilities and have confidence that he can be a great asset in our state. We said this long before he became lieutenant governor." The editorial noted that Simon was a likely opponent of Ogilvie for governor.

The paper complained that Simon had six aides, one a publicity man earning $17,000 a year. It noted Simon's budget request "is the largest in history, $300,000." The paper concluded by expressing doubt that Ogilvie and Simon could maintain a civil tone in their relationship. "If Paul Simon intends to use his massive office staff to improve Illinois, well and good. If it is going to be used to build a campaign machine which will begin moving long before the next election, then it's time we blew the whistle and reduced the team to standard size, and let the lieutenant governor have as his major assignment the presiding over the Senate."

Simon could not let the letter go without an answer. First he "corrected" the comment about a full-time "publicity man." Gene Callahan, Simon said, "is a former newspaper man and one of the things he does is take care of inquiries from newspapers. But he also has many other responsibilities. His responsibilities in our office include the fields of agriculture, conservation, highways and personnel."[5] He admitted having a larger staff than previous lieutenant governors, adding, "For obvious reasons [a small staff] is no longer possible. Secondly, we are moving to annual sessions, and this means a greater budget and work load." Simon rarely let critical commentary go unanswered.

Republicans, suffering a major case of denial about the election outcome, resorted to treatment of Simon that led to backlash and cast Simon in the role of victim. From the outset, W. Russell Arrington, the Republican majority leader of the state senate and the most powerful person in the General Assembly, did not like the idea of having to share responsibilities when the senate met. As senate leader, Arrington got his way on how to run the chamber. Simon had responsibility for presiding. They obviously disagreed on many subjects and resolved most of those out of sight, with one major exception: office space for the lieutenant governor.

Since the 1870s, lieutenant governors had used the same large office space in the capitol building. When Shapiro moved to the governor's office before the end of Kerner's term, Arrington took the lieutenant governor's office for his own. He assumed the next lieutenant governor would be of the governor's party and the rightful occupants would resume historic locations.[6] Simon upset that thinking, and Arrington refused to move, exercising his position of power and citing the need, however weak, for space to accommodate staff and the flow of senate business. This left Simon to occupy the much smaller space Arrington had evacuated.

Simon's friends urged him to protest loudly, but Simon turned the other cheek, choosing only to express his disappointment at Arrington's arrogance. However, Simon's friends in the press made the disagreement sound as if survival of the ship of state depended on Arrington giving Simon the office. Variously, columnists belittled the majority leader, calling his refusal a "sit-in." Quietly, Simon assumed the role of victim and moved to the smaller office. Arrington never backed down. Two years later when Democrats took control of the senate, Simon finally moved to the lieutenant governor's historic location.

The keystone in Simon's plan turned out to be the ombudsman program. Callahan, intending to make the idea sound exotic, said he had never heard of an ombudsman, "and I didn't even know how to spell it."[7] Simon described the term as of Swedish origin, "meaning a complaint officer who assists people seeking help in their dealings with governmental agencies." While it may have had different interpretations around the globe, that definition fit the model used by Simon. The shorthand description often used was "cutting red tape." From the beginning, the program had few limitations. The only subjects excluded were matters before the courts or the result of court judgments.

Staff did not promise to achieve favorable results. If after an initial inquiry workers found governmental or private agencies made equitable and proper decisions, citizens were so advised. Simon also did not promise to protect the state from criticisms of citizens, describing his mission as a "man who tries to cut red tape in helping the citizens with their problems with government and private agencies."[8] Not all claims were justified or reconcilable, but "they all get heard and that in itself brings government closer to the people."

Citizens all over Illinois inundated the Springfield and Chicago offices with phone calls, letters, and personal contacts about issues that needed sorting for action. As Simon made his way around Illinois for personal appearances and political activities, he collected many requests in person.

People with concerns called Simon at his home in Troy. Staffers preferred receiving requests in writing, which saved time in handling, and they found that people tended to be more accurate and less prone to exaggeration when they put their concerns on paper. Keeping count of contacts was difficult because of the huge numbers and limited staff time. Simon's staff never became larger than ten to handle all the activities of the office. Over the first seventeen months of the program, until June 1970, Simon estimated receiving 22,000 complaints and requests.[9] That number rose to more than 42,000 over three years. He figured letters came at the rate of 100 to 130 a day.

With reach into all the corners of the state, it was only a matter of time before opponents attempted to clip Simon's wings and nullify his ombudsman role. After only three months of operation, jealous legislators, egged on by Republican leadership, tried a pincer movement.[10] First, the Legislative Budgetary Commission sent Simon's request for operating funds to a committee of two Republicans and one Chicago Democrat. They threatened to reduce Simon's budget that provided mostly for staff. Simon said he needed the people regardless of the ombudsman program. Legislators took another approach by submitting a bill that would have given the governor authority to appoint an ombudsman. These actions created a howl from media across the state, so loud that critics of Simon backed away from reducing the budget or creating a different ombudsman program by law.

Because of the volume of requests for help and the number of success stories, Simon always had examples at hand to demonstrate the plight of people and how his office helped. If nothing more, they showed that people had ongoing issues with their government at all levels, and the cases multiplied as government grew and population expanded. Many complaints required little more than a telephone call or conversation to fix. A woman called to complain that government agencies were bickering among themselves and could not decide how to correct problems caused by a flood.[11] Several telephone calls later, taking about ninety minutes, agency efforts were coordinated and relief was on its way to suffering citizens.

Staff members could not solve all problems as easily. After a complaint by a mental health association about unlicensed homes into which mental patients were placed, Simon made an unannounced visit to several of the locations and found horrible conditions. Simon visited one immobile man in a filthy room who could not get downstairs for food, and he immediately summoned an ambulance. Malnutrition was the verdict after a medical examination. Simon's staff received assurances from the Department of Mental Health that efforts would be made to improve living conditions for patients.[12] Other issues seemed so complex that no simple answer could be found. Simon told the story of a rural township of 12,000 population, almost entirely black, in northern Illinois:

> The community leaders had banded together to raise $70,000 for a supermarket—the first in the community—and had the shell of the building complete when they were unable to secure the additional financing which had been promised. Through our office, we helped secure private financing to complete the building and stock it, with final details still pending. We also organized a task force headed by a volunteer, a Chicago attorney. He and his fellow volunteers are doing what they can to assist these citizens who are trying to secure adequate roads, sewer facilities, public health services, and industry. The citizens of this township have not asked for handouts. They seek only advice and direction.[13]

Simon found that government was not prepared to provide instant responses. In these cases, his staff gave temporary relief until government machinery met its responsibility. He told of a woman from a small southern Illinois town that was without food or heat because her public aid check had not arrived on time. He wrote, "She could not wait until Monday for her check. We contacted a local church which delivered a sack of groceries to her and gave her a small amount of money to see her through the weekend."[14]

Some of the stories made readers or listeners feel warm all over. The state had purchased homes to accommodate a highway through a suburban Cook County community and then canceled the project. Many people dislodged by the original plan wanted to buy back their homes, but were told it could not be done legally. Simon's workers asked for the introduction of a bill permitting the Division of Highways to sell homes and property to the original owners. The bill passed and was signed by Governor Ogilvie.[15]

Another feel-good story concerned an elderly man who provided money toward the burial expenses of his brother. The brother had died while a recipient of public aid. Simon wrote about the case: "The funeral director was supposed to reimburse the man after the state agency paid the funeral bills. The mortuary neglected to do so despite numerous pleas from the elderly man. He wrote to us. At our request, the state agency notified the funeral home that it would be removed from an approved list maintained by the department unless reimbursement was made immediately. They paid quickly."[16]

One case involved building support for a community of people instead of solving a single problem. More than 400,000 Spanish-speaking citizens of Mexican and Puerto Rican background living in Chicago without direct representation on the Chicago City Council needed help. Simon went to state universities for ideas and programs that would provide programs of assistance. Noting that this group had the highest school dropout rate of any in Illinois, Simon said, "We are exploring ways of meeting some of the immediate, pressing needs of the community."[17] The effort received widespread media attention.

Inevitably, Simon got drawn into controversies. One of the first and longest lasting involved racial troubles in Cairo, a town of more than 8,000 people at the southern tip of Illinois, about 40 percent African American. A few weeks after the ombudsman program began, Simon received a telephone call from Martin Brown, editor of the *Cairo Evening Citizen,* that set in motion the lieutenant governor's involvement as a mediator.

The community at the confluence of the Mississippi and Ohio rivers had known racial conflict for years. Attitudes of the Old South were part of the culture and community tradition. Once a thriving town, Cairo had fallen into economic distress, unable to provide opportunities for lifting blacks out of poverty. A *New York Times* reporter described the town this way: "Rows of dingy stores stand vacant. Unpainted shacks house many of the 4,000 Negroes. Most of the whites, who have always held all the economic and political power in this Southern-oriented city, live in modest but much more adequate frame houses."[18] In a written statement about living conditions, the Chamber of Commerce stated, "Our image has been devastated, our economy is crippled and our future, if there is one, is dark."

On the first day and night of April 1969, the residents of Cairo experienced sporadic gunfire and protests.[19] Tensions cooled temporarily after a thunderstorm drenched the area with rain. The mayor implemented a curfew. Attempts to schedule meetings of opposing forces failed, and curfews remained in place. Anger prevailed between blacks who organized to demonstrate for greater tolerance, jobs, and civil rights and a group known as the "White Hats," enlisted to augment understaffed law enforcement and to help keep the peace. County and local officials, seen by protestors as part of the problem, had lost control.

In the next two weeks, tensions ebbed and flowed. Shootings continued, police arrested a few people, and inflamed rhetoric shattered any chance of peace talks. During this time, Editor Brown called Simon to report that the governor and Attorney General William Scott had not responded to his request for assistance in a worsening environment.[20] He feared the town would explode without a third party's involvement. Simon agreed to send staff members and visit himself in an effort to apply pressure for talks. Early in the week of April 14, three of Simon's staff members arrived in Cairo. They were Gene Callahan, Dick Durbin, and Yvonne Rice, an African

American assistant to Simon. Callahan recalled never being as scared as he was during those days.[21]

Simon joined staff members in Cairo on Thursday and stayed through Friday. During the week, they interviewed "literally hundreds of citizens, both white and black," according to Simon.[22] He met with city and county officials, ministers and Catholic priests representing all the city's denominations, black leaders and private citizens, bankers, members of the Chamber of Commerce, and school and housing authorities. Many residents attended a meeting called by Simon where they candidly expressed their views.

Simon's intervention drew cautious enthusiasm. A Catholic priest at the center of protests said he was "very thankful the lieutenant governor came to our community. It would be naïve to say we're going to solve our problems in an hour and a half meeting." Brown, in an editorial, thanked Simon for appearing. He wrote, "Simon, a most sincere young man who prior to his election to the state legislature published several weekly newspapers, admitted that the situation was a most complex one."[23] Simon promised a report and recommendations.

Four days after leaving Cairo, Simon released a seven-page document of observations in the form of recommendations.[24] The *Citizen* published the report in full that day. The headline item across the state was Simon's call for Police Chief Carl J. Clutts to resign or be replaced. Simon wrote, "A change in the position of chief is essential, and that must be done quickly. The man brought in should be an experienced police officer who is fair, courageous and decisive." Protestors had targeted Clutts and called for appointment of a black chief.

Simon acknowledged accusations against the White Hats but wrote, "This fear appears to be largely unwarranted . . . The organization appears to have grown out of fear, resulting from the poor enforcement of the laws in Cairo." He called for leadership of the organization to "assure the black community that they intend no hostility." Simon said disbanding White Hats would benefit the community, "but it is unrealistic to hope for this in the immediate future."

Simon called for inclusion of blacks on the city council, at the fire department and the police department, in the local unit of the National Guard, and on the newspaper staff. He said blacks would be willing to serve on community committees. He asked community leaders, clergy, school officials, and others to "weigh their words with care" and accompanied this with a suggestion for a "rumor center" where people could call with rumors they heard and where the truth could be provided. He said the Human Relations Commission of the city "appears to have done nothing to bring about reconciliation in the community. It either should act or a new commission should be appointed."

Simon's report mixed mild cheerleading about the community's future with encouragement and scolding. He did not place blame directly on anyone, except the police chief, and addressed his comments to people who wanted to resolve problems. He condemned violence but offered no ideas that would turn matters around overnight. Problems in Cairo had lasted for years. "The recommendations are not intended to please anyone for the situation demands not comfortable answers but honest answers," he wrote. Simon directed recommendations toward improved communications, his often-used approach in settling high-octane disagreements.

Addressing the role of state government, Simon said, "The state must provide leadership in helping Cairo solve its problems . . . The state has the obligation to quit treating the deep, southern part of the state as a stepchild. In part the problems which Cairo faced have been caused by state indifference."[25] In turn, the *Citizen's* editor praised the lieutenant governor in an editorial, stating, "We at the Cairo Evening Citizen applaud Paul Simon for his willingness to help Cairo solve its problems and thank him for his courageous and forthright approach. We need more representatives in government who display these rare talents of honesty and courage."[26] This was the same editor who earlier in the year had questioned whether Simon would use his office for political gain.

Henry Bolen, president of the town's Chamber of Commerce, told the *St. Louis Post-Dispatch* that the board of directors "read Simon's report and concluded that he sincerely, honestly tried to make a report that he thought would be helpful. It was a down-the-middle report. The Lieutenant Governor said our chief has been ineffective, and the evidence shows he has been ineffective. But the mayor and the council appoint the chief. As long as they are satisfied, nothing can be done."[27] Local elected officials, especially the sheriff, mayor, and prosecuting attorney, resented Simon's involvement and recommendations.

After the report, violence and lawlessness continued, compelling the governor to send National Guard troops and state police to keep the peace. A committee of the state house of representative held hearings in Springfield and in Cairo, with officials and representatives of the protestors testifying. Simon appeared before the committee and reiterated his recommendations, calling for ouster of the police chief.[28] Late in May, the chief resigned and the council appointed an experienced lawman from Alton. However, continued conflict throughout the community resulted in his resignation after a few months.

In May, Simon received a letter from Oldham Paisley, publisher of the *Marion Republican,* questioning whether the responsibilities of the lieutenant governor included involvement in places like Cairo.[29] Paisley was representative of critics who wondered if Simon should be trying to solve Cairo's long-standing racial problems. Simon defended his actions in a letter to Paisley: "The recommendations prepared by our office have been endorsed by the Cairo Chamber of Commerce, the *Cairo Evening Citizen,* which is Cairo's only newspaper, and the clergy of Cairo; Protestant and Catholic." Regarding Paisley's concern about the governor's attitude toward Simon's role, Simon said, "The governor and I have had no disagreement regarding Cairo." Simon ended the letter, "Yes, I am proud of the fact that I have had newspaper experience. I believe being a newsman is one of the most noble of professions, and I assume that on this issue, your newspaper and I agree."[30]

With trouble continuing in Cairo, Simon sent staff member Durbin in June to consult with community leaders about organizing a police-community program. The *Evening Citizen* reported the reaction of leaders in the white and black communities: "Leaders in the white community accepted the concept of such a committee and offered suggestions as to local citizens who might serve. Leaders in the black community felt that such a committee would be powerless to enforce its decisions and as such would be of little use to their community."[31] In a memorandum to Simon, Durbin listed his observations about the meeting, the unstable law enforcement, quarrels that continued in the town, and threats to individuals. He offered little optimism.[32]

The summer wore on and Simon periodically surfaced in news accounts about Cairo. At one point, the *Alton Evening Telegraph* contacted Simon at his home in Troy. He told the paper that each side in the Cairo conflict should participate in a written agreement with time limits to accomplish certain goals. "Then if either side violated the agreement, state officials would make a public reprimand by pointing out the written pledge that had been broken," Simon said.[33] He remained willing "to drop everything" and take part in a peace meeting.

The situation in Cairo remained unsettled and Simon continued to receive mixed reviews in the state's press. Chief among the critics was the *Illinois State Journal* in Springfield, whose editorial page routinely leaned toward Republicans. An editorial in August stated, "Simon has embarked on an independent and reckless course of his own."[34] The paper noted efforts by other state officials—presumably the governor—to bring calm to Cairo but expressed alarm over Simon's acceptance of an offer to mediate from the United Front, an activist organization viewed by many as one cause of the unsettled conditions.

The editorial noted that two weeks prior the United Front had refused to meet with Ogilvie in Springfield. "It is difficult to reach a conclusion other than that Simon, knowingly or unknowingly, is permitting himself to be used as a tool by the United Front in its attacks on Gov. Richard B. Ogilvie," the paper said. The *State Journal* claimed Simon's actions threatened to rupture the close relationship between Simon and Ogilvie, adding criticism of the lieutenant governor as "a self-appointed ombudsman and trouble-shooter."

Simon tried to mediate the almost untenable situation at a meeting in Cairo on March 14, 1970. In order to minimize disruptions before the session, Simon and staff worked to avoid advance publicity.[35] When word of the meeting leaked, Simon acknowledged the planned meeting and said he hoped it would be held behind closed doors. That wish was granted by participants, leading to what Simon called "frank and open discussion."[36] At the session, Simon requested detailed statements of demands and responses from the United Front and merchants. After the meeting, he asked city officials for a "detailed profile of vacancies on city boards, agencies and commissions, as well as thoughts on the city's role in resolving Cairo's difficulties." Each party responded with information and a critical assessment of problems. The papers revealed the depth of tensions.

The parties remained distrustful, and responses to the meeting did not give Simon much encouragement. A month after the meeting, Darrell E. Kirby, chairman of the Chamber of Commerce, provided fresh proof of existing frustrations. He wrote to Simon, "The March 24th meeting really proved nothing, there was much misunderstanding from the start . . . The City of Cairo has tried, tried and tried again to do the right thing and as one of our members has stated, 'All we have gotten so far from the Federal Government is a lot of promises, confusion and red tape.'" Kirby concluded, "We welcome and solicit your help as long as it does not entail injury to the white and black citizens of our town working together for a better Cairo."[37] In a report to the public in June 1970, Simon assessed his ombudsman work in Cairo:

> A great deal of time has been spent working to ease tensions and improve the situation. After more than a year of efforts we were able to get all factions in this community to sit down and meet with one another for the first time. There is a long way to go yet in Cairo. Our efforts have not resulted in any "success story." But a community long neglected by the state knows that there are leaders concerned, and willing to work toward a better tomorrow.[38]

Work of the ombudsman continued through 1969 and into 1970, when Simon made a budget request for the lieutenant governor's office that was an increase of previous appropriations by 16 percent. The dollar figure paled when compared to expenditures in other constitutional offices. He requested one additional employee, bringing the total to thirteen, including three people working part-time. A year earlier the legislature approved an increase of 70 percent in recognition that the office needed to be independent of the governor and other state officials. Simon said even with an increase the office had far fewer employees than lieutenant governors in other large states. He noted that the lieutenant governor's budget had not increased state government costs appreciably.

During public discussions of the budget, a newspaper columnist suggested Simon issue a public report on the activities of ombudsman so the public could evaluate the work.[39] Simon agreed, and before the end of the legislative session and settlement of the state budget, he offered a report that included some statistics, examples of people and organizations served, a brief mention of Cairo, and a concluding comment on suggestions for the continuation of the office. He asked whether an ombudsman office was needed on a permanent basis. "The evidence is overwhelmingly in the affirmative," he answered. Even with various "action lines" run by newspapers, Simon said the need was not met. "And that need will grow, not diminish, for government will grow more complex not less so in the years ahead."[40]

Simon said there were both advantages and disadvantages in having the office affiliated with the lieutenant governor. "The disadvantage is that no matter how non-partisan the approach—and we have gone out of our way to keep it that—there inevitably will be charges of politics . . . The advantage to keeping it with the lieutenant governor's office is that he is in a position to open doors in both government and private sectors which otherwise would be unopened." A final option, he said, was to create a separate office of ombudsman. Simon promised to make a recommendation by the end of his term. Meanwhile, ombudsman work continued and with it concern over how much Simon's work would be a factor in a race against Ogilvie for governor in 1972. Simon wrote, "I enjoy helping people, and I also know that providing assistance could be meaningful politically."

While Simon and staff worked on the Cairo issue in 1970, their attention was diverted to violence in the streets of Carbondale where law enforcement personnel and students at Southern Illinois University clashed over a myriad of national and local issues. Leading up to May, students expressed concerns about racism, university policies such as curricula and poor communication with administrators and faculty, and expansion of the Vietnam Studies

Center.[41] Shooting deaths on the campus at Kent State University in Ohio added to tensions at SIU. Demonstrations, protests, and police reactions resulted in students occupying campus buildings, surrounding the home of President Delyte Morris and threatening to burn it to the ground. On May 12, with no resolution of differences in sight, Chancellor Robert MacVicar announced closure of the campus for an "indefinite" period. The campus reopened for the summer quarter.

Accusations flew in the wake of open hostilities. Neither side trusted the other. Police used tear gas on protesting students, and students claimed they had to react in self- defense. On the day after the closing of the school, Simon wrote to Brian Whalen, administrative assistant to Governor Ogilvie, "I have just received a telephone call from the editor of the *Southern Illinoisan,* the daily newspaper in Carbondale, and he says that the difficulties in Carbondale tonight can be reduced if the situation is handled by the National Guard and city police, keeping the state police out. He says that because of some excessive action by a few state police that student irritation with the state police is running at a very high level. I am not in a situation to evaluate this, but I respect the editor."[42] At the request of city officials, Ogilvie dispatched National Guard troops and state police to reinforce local police.

John C. Gardner, editor of the *Southern Illinoisan* newspaper during the protests, elaborated in a communication with the author about the concern over state police activities.[43] He wrote:

> The state police were a particular target of the students. On one of the initial nights of the rioting, state troopers had pursued students, some of whom, at least, were just trying to get out of the way of the melee, into the towers [dorms]. The troopers tossed tear gas into the buildings, discomforting many who were trying to avoid trouble, not make it . . . The state troopers also had rather recently formed a special unit to deal with major disturbances and they appeared on the SIU scene with a bit of self-promotion. Their technique resembled a Roman legion square and they plunged, so formed, into the middle of a crowd, only to find themselves seriously outnumbered and surrounded. Much to the rioters' delight, the state troopers remained for some time thus trapped until the National Guard came to their rescue. Much taunting over the incident continued whenever the troopers showed up after that. These troopers in the special corps, many from areas that had no universities and had seen no such actions, were felt to be more aggressive in dealing with the protestors than either the National Guard, the campus cops or Carbondale police and Jackson County deputies . . . My opinion was that the less visible the state troopers were the better.

Fearing more trouble, the Jackson County state's attorney, Richard Richman, a Democrat, asked Simon to appoint a committee to investigate the May upheaval in Carbondale and issue recommendations for reducing troubles in the future. Simon named twenty-three people to the Lieutenant Governor's Committee on Southern Illinois University with Paul Verticchio, chief judge of the Seventh Judicial Circuit in Illinois, as chairman.[44] Members were from Carbondale, Jackson County, and SIU, representing every possible interest group. Eight were SIU students, three were members of the faculty, and two had jobs in the SIU administration. The remainder held official positions in Carbondale or the county, and a few represented businesses. The committee held six meetings and heard three days of testimony before issuing its report in September with twenty-six recommendations. Twenty-two of the twenty-three members signed the report, with one student leader leaving his signature block blank.

On at least two occasions during deliberations of the committee, Simon commented on campus violence. In a column circulated to a mailing list of more than 300 media outlets, he offered answers to the general question "Campus Violence: What Can Be Done?"[45] He condemned violence and called for all sides to sit at a table and resolve differences. More specifically, he listed these recommendations:

1. Listen.
2. Examine whether some universities are too big, whether some have been permitted to grow too rapidly.
3. Give students a meaningful role in determining policy.
4. Make university rules clear so students will know that violation means expulsion.
5. Encourage student participation in the processes of government, in helping to meet the problems which society confronts.
6. Screen faculty more carefully to make sure that instructors are emotionally mature.
7. The military draft should be changed.
8. The few who are bent on violence who live off campus, who are not students, must be restrained.

Simon's separate report titled "Southern Illinois University: The Challenges of 1970," spoke to all sides in the controversy but was aimed primarily at students.[46] In an appeal for nonviolent days, Simon expressed his own misgivings about Vietnam policy and the expansion of the war into Cambodia, both issues with the protestors. He added, "Closer to home, I, too, realize the student grievances regarding problems at SIU must be given attention, and where proper, remedial action." In spite of his sympathy on those counts, Simon decried destruction of property as a means of redress. "Havoc in the streets invites, through reaction, public support of political extremists."

Well into his comments, Simon spoke to public officials. "Even as I urge students to remain calm, however, I hope that public officials can exercise restraint of their own in what has too often been inflammatory rhetoric." Addressing SIU officials, Simon said, "Students must be given a meaningful role in determining policies . . . I am not suggesting that students should run colleges; sensible students are not asking for that. But they do want to feel that their voice is heard." Mostly, Simon spoke words of reconciliation, communication, and attempts to understand the concerns of other parties.

The study committee addressed most of the charges in language that avoided accusations or demands. In fact, a close reading might have caused some people to wonder if the committee had been too general and accommodating. Editor Gardner did not recall the study group's contributions to resolution of the protests. He believes calm returned to the campus with the departure of MacVicar and the diminishment of President Delyte Morris's tenure. Most of the committee's suggestions asked for conversations between community and university interests.[47] Its recommendations included:

- Define methods by which members of the university committee can address the SIU Board of Trustees.
- Include faculty and students in formulation of university rules and policies.
- Review university procedures for the suspension and dismissal of students.
- Expand the system of legal aid to include students as well as area residents.
- University and the City of Carbondale should work together on a comprehensive physical and social plan for the entire community.
- Provide adequate housing for students.
- Encourage regular official contact between city officials and student government officers.
- Establish town meetings every quarter.
- Develop a standard operating procedure for community crises.

While the Cairo and SIU disturbances were the high-profile exceptions among the thousands of ombudsman cases, they required special handling by Simon and staff and added an element of political risk. Quick-fix solutions were not welcomed by those directly afflicted by the troubles nor would they have worked. Simon's opinions were solicited by some and rejected by others. Gardner, for example, did not recall Simon's efforts as significant to a truce on campus and in town. Simon's voice was directed toward long-term answers reached by those involved. Presenting his ideas as an enabler allowed Simon to take the high road and hand off to others a suggested roadmap. In Cairo, he issued a report that provided ideas for others to pursue. Regarding SIU, he issued statements and wrote columns but gave the main responsibility to a committee of local people who had a stake in finding answers. This approach denied him any claim of solving the problems but had two advantages: he was not blamed if others failed to reach an agreement and he could say that he tried. Moreover, he demonstrated a willingness to tackle tough issues.

Decades later, it is difficult to assess the full value of his participation. He elevated the need for concern and action in Springfield among executive officials and the legislature. He gave voice to all sides: well-meaning blacks and whites in Cairo, students and responsible adults in Carbondale. In both cases, he condemned extremists and spoke to the large middle ground. Simon's involvement empowered all sides and gave them an opportunity to attack his ideas rather than fight only among themselves. Inevitably, critics cried "politics" and accused him of making a personal pilgrimage. Simon was the last person to deny that politics played a role. The ombudsman project had enormous political implications. Simon's ability to deal with critical issues, not take sides, and make a quick exit from the scene minimized political criticism and built respect among citizens across the state. With this approach, Simon got close to a political win in each situation.

On the heels of Cairo and SIU, Simon's longtime nemesis, Secretary of State Powell, was found dead on Saturday, October 10, in Rochester, Minnesota, where he had gone for treatment of a lingering heart ailment. Marge Hensey, Powell's secretary and traveling companion, discovered the body in their hotel suite. So began one of the state's most bizarre public mysteries.[48] While none of the events as they were revealed involved Simon in a major way, he could not help but be in the background. Because the story involved a man who Simon had battled publicly during four terms in the house and six years in the senate, a curtain dropped on a significant chapter that might be titled "the good, the bad, and the ugly."

On the night of Powell's death, Simon received a telephone call from a member of the state police asking the whereabouts of Governor Ogilvie. Simon did not know where to locate the governor.[49] As it turned out, Ogilvie was in the Chicago area and did not learn of the death until a day later. The following week, a host of public officials, including friends and enemies, attended services for Powell in Springfield and at his home in Vienna. Simon joined the mourners.

In an interview years later, Simon told of a conversation with Mayor Daley at the Vienna services. Aside from being an amusing anecdote, it shows a side of Daley that might have been missed. Simon said, "There I am talking to Daley next to the open casket. Daley said, 'You know I believe if you're honest, then the people below you are going to be honest.' He said Powell took money and everybody took money. I thought Powell would rise up at that moment. Daley knew he was a crook. And Daley did try to promote people who were honest."[50]

Unbeknownst to Simon, Ogilvie, or any state officials, a drama played out in the hours and days after Powell's death that would not become public for almost three months. It involved Hensey, John Rendleman, chancellor of Southern Illinois University at Edwardsville and Powell's executor, and a handful of aides close to Powell. Centerpiece of the story was the discovery of more than $800,000 in cash Powell had most likely kept at his office in the capital building.[51] The money was transferred by Hensey and friends to a suite Powell kept at the St. Nicholas Hotel. Rendleman said he discovered the stash at that location and turned it over to officials of a Springfield bank. Instead of making the discovery public, Rendleman maintained tight secrecy until he revealed details to *Southern Illinoisan* editor Gardner weeks later at a Christmas party.

Before the November elections, Simon received a telephone call from Rendleman who divulged details of the discovery and acknowledged attempts to keep the matter quiet. Simon told an interviewer, "John said there was a strong feeling that Powell had stashed more cash other places, and he wanted to know if I could suggest some spots to look."[52] The request of Simon was absurd because no one could have known more about Powell's financial affairs than Rendleman. Simon said he could only think of looking at Powell's home in Vienna, which Rendleman had done.

The conversation might have gone unnoticed except that Ogilvie did not learn of the money and Rendleman's involvement until the story became public in newspapers on December 30. The governor resented not being told of Powell's death immediately and then was embarrassed by being in the dark about the $800,000.[53] When Ogilvie learned that Rendleman had called Simon and that Simon also had been among the first to learn of Powell's death, the relationship between the governor and lieutenant governor cooled. In time, Ogilvie realized that Simon had no role in keeping the secret nor did he play any part in the strange events. The Powell issue surfaced again, however, during Simon's campaign for governor.

10

A Louder Voice

While Cairo and SIU occupied much of the time of Simon and his staff, the tactic of providing regular commentary on state affairs continued. With a ready-made mailing list and fresh subject matter, Simon began his column "From the Statehouse" as soon as he was sworn in as lieutenant governor. He wrote nineteen columns in 1969, nine in 1970 when he was consumed with Cairo and SIU, nineteen in 1971 when his campaign for governor built steam, and four in 1972.

Simon plowed new ground with his column.[1] No lieutenant governor before bothered to write a column because it would have been presumptuous, to say the least, while serving with a governor of the same party. Governors had sent columns to newspapers across the state, but they were written primarily by staff members. Simon always wrote his own columns. He wrote primarily to establish a voice as commentator on the affairs of the state and occasionally the nation. As presiding officer of the state senate, he knew legislative affairs in detail and could comment on them, but he saw an opportunity to tackle subjects facing the executive branch of government not just the General Assembly. Governor Ogilvie provided a fresh target as well. What made the situation unusual was that Simon had no official role or responsibility in the operations of state government except to preside over the Senate.

Some column subjects came to him through the ombudsman program. Also, it was fair game for Simon to comment on projects and programs put forward by Governor Ogilvie. He avoided personal comments or harangues and chose the subjects carefully. When criticizing an Ogilvie initiative, Simon usually offered alternatives. In this way, Simon established his credentials to participate in debates at the same level as the governor and the governor's aides. He wrote on many of the same good government subjects that he had addressed in his legislative columns. Periodically, he returned to a subject with a fresh approach or additional comment.

A number of familiar themes surfaced, especially those connected to current events in state government. During the first half of 1969, when the legislature and Governor Ogilvie wrestled with proposals for a state income tax, Simon wrote seven columns on various aspects of state revenue. He reiterated a preference for an income tax early in the year. His strong belief, developed early in his legislative career, was that Illinois had significant social needs that could not be met, and should not be met, by increasing sales, corporate, or property taxes.

During the 1969 discussion about sources of revenue, Ogilvie submitted a budget that included an income tax. As a proponent, Simon did not take issue with Ogilvie on the idea but suggested changes that would have affected other taxes. Ogilvie's plan, a flat percentage income tax on individuals and corporations, did not include any reduction in other taxes. Simon proposed removing the sales tax on food and eliminating the corporation franchise tax, "since corporations are paying their fair share under this proposal."[2] As further relief on property and personal property taxes, he suggested an income tax credit for payment on real estate and personal property taxes. When Simon figured the impact of the givebacks on Ogilvie's proposal, the bottom line showed about $81 million more than the governor's revenue estimate. Simon called this "much fairer."

As legislators reached a critical moment in the final weeks of the session, those opposed to an income tax proposed a higher sales tax. Simon had only to rely on his memory for a reply, reflecting the many times he had opposed adding to the sales tax. He recalled, "When I first was elected to the legislature in 1954, the Illinois sales tax was 2 cents. It has climbed steadily—always without my vote." At 5 cents on the dollar, the Illinois tax ranked among the highest in the nation. Simon argued that a sales tax put a larger burden on those in lower income categories. "The lower your income," he said, "or the bigger your family, the higher the percentage of your income is paid by a sales tax. The greater your income, the less you spend percentage-wise on a sales tax."[3] He called it a "soak the poor" tax. After many changes in the original proposal, the legislature passed an income tax of 2.5 percent on individuals and 4 percent on corporations.

Another of Simon's long-held policy positions was opposition to state bonding programs that required taxpayers to pay billions of dollars in interest charges over many years. He preferred a pay-as-you-go approach to construction of highways and buildings on university campuses, the cost for which would be carried in annual budgets as the work was done. While this would have required tax increases to pay the bill, Simon preferred that to delayed interest charges that would lead to higher gasoline taxes long after current state officials had left office. For anyone who would listen, Simon spoke and wrote against bonding during the legislative years, but nothing matched his fierce determination to derail specific programs during the first three years of the Ogilvie administration. Simon was accused of grandstanding and attempting to thwart the public's desire for more and better roads. Simon saw his tussle with Ogilvie as a matter of principle, but it gained him few friends.

As part of an appeal to downstate voters in the 1968 campaign, Ogilvie pledged to improve existing state roads and upgrade airports and mass transportation. He used ideas presented by a highway study commission to form a bond plan. While much of the press and public attention was directed at resolving a serious shortage of state revenue—leading to an income tax—the bond program made its way through the General Assembly almost unnoticed. After revisions in the original bill, the plan called for an Illinois Highway Trust Authority that would issue $2 billion in bonds without referendum. It provided for increases in the gas tax and vehicle registration.

When Simon got wind of the proposal, he blew a gasket. On May 6, he addressed a memorandum to "Editorial Writers of the State" calling for condemnation of the proposed bond program.[4] In a breathless tone, he expressed support of an increase in the gas tax for improving highways but drew the line at Ogilvie's bond issue idea. He listed these defects in the legislation:

- Interest alone could reach as much as $150 million per year, or more than three and a half cents a gallon just for interest.
- If the present apportionment formula is continued, returning a portion of the tax to local governments, it would take seven and a half cents per gallon just to meet the interest on the bonds.
- There is no requirement for competitive bidding on the bonds.
- Payments on the principal would amount to more than $83 million per year, or two cents per gallon of gasoline tax used for no other purpose.
- The result could be a system of toll roads throughout the state.
- Like most evils, it has a very inviting temptation built into it: Those who serve now can build the roads, while others pay for them later.
- In our fast-moving society in which there is much new research on transportation, it would be unwise to invest billions for a road system that fits the cars of 1969 but may not accommodate the cars of 1979.

He concluded, "If we want more highways, let's build them, and let's pay for them."

Three weeks later, after amendments to the bill, Simon said the proposal "continues to remain a major threat to a sound highway program in Illinois."[5] The revised language reduced the indebtedness from $2.5 billion to $2 billion, but raised the interest rate from 6 percent to 7 percent. It also provided salaries for the chairman and members of the highway trust, although it did not appear there was much for them to do.

He reiterated opposition. "It would inaugurate a needlessly expensive build-now, pay-later highway system from which the state could never extricate itself." His objections failed to stop passage by the General Assembly. Simon called the bill "undoubtedly the most ominous bill for the future of Illinois roads and finances which has advanced this far in my 15 years in state government."[6]

Vocal opposition failed, but after the bill's passage at the end of the session, Simon took a course that confused the situation and looked to many like an attempt to grab headlines. On July 9 he refused to sign the bill until Attorney General William Scott clarified a "serious legal question."[7] Observing that the lieutenant governor, as president of the Senate, had to sign all bills before they went to the governor, he stated the bill did not contain a fiscal note estimating the effect on state revenues or expenditures. He referred to a law requiring fiscal notes when applicable. Simon used the announcement to repeat his objections to the plan.

Simon observed that Ogilvie attended a ceremony purporting to sign the bill into law. He complained, "Since I had not—and still have not—signed the bill, the Governor did not sign the actual bill. Obviously, this is somewhat of an embarrassing situation and one which I wish would have been avoided."

Within less than a day of receiving Simon's letter asking for an opinion, Scott wrote, "I have informed the Lt. Governor today that it is mandatory for him to sign the road bill in his position as presiding officer of the senate. A presiding officer cannot thwart the will of the legislature by refusing to execute his ministerial function. It is up to the courts to determine the constitutionality of this legislation."[8] Simon signed the bill.

Nine months later, in 1970, the state supreme court unanimously declared the law unconstitutional.[9] The primary issue for the court was the highway authority. Ogilvie contended the authority was independent of state government and the bonds did not have to be approved by vote. The court disagreed about the connection with state government, making a vote required. Ogilvie said the decision "set back highway improvement for years." After the decision, Simon wrote, "Now the people of Illinois can proceed on a pay-as-you-go road program. Highways in Illinois need to be improved, but we can do it in a fiscally sound way."[10]

Simon's joy lasted only a short while. The 1970 Constitutional Convention eased restrictions on state bonding that allowed Ogilvie to resurrect the highway plan for the 1971 session, including a proposal to form the Illinois Department of Transportation. Simon continued his campaign against the idea with back-to-back columns sent statewide in which he raised most of the objections put forward in 1969. He called the bill "the worst bill of the current legislative session," and "a road of no return."[11] He mentioned again one of his frequent arguments: "Those who hold public office now can 'point with pride' to roads we have built, and presumably the office holders are out of office before the awful truth and high taxes hit the public. Illinois needs better roads, but we should pay for them as we go." The legislature approved bond issues totaling $900 million for highways, aviation, and transit. It called for no increased taxes.

Simon heard from many readers in 1970 when he wrote in support of public aid for nonpublic schools. He began the column with an anecdote about a visit to Christian Brothers High School in Quincy. "Before introducing me, the principal of the high school, Brother Pius, said he had an important announcement to make, an announcement he would make with great reluctance. He proceeded to tell a hushed and stunned student body that at the end of the school year the Christian Brothers order would have to abandon the high school because of the heavy deficit in operating the school each year."[12] Simon said similar action was occurring across the state.

Simon said the number of students in nonpublic grade schools and high schools dropped by 51,000 from a year before, while public school figures rose "dramatically." He added, "If the present trend continues, as many as 70,000 of the 477,000 now enrolled in private schools may transfer to public schools. Regardless of what your feelings may have been in the past, it is clearly desirable from an economic viewpoint to avoid that tremendous shift of tax burden to the public." Proposals in the legislature called for state assistance on a per pupil basis to nonpublic schools. Simon said this would save private schools at a cost much less than state aid per pupil for public schools.

He recognized that not all private schools met the minimum state standards for public aid. "These young people should not be denied quality education. One good way of increasing quality is to say that state aid is available only to those schools which meet minimum state standards," he wrote. Simon also said maintaining a strong private school system provided a "healthy, but restrained competition to the educational field . . . There is no question that in some areas the non-public schools are superior to the public schools, and the existence of these superior schools within a school district has to be a healthy goad to the public schools there."

A negative response to the column prompted Simon to address the subject again a week later, under the heading, "Important Questions—Important Answers."[13] He listed three questions raised by comments and his replies:

"Aren't you exaggerating in suggesting that as many as 70,000 non-public school students may be transferring to public schools next year?" He responded that in the 1967–68 school year enrollment in nonpublic schools dropped 30,142 from the previous year, adding, "This year the drop is 50,530 over last year, and the trend will continue to accelerate if something does not happen to change the pattern." He cited an increase in public school enrollments at 58,189, of which only 7,659 was due to normal population growth. He said, "Put another way, that portion of your tax increase which was caused by additional public school enrollment was divided this way: 13% caused by normal population growth, 87% caused by transfers from non-public schools."

"But aren't some non-public schools failing to meet minimum educational standards? Why should we help them?" He acknowledged that some did not meet state standards, adding, "I do not favor giving aid to any school which does not meet minimum standards. State aid is one practical way of encouraging the meeting of standards."

"Doesn't this violate the absolute separation of church and state which is part of our constitution?" Simon said there has never been an "absolute separation of church and state. If the local Methodist church is on fire, you call out the fire department. No one says, 'separation of church and state, we can't call out the fire department.'" He explained that the Constitution prohibits an established state church. He expressed confidence that an Illinois provision for aid to nonpublic schools would be constitutional.

Reflecting his long-standing crusade for income disclosure by public officials, Simon twice wrote columns on the subject in 1971. His columns followed on revelations about the estate of Paul Powell—which by the time of settlement in 1978 reached $4.7 million—and attempts by legislators to pass a disclosure bill. Powell fought disclosure proposals as long as he served in the legislature. Simon wrote in January on "Public Confidence Shaken," then returned to the subject in September before the convening of a session in October. At that point, the Senate had passed a measure that was still pending in the House.

Calling the situation "a crisis of confidence," Simon said, "If political leaders refuse to meet this crisis head-on, we jeopardize our system of government. And disclosure of income in detail, as well as disclosure of economic assets and liabilities, is the only way to meet it head-on."[14] The words were similar to those Simon used from the time of his first election to public office in 1954. He wrote, "It is the only way to meet the complex problem of conflict of interest. Put the matters on the table in public view and then the citizenry can make reasoned judgments, whether we are serving ourselves, or serving the public."

Simon concluded the column on a personal note: "I have disclosed all of my income and the sources of that income during my 17 years of public life. My wife and children are part of that disclosure . . . Disclosure of income hasn't hurt any of us. And it lets the public make informed judgments about our motivation in dealing with the issues which come before us."

Simon wrote about a number of social issues facing state government, especially the system of providing public aid. He reported in one column on an experiment by his family of eating on a budget according to public aid allocations. For the family of four, the aid budget was $19.15 per week. They tried, but spent $26.77. "The lesson for us was clear. Those who think that public aid dollars are just thrown away wildly are wrong," he concluded.[15] In another column, he called for changes in the state public aid program but did not have a specific plan.

Another familiar subject was providing a school aid formula with additional funds for the state's most depressed counties, a number of which were in southern Illinois. He argued against a state lottery to provide additional revenues, saying it was unconstitutional and, based on other states' experiences, an undependable plan for providing money. He promoted a pamphlet on environmental lifestyles put together by his staff. There was a column on the rising rates of crime in U.S. urban centers. A few stories from his ombudsman experiences made their way into columns. Simon did not ring a bell with every column, and some read as if he had dashed them off in haste or had reached for a meaningful subject and missed. One staff member called some of them "weak." Nonetheless, they transmitted his opinions and thoughts across the state as he prepared a run for governor.

Under the heading of pure public relations, Simon's office issued a semiannual newsletter starting early in 1969.[16] The publication made little pretense of being anything but a promotional device for the officeholder. The first issue carried a message from "Paul" on the cover announcing the newsletter, mentioning his pledge to be an ombudsman, and his willingness to cooperate with Ogilvie, although he disagreed with the governor on many issues. He mentioned the newsletter would not cost taxpayers any money, announcing the formation of a "Friends of Paul Simon" committee to defray the costs of the newsletter—$16,000 per issue—advertising, and other promotional expenses. In keeping with his attitude about disclosure, he said the names of donors would be revealed but not the amounts. He added, "We will also make public an annual statement of how much money was contributed and how it was spent."

Simon discussed the work of an ombudsman and tackled the issue of the $2 billion bond issue for highway projects passed by the legislature and signed by the governor. "From a fiscal point of view, it is the worst bill to pass and become law since the Internal Improvements Act of 1837," he stated. He called it a "massive step backward from pay-as-you-go government." In a list of the bill's bad features, he said payment of principal would not start for ten years. "In this respect, this bond issue is unlike any other ever passed. The governor and others will cut ribbons, get their pictures taken and bask in the sunlight of all kinds of publicity—and 10 years from now you will get the bill in the form of 6 to 10 cents additional tax per gallon on your gasoline."

The newsletter carried a notice about the opening of Simon's Chicago office, disclosure of staff income, Simon's appointment to a Democratic committee to formulate party policy between conventions, the death of Simon's father, Martin, a notice about the 1970 state Democratic ticket, and the appointment of a lieutenant governor's task force on the environment.

At the end of 1970, the busiest in terms of high-profile matters of state projects and the death of Paul Powell, the newsletter trumpeted the achievements of Simon and his family.[17] It noted his work in behalf of Democratic candidates who won elections—Adlai Stevenson as U.S. senator, Michael Bakalis as superintendent of public instruction, and Alan Dixon as state treasurer. A front-page piece told of Simon's election as a regional vice president of the national lieutenant governors organization. The death of Powell received three paragraphs. An article with pictures introduced the five secretaries in Simon's office and their myriad duties. A short item noted the mention of Simon in national publications such as *Newsweek, Wall Street Journal,* and *New York Times.* It also acknowledged an interview with host Hugh Downs on the NBC *Today* show.

The newsletter reprinted a column in the *Chicago Tribune* by reporter Robert Wiedrich that went into considerable detail about how Simon handled the relationship with Governor Ogilvie:

> Just last Tuesday, we reported the thesis of leaders of both political parties that, had Illinois Secretary of State Paul Powell died just 48 hours later, Gov. Ogilvie would have been out of state on business and Lt. Gov. Paul Simon could legally have named any Democrat he chose to fill the vacancy, thereby saving for his own party some 4,000 patronage jobs in an election year. Simon agrees that that is precisely what he could have done. He also could have acted to appoint a Democrat to the late Sen. Everett M. Dirksen's seat on Capitol Hill in 1969, when Ogilvie was in

Washington attending the Dirksen rites. But he didn't and here's why. Soon after their inauguration, Simon voluntarily gave his word to Ogilvie that he would never take advantage of a temporary ascension to the governor's chair by filling vacancies that were constitutionally Ogilvie's responsibility. The men reached this gentleman's agreement because it was the first time in Illinois history that candidates of opposing political faiths had been elected to the two top posts in state government.[18]

If Wiedrich had stopped there, he already had done Simon a substantial favor with the readership of the most Republican-leaning newspaper in the state. But he continued: "In doing so, Simon was assuring the voters who elected Ogilvie governor that their mandate would never be violated by political opportunism, whatever the pressures of the moment. We would have expected no less of the lieutenant governor. But again, just as importantly, Simon proved himself a man of his word, and in these days of eroding values, we find that a prized quality in one holding public office." Simon often mentioned the understanding with Ogilvie, but when a political reporter said it, the message added to the image Simon had worked hard to create.

Readers had an opportunity to read some good news about people other than Simon or his friends. In an article on the ombudsman program through the end of 1970, Simon reported receiving more than 28,500 contacts in twenty-two months. The stories put life in the statistics.

The office received a note from a working mother whose husband suffered a diseased nervous system while in the military and could not work. The Veterans Administration denied their petition for disability benefits, and she turned to the ombudsman. The VA reviewed the case after being contacted and awarded the family a lump sum covering the previous year and a half. Additionally, the VA put a monthly payment of benefits connected to the disease in place for the future.

Simon received a letter from a truck driver from Peoria who wanted to educate the lieutenant governor on the need for improving the state's highways. He invited Simon to have dinner with his family and ride with him from Peoria to Albia, Iowa, a trip the driver made each night starting at 6:30 P.M. After taking the ride, Simon said, "I learned to appreciate the problems of the truck driver as I bounced through Illinois to the central part of Iowa. I also came away with several practical ideas, including the desirability of placing 'no passing zone' signs on the left side of the road, as Iowa does." Upon hearing from Simon, the Illinois highway department moved the signs to the left side of the road. What Simon did not mention in the newsletter was that press aide Gene Callahan contacted the NBC *Today* show and the program staff sent four camera operators to cover the dinner and the truck ride.

A resident in a small community whose relative lived in a nursing home contacted Simon to express concerns about building safety. The office contacted the Department of Public Health and requested an investigation. The department learned the nursing home was "not fireproof and in the event of a fire it could be a calamity." In a report to the ombudsman, the department said the building owners had since installed an automatic sprinkler system with flow alarm, which investigators said made the building fire safe.

Not all the beneficiaries of the ombudsman were Illinois residents. In one case mentioned in the newsletter, a man from Oklahoma was involved in a car accident while driving in St. Clair County. He lost his glasses and was unable to use a pay phone to contact the other driver's insurance company. Someone directed him to the ombudsman, and a call was placed to the other driver's insurance company in Chicago. In a short time, the company sent an adjuster to meet with the Oklahoma man. The adjuster saw that the man had lodging and new glasses while he waited for repairs to the car.

In April 1971, during discussions of disclosure legislation in the General Assembly, Simon provided a report on income and assets for 1970. When he became lieutenant governor, Simon required disclosure by his assistants, Callahan, Durbin, William Colson, and Craig Lovitt. The report revealed a total income of $46,137.42 for his family, with the largest portion a state salary of $34,375.[19] The next largest sum was $1,535.15 in royalties on books he had written before becoming lieutenant governor. Another $1,084.45 came from interest on the sale of weekly newspapers, and his assets listed $6,800 still due for the sale of the papers.

Simon mentioned every amount received for forty-nine talks, of which five were out-of-state appearances. The disclosure did not list talks given for which he received no payment, of which there were many. The out-of-state talks produced the largest sums: $1,299.85 for lectures at Hunter College in New York City; $400 for a lecture at the U.S. Air Force Academy; $350 for a talk at Grace Lutheran Church in Eugene, Oregon; $250 from St. Thomas Aquinas Church at Purdue University; and $450 for a lecture at Bluffton College in Ohio.

The payments for Illinois talks ranged from $15 to $250 and represented locations throughout the state. In a footnote, Simon said, "In no instance did I request an honorarium for a speaking engagement within the state. In most instances there has been none. However, when one is voluntarily paid I then reimburse the state for the travel, even if I was going to that area of the state on other state business." He received payment for one article during the year, $50 from the *Chicago Tribune* for a travel story.

Jeanne Simon was paid for nine talks and one magazine article. Fifteen of Simon's talk payments came from churches or church organizations, and fourteen from colleges and high schools. Four organizations representing industry groups were listed: Illinois Association of Tobacco Distributors ($250); Illinois Savings and Loan League ($200); the Henry, Illinois, Chamber of Commerce ($40); and the Illinois Oil Council ($100). Simon received dividends from stock holdings in thirty-four corporations. The largest was $215.88 from National Aviation and the next largest from International Harvester. Twenty-five of the dividends were for less than $10 each. He also listed the dollar amount of shares held in each company, totaling $18,132.

Simon estimated the value of his house in Troy at $35,000, with a mortgage of $12,345.55. All assets listed totaled $93,253.31, with liabilities of $18,863.66 and a favorable balance of $74,389.65. Among the assistants listing incomes, the largest revealed was $19,001.41 for Colson, a lawyer who received $2,186 in fees. Assets for each assistant were also provided.

Reaching for the Ring

Simon's efforts to keep his name in front of the public during the first three years as lieutenant governor set records not easily matched by any state officeholder. While the program had the unmistakable appearance of public relations and self-promotion, negative impressions appeared not to stick with the public or members of the press. The primary reason was Simon. He came through the occasional media puffery as a politician of substance who spoke to the public and in many cases for the public. There was no way to assess the impact of his opinions on business in the legislature or the governor's office.

The ombudsman program and his columns on public issues of the day generated much of the attention. Behind the scenes, Simon's high energy and a willingness to appear before large and small audiences built grassroots support. His attention to the subjects of open government, full disclosure by politicians, and pleas for higher ethical standards sounded reasonable and logical to many. Those less enamored of Simon complained that the press gave him a free ride and claimed his record as legislator and lieutenant governor counted for little. Regardless, he seemed primed to take on Governor Ogilvie in the 1972 election.

As 1970 and 1971 progressed and the election drew closer, four Democrats said they would like to run against Ogilvie. Simon made no secret of his desire and let it be known that he would run even if not endorsed by Mayor Daley and the Democratic State Central Committee.[1] Chicago newspapers reported Simon's statement as a shock to organization Democrats, many of whom predicted Daley would anoint a less-independent candidate. Also in the wings were Auditor Howlett, a proven statewide vote-getter and a widely liked and honest office holder, and Thomas Foran, former U.S. attorney for the Northern District of Illinois and famously the chief prosecutor of the Chicago Seven. The seven defendants were tried for their actions during the 1968 Democratic National Convention. Notably, Foran and Daley were close friends, and Foran had served as assistant corporation counsel for Chicago. He had not held elective office.

The fourth candidate, considered a long shot by almost anyone with an interest in the election, was Daniel Walker, a successful corporate attorney and activist for an open Democratic candidate selection process. Notably, Walker had directed a thorough study on Chicago police activity at the 1968 Democratic convention titled "Rights in Conflict."[2] The title drew little attention, but the report included the term "police riot," which gained widespread usage and put Walker on the map among those who denounced Mayor Daley's actions during the convention. That served Walker well, because he intended to make Daley and his tight grip on state politics the campaign target.

Walker also had served as Adlai Stevenson's campaign manager in the 1970 race for the U.S. Senate. The experience caused a rift with Stevenson over compromises the candidate made with Daley. As one published account stated, Walker "couldn't buy that, because he is too much a creature of his own discipline to bend on matters of principle."[3] Walker intended to run in the primary and assumed the party leadership would not support him.

Simon anticipated Walker's entry into the race and received a memorandum in November 1970 that accurately spelled out the dangers Walker presented. It warned Simon against being too cautious. Written by Robert Weinberger, the memo evaluated reaction to the Walker candidacy in the liberal community, among the general public, and in the Democratic party organization.[4]

Liberals would be drawn to Walker because they viewed him as pure and uncompromising, the report said. They would view Simon as a "hardworking, bright politician who has made, or is making, his peace with the Democratic machine." Liberals would lean toward a candidate "who is outspoken against evil and injustice and Mayor Daley." The danger for Simon, Weinberger wrote, was in maintaining a safe posture. If that happens, he said, "you will lose liberal support. Walker will ride the white horse, and you will be on a light grey, but grey one nonetheless." The report identified rallying phrases Walker was likely to use—"fundamental change" was the centerpiece—and concluded, "Deep trouble: the initial loss of the core of Chicago liberal, independent Democratic activists."

While less widely known among the general public, Walker still "will be appealing," Weinberger wrote. The report raised doubts about Walker's ability to raise money and maintain a viable campaign organization for the duration of the primary campaign, and suggested that Simon's appeal as a "middle of the road" moderate would be successful.

As for the Democratic organization, the paper said Walker's candidacy would help Simon with that constituency. However, it stated, "The question here is whether Walker will succeed in either forcing you to become an apologist of machine politics or in joining him in urging massive reform. Unlike some issues, a middle of the road position here . . . will alienate both liberals and regulars. If Walker 'smokes you out' on the issue, you will be in difficulty, likely to satisfy no one."

The writer urged Simon to consider stepping away from his present course of a "low profile." He urged Simon to become "more visible publicly and speak out more often on questions of public concern." While Weinberger could not predict the future, he cited the threats that Simon needed to watch and recommended a plan of action to neutralize Walker. As a result of the analysis, Simon had plenty of warning about the prospect of a Walker fight.

Simon was the favorite hopeful among political editors and editorial writers on Illinois newspapers. However, columnists did not pick the Democratic nominee. Almost all pundits assumed Simon was the strongest candidate to oppose Ogilvie, but they wondered if Daley could swallow his pride long enough to support the lieutenant governor. After all, there were issues between Simon and Daley, mostly having to do with differences over openness of the Democratic party. Many thought Simon too independent to get the nod. And some of the old bulls in the party feared what Simon might do if elected governor.

Howlett and Foran had good public records but did not appear to be contenders for a showdown with an incumbent governor. Still, Daley had a record of choosing candidates to reward loyalty, not popularity with voters. As Simon considered the odds of a primary fight, he thought Walker would be a threat only if there was a three-way race among Daley's choice, Simon, and Walker. He believed Walker would cut into his potential to upset the party choice. Endorsements of Simon fell in place by fall, including Paul Douglas, labor union officials, and corporate leaders. A poll by the *St. Louis Globe-Democrat* and the *Chicago Sun-Times* indicated Simon would beat Ogilvie in a general election.[5]

But Walker's campaign would not go away. And the level of intensity rose throughout 1971. Simon got an early message of how forcefully Walker intended to carry the fight to the lieutenant governor. A letter dated April 13, 1971, from Victor de Grazia to Gene Callahan should have set off alarm bells.[6] De Grazia was the guru behind the Walker candidacy, and absolutely nothing happened in the campaign without his stamp of approval. Preceding the letter from de Grazia, Callahan raised concerns about the tenor of the Walker campaign and suggested the battle should be conducted honorably.

An issue that concerned Callahan was Walker's claim of improper behavior by John Rendleman, Paul Powell's executor, and Simon regarding their telephone conversation about the discovery of $800,000 belonging to Powell. The Walker campaign criticized Simon for not informing the governor of the call, and de Grazia explained the reasons in the letter. "The fact that Rendleman told Paul in confidence is really immaterial. Paul is not a priest, he is a public officeholder. As Lieutenant-Governor, he had a responsibility to the Governor and to the people of Illinois to make public that knowledge." He accused Rendleman "and others" of "violating the state inheritance tax laws, under which all openings of boxes, etc., has to be done in the presence of a representative of the attorney-general or treasurer." De Grazia punctuated the comment with a hint that the $800,000 might not have been all the money found. Regarding Attorney General Scott's knowledge of the money, de Grazia added, "We have and will continue to rebuke Scott for his silence." This was going to be a tough campaign.

Questionable behavior was an issue in both camps. Simon told of an incident during Walker's tenure as Stevenson's campaign manager. He said, "During Adlai's campaign Walker asked for my list of contributors, and with both spoken and written assurance that no one else would get it, I gave it to him, wanting to help Adlai. After Walker announced, we quickly learned Dan had violated his word and used my list for his own campaign."[7]

The point at which Simon and his staff took Walker seriously as a competitor for the nomination occurred in the summer of 1971. Walker had difficulty raising campaign funds and getting the attention of newspapers and influential individuals. He needed a spectacular event that would shower him with publicity and catch the other candidates off guard. He decided to walk the length of Illinois—later calculated at 1,197 miles—to publicize his candidacy, discuss his version of the issues facing Illinois, and criticize the party selection system.[8] By any measure, the walk across Illinois was a stroke of political genius, likely to live in state political history as decisive. It might have been unique as well except that a year earlier Lawton Chiles, a Democrat seeking a seat in the U.S. Senate, had walked across the state of Florida en route to victory.

Suffering blisters on his feet, perspiring in the hot sun, wearing a signature red bandanna all the way, and including members of his family on the trail, Walker fed his story to the press and therefore to citizens for 118 days. Major daily newspapers followed the trek and sent reporters to talk with Walker. As he passed through small towns and areas served by weekly and small daily newspapers, reporters and editors splashed his picture and comments across page 1. Television reporters loved the visual story and spread it to all corners of the state. Political columnists in Chicago and national pundits ridiculed the walk as a meaningless stunt.

However, the walk encouraged the defection of Simon loyalists who for years shared a common objective: breakup of Mayor Daley's tight-fisted control over whom the party would support on the statewide ticket. Through the remainder of 1971 until Mayor Daley chose Simon as the party's gubernatorial candidate, people began to consider Walker as the puritan, not Simon, when it came to defying Daley. At first Walker did not win over many anti-Daley true believers, but as he pounded the mayor day after day in public comments and Simon did not, doubts arose about who would be most likely to carry the fight to Chicago.

Mikva and Scariano remained loyal to Simon regardless of apparent mixed feelings. Mikva and de Grazia, Walker's campaign guru, had a long history in liberal Democratic party circles. One newspaper writer said, "De Grazia put Abner Mikva on the map" in his role as leader of the independent Democrat movement.[9] Mikva's endorsement of Simon made conversation difficult between Mikva and de Grazia. Scariano said to a Chicago reporter, "If Paul Simon weren't the candidate, I'd be Dan Walker's running mate right now."[10] In the same article, Mikva said, "Dan would make an excellent governor; any other time and I'd work hard for him, but Paul and I were roommates in Springfield, remember. You don't just turn your back on that."

Those falling away included people not among the elite of the party or the independent movement. An East St. Louis lawyer who signed up with Walker told a reporter, "We had both candidates down to talk, asked them the same 20 questions. Dan not only has the independence, but he spoke on the issues. Simon really flopped. We asked him what he thought about Daley. He said he was a warm, honest fellow."[11]

Among those with close philosophical ties to Simon who drifted to Walker was Dick Mudge Jr., a compatriot from many Madison County wars and a Northwestern University Law School classmate of Jeanne Simon.[12]

Mudge interrupted a college education aimed at becoming a lawyer to enter World War II. He flew eighty missions in a fighter plane before being shot down and held as a prisoner of war. After the war, he followed his father into an Edwardsville law firm and worked there until he developed an interest in Democratic politics and public office. Mudge picked a difficult time and place to start. In the 1956 Madison County primary election, he ran against incumbent State's Attorney Austin Lewis, a longtime target of Paul Simon and the *Troy Tribune*, who had a history of winning elections.

Running on a shoestring against Lewis, the party choice, Mudge tried several public relations gimmicks that gained him widespread publicity and a following. He "bombed" the site of a gambling operation with 8,000 pamphlets dropped from an airplane. When that got headlines, he dropped another 30,000 on cities in the county. Saying he would clean up gambling operations and bring a breath of fresh air to the state's attorney's office, Mudge defeated Lewis by 3,000 votes.[13]

Simon and the *Tribune* supported Mudge against Lewis, and a few months after the election said in an editorial, "You may have noted in the newspapers that there were only six from Madison County who purchased federal gambling stamps, evidently in the hope that things might 'open up.' Compare this with the 'old days' in Madison County and you get to see that our new state's attorney is keeping his pledge to the people for good, honest government. The old alliance between criminal leaders and public officials in Madison County can be a thing of the past if we continue to elect officials like Dick Mudge, Jr."[14]

Mudge served two four-year terms in the office, concluding in 1964. During that time, his rhetoric on gambling, corruption, and open government could have been taken from the Paul Simon playbook. While Simon did his crusading with a newspaper, Mudge held a bigger legal stick, and soon gambling operations shut down rather than risk becoming targets of the state's attorney. Mudge said with satisfaction, "After I got elected, gambling collapsed . . . period. The only thing I did to stop it was to say it had to stop. Apparently, the people involved believed me."[15]

Pursuing his personal fight against Democratic party machines, Mudge ran for a seat on the state Democratic Party Central Committee in 1958 in an effort to unseat incumbent delegate Alvin Fields, East St. Louis mayor and head of the most influential party organization outside Chicago. He took the fight directly to Fields as the symbol of everything wrong in the party. "Illinois Democrats have learned through bitter experience that the Democratic party cannot carry the load of Mayors Daley of Chicago and Fields of East St. Louis and expect victory in any November election. These co-captains of defeat must be neutralized before they cause Democrats in other counties to desert the party as has been the case in the counties of Cook and St. Clair," he said.[16] Fields won reelection easily, although Mudge outpolled all candidates in Madison County.

When Mudge ran for reelection to the county position in 1960, Simon led cheers from the *Tribune.* He wrote, "The big fight in Madison County for county office will be for the office of state's attorney. Here the fine record of Dick Mudge Jr. in that office should speak for itself and should result in his election by a big majority."[17] Mudge won handily. Two years later, he tried again to unseat Fields for the state central committee and failed. In a letter to the *Tribune,* Mudge used the same anti-Daley rhetoric as in 1958 but included a comment that later would have meaning in his relationship with Simon. He said, "Let's not blame the Senator or the Governor or other elected officials when they obey the mayor's command on political matters. His is the only voice they can hear—loud and clear."[18]

In 1968, Mudge was elected as a delegate from the twenty-fourth congressional district to the Democratic National Convention in Chicago. Simon was an appointed delegate and supported Mudge's election. Continuing his activity as a party contrarian, Mudge backed the nomination of antiwar candidate Eugene McCarthy. In an interview after the chaotic convention, Mudge said he would support nominee Hubert Humphrey, "because, after all, I am a Democrat," then issued another blast at Mayor Daley and his control over most of the Illinois delegation to the convention. When asked about supporting Democratic candidates on the 1968 state ticket, Mudge said, "State Sen. Paul Simon, and Atty. Gen. William Clark, both voted for the peace or minority platform on Vietnam and Simon voted for the [Georgia] delegation. If either asks me to campaign for them, you can bet I will."[19]

The mutual admiration between Simon and Mudge changed during the 1970 state senate election for the district that included Madison County. In the primary to fill the vacant seat, Mudge faced popular two-term state representative Sam Vadalabene, who had support of the party organization including Simon.[20] Predictably, Mudge attacked his opponent and the Democratic party machine structure. Mudge lost to Vadalabene.

If that did not completely erode the relationship with Simon, the rise of Walker did. In announcing his support of Walker, Mudge told reporters, "I don't think every politician has his price, but Paul's price is power. It's his ambition that has caused him to rationalize that Daley's one-man rule of the Democratic Party is all right. Simon isn't dishonest financially. He won't take a bribe, but he will make whatever compromise in principle that is necessary to get Daley's support."[21] Those words were sweet music to Walker.

Formidable as these and other threats became, Simon and staff continued their own tactics, seemingly reluctant to carry the fight to Walker. Simon's main concern was getting Daley's nod, and editorial pages gave support to the cause. The *Chicago Daily News* in a November 6 editorial typified the rallying of press for Simon: "In a field of strong candidates seeking the blessing of the regular Democratic organization for governor, Paul Simon is clearly the best qualified. The Daily News urges his selection by the Democratic slatemakers when that body meets next month."[22] The paper dismissed Walker's effort, saying, "Historically, it's the regular organization that packs the political punch." In brief, the editorial also scanned the backgrounds of

Foran and Howlett, then added, "Simon has earned his credentials as the class of the field." Predictably, the paper mentioned his military service and success as a newspaper publisher and bragged about his legislative service and work as lieutenant governor.

The *Daily News* mentioned that Simon had criticized Mayor Daley, saying he "has followed the broader path of public man rather than the more comfortable one of politician's politician . . . Simon, while not hesitating to criticize his party when he thought it was wrong, has—partly for this very reason—brought great strength to an organization that has sometimes seemed on the verge of cracking under its own rigidity." The paper might have substituted Walker's name for Simon and reached the same rhetorical conclusions.

In December, the central committee deliberated, and Daley gave his nod to Simon as candidate for governor. The Illinois Democratic Central Committee met with potential candidates for office behind closed doors, but leaks to the press were inevitable as were errors in reporting. One story about Simon's 1964 *Harper's* magazine article claimed Simon said he had been misquoted by coauthor Al Balk in the article as it appeared. In a letter to the author, Simon said, "The reality is that I did not say that, but the item has reappeared in newspaper after newspaper."[23]

Another issue during the session dealt with Simon's attitude toward patronage. He had spoken frequently against the party patronage system, which caused a huge displacement in state employees when governors and state department officeholders turned over after elections. Party leaders were concerned that Simon might do away with patronage altogether if elected governor. He wrote after the meeting, "I told the political leaders that I would generally be cooperating with the party on patronage matters. That has always been my policy. But I also made clear that some changes must be made, and I specifically suggested that unemployment compensation coverage must be given state employees . . . I do not believe in people holding a job in name only; I do not believe unqualified people should hold jobs. But there are jobs which a state administration should have the power to fill."[24] These differences might have been avoided if, as Simon believed, the question sessions with candidates were open to the public and party leaders discussed the selections in private.

No sooner had the endorsement deal been sealed with Daley than Walker began the inevitable attack on Simon as a puppet of the mayor. Walker talked to a reporter about "a good man brought to his knees" by "having to go before that slate-making charade and beg, 'Please, please, may I be governor?'"[25] That brought a quick response from Simon that Adlai Stevenson and

Paul Douglas had obtained their opportunities at state offices in the same manner. He added, "This kind of Joe McCarthyism is not a public service." So went the response and counterresponse between the two. During his attacks on Simon, Walker failed to mention that on one previous occasion he had sought the mayor's endorsement. Prior to the 1960 election, Walker appeared before Daley and the state central committee seeking the nod for state attorney general. He was not slated, although in his autobiography Walker said he was told that he had been chosen only to learn quickly that was not true—William Clark got the blessing.

Walker always seemed to be on the offensive. When efforts to work out a series of debates failed, he "debated" Simon's tape-recorded voice. Simon met Walker's fierce criticisms with "I'm sure he's sincere but he's wrong." That did little to thwart Walker's thrusts. A later assessment of Simon's approach to Walker's accusations came from Richard Durbin, who left the lieutenant governor's staff to work on the campaign team. He said, "He ran more as a preacher's son" and did not react aggressively when attacked by Walker.[26]

A pivotal issue late in the campaign arose from comments Simon made about taxes. Speaking at a press conference in mid-February, Simon discussed making the state tax policy more equitable, echoing comments he had made numerous times. He criticized the weight given to property taxes for financing education. He proposed taking the sales tax off food, eliminating the personal property tax on non-income-producing property, and reducing the real estate tax that paid for education. Those changes would require an increase in the income tax to maintain a sufficient flow of revenues, he said.

Always quick to characterize Simon's proposals in a few sound bites, Walker said the plan would triple the state income tax. He offered no backup statistics to prove his point, but he did not need them. Walker bought television advertising time to urge voters to "stop Paul Simon from tripling your state income tax."[27] Simon called it a plan for a fairer tax not an increase in taxes. Regardless, the damage was done on an issue critical to certain constituencies such as seniors. Many citizens still resented the income tax passed by Ogilvie and the state legislature in 1969. Although Simon had no direct role in passage of the tax, he supported it, and in the race with Walker he became the target for angry taxpayers.

The Simon communications machine worked until primary election day in an attempt to turn the Walker tide. In a column for use in the first week of March, Simon explained again that his state financial plan was designed for fairness and would require a "modest increase in the income tax."[28] He lamented headlines that stated, "Simon Favors Tax Hike." He repeated his pledge to veto any income tax increase unless it included a decrease in other taxes. He acknowledged unhappiness across the state with his statement. Friendly editorialists wondered in print if Simon was honest to a fault and should have kept a low profile on the tax question. The title of a Simon column expressed much of that sentiment: "You're Right, But Don't Say It." Simon stated his preference for speaking candidly, no matter what the cost. The column failed to take the fight to Walker.

Simon timed the release of his 1971 income disclosure statement for the week before election day.[29] He included a list of assets and income and assets for seven staff assistants, including Callahan, Colson, Durbin, Johnsen, Lovitt, Michael Pollak, and Michael Stone. Simon's total income was $43,155.01, about $3,000 less than for 1970. The total included $6,874.73 in capital gains on money owed for his sale of newspapers; $1,326.84 in royalties, which included $500 from the University of Illinois Press for a reprint edition of *Lincoln's Preparation for Greatness*; and $726.51 in interest on sales of newspapers. He showed income from twenty-four speaking engagements, dividends from stock holdings, and sales of stocks. He valued stock holdings at about the same total as in 1970.

His net worth in terms of assets minus liabilities was $74,750.65 and reflected little change from year to year. An addition to assets was thirty acres of land in Fayette County, purchased for $7,500. He took a loan of $2,400 from the First National Bank of Vandalia to start building a cottage on the property.

The income disclosure, his nineteenth since election to the legislature in 1954, always provided interesting information about Simon's financial situation although rarely any surprises or shocking revelations. While Simon reminded voters that he was no "Johnny-come-lately" to disclosing income and assets, it had little impact at the tail end of a hard-fought campaign. The only difference from other years was a news release accompanying the information. It contained some of the toughest campaign language to date from Simon. To make sure no one mistook the press release as written by someone other than Simon, the entire statement was in quotations. After reminding the reader of his disclosure record, Simon added:

> However, dollar honesty in government is not enough. Campaign honesty is equally important. If we are to trust our public officials we must demand that they live up to their campaign promises. A public official who lies to the public, is just as deceitful as a public official who has his hand in the till . . . In the last few weeks I have watched my opponent deliberately misrepresent to the people of Illinois my proposals for tax reform . . . I

have listened to my opponent's pie-in-the-sky promises where they will increase services and reduce taxes . . . In fairness to my primary opponent, he has never run before for public office. If he understood government, he wouldn't be making the wild charges he is making.

After taking jabs at Ogilvie's budget proposal—a $4.3 billion annual increase since taking office—Simon concluded, "Anyone who knows my record in Springfield knows there will be a belt-tightening when I am governor. But glib speeches about easy cuts in taxes with more services elsewhere are political baloney." For Simon, those were tough words. However, they came too late to reverse the tide.

In an interview years later, Gene Callahan related an anecdote that illustrates how tense it was in the final days of the campaign, when it became obvious Simon and Walker were fighting to the wire. As spokesman for the campaign, Callahan had referred to something Walker said as a "deathbed confession." At a staff meeting, Simon upbraided Callahan for the comment. Callahan came back at him, explaining he would say it again because Simon needed to be tougher with Walker. Callahan said Simon later agreed Callahan was right. "It happened two days before the election," Callahan said, "What was Paul going to do, fire me at that point?"[30]

Endorsement editorials flowed for Simon. Many commented on Walker's charisma and lively campaign but noted he had done little to put meat on his accusations that Mayor Daley and his organization were threats to good government. Walker's sweeping generalities and little detail about what he would do as governor did not sway the editorialists. As for Simon, the commentary pointed to his record as legislator and lieutenant governor, experience in government—which Walker did not have—and campaigns for open government and disclosure of information.[31] Most of the editorials discounted Walker's criticism of Simon's tax proposal but wondered if Simon's candor would have been better left unsaid.

Alan Dixon, who served as campaign chairman, strategist, and campaigner for his friend Simon, joined the candidate, key staff people such as Callahan, and family to watch election returns. Simon recalled, "The first sense that we might lose came from Alan, who said he heard bad reports from two precincts in Belleville that should have been for me. Gene Callahan . . . said it did not look good."[32] Walker won by 40,293 votes, with a strong showing in Chicago and its suburbs. He cut Simon's margin in Cook County to only 20,957 votes. Walker carried 52 of the 101 downstate counties, many along the route of his walk across the state. Mostly, though, he defeated Simon on ground the lieutenant governor should have won. Most embarrassingly, the winner whipped Simon at his own public relations and communications game. In his concession statement, Simon took the high road:

> It is easy in defeat to blame others; that is rarely accurate. And after a strenuous campaign, it is not easy to lose. I am sorry that I have let my supporters down. I regret the inadequacies of my campaign, inadequacies which others may see more clearly than I do. But I do not regret telling people the truth. I hope I never become so eager for any prize that I corrupt the truth, as vile a corruption as any other. To those who fear that all is lost, let me remind these good friends that what you supported was not only a man, but a cause. The cause of decency in government of dignity for all men, needs your continued support, as it will have mine.[33]

Simon wrote a valedictory in the newspaper column circulated at the end of April, admitting that "losing an election is not easy—particularly when you expected to win." He added, "There is unhappiness in losing, obviously. When you read things said about you which are not true, but which many people must have believed, obviously it hurts some."[34] After the primary, Simon said he would support Walker, and he thanked Mayor Daley.

Walker completed his stunning run for governor by defeating Governor Ogilvie in the fall election. Walker proved to be a giant killer unlike any in modern Illinois political history. Not only did he defeat the sitting lieutenant governor and the incumbent governor, he did it in a presidential election year when Richard Nixon won an overwhelming national victory that included Illinois's electoral votes and returned Republican Senator Charles Percy for a second term in Washington.

Toward the end of his lieutenant governor term, Simon prepared a farewell to Illinois state government for the *Chicago Sun-Times*. He reviewed changes in the General Assembly beginning with his first term in 1955. He stated, "There has been a gradual lifting of the caliber of legislator elected, better legislative procedures, and improvement in the ethical tone. . . . But there remains substantial room for progress."[35]

Simon said when he entered the legislature, "corruption was blatant and even accepted as inevitable by those who did not participate." He credited Orville Hodge and Paul Powell for the headlines they made that shocked the public and forced reform. He also referred to his *Harper's* article in 1964 as contributing to improved ethical standards.

On his list of needed improvements, Simon included full-time legislators and two of his favorites, detailed public disclosure of income similar to what he had done for seventeen years and public financing of election campaigns. "Had I been elected governor, one of the proposals I intended to make called for an experiment in public financing of General Assembly races," he said, adding, "The more light which can be shed on the General Assembly, the more public understanding there should be, and the less likely will be abuses of the public trust."

In his concluding sentences, Simon called for leadership to create long-term answers to difficult questions:

> By its nature, politics is a short-range business. But there must be at least a minority of public officials and a minority of citizens who look for fundamental answers, rather than easy, politically satisfying, superficial ones. That involves leadership, not in name, but in fact. It is still politically attractive to follow the crowd, no matter where it leads. That was true in 1954 when I first entered the political arena. It is true in 1972 when I exit as a public official.

Political scientists, historians, and pundits have speculated about the 1972 gubernatorial contest that never was. What would the issues have been between Ogilvie and Simon? How would the campaign have unfolded? Who would have won? Such questions are intriguing. The two were political achievers with an eye for ideas and public policies.

Ogilvie would have been a tough opponent for Simon. He had scrambled uphill in Cook County against entrenched Democratic rule and, once elected sheriff and then county board president, turned in an admirable record of reform. As governor, he initiated serious expansion and reforms of state government rivaled by few previous state leaders. Among them was enactment of the state's first income tax, which provided fresh revenues for education, public aid, and a variety of social programs. He created the Department of Transportation and spearheaded a massive program of road building and capital expenditures.

While Simon had serious differences with Ogilvie on public policies, he admired the Republican's initiative, drive, and success with the legislature. Simon supported many of Ogilvie's ideas for governmental organization and expenditures on social programs but that would not have restrained him from criticizing the governor. Regardless of areas of agreement, Simon had a reservoir of public policy ideas ready. Also, his four years as lieutenant governor, during which he talked continuously about policies of state government, provided a familiarity with the governor's office not available to others. He would have talked at a level never before reached by lieutenant governors. It would have been a close and fair fight, perhaps with a slight edge to Ogilvie.

Part Four

Beyond Defeat, 1972–97

12

Interregnum

Paul Simon could have lost much more than an election in his 1972 defeat by Daniel Walker. It could have been the permanent end of Simon's storybook rise from small town weekly newspaper editor to one of the best-known Illinois politicians of his time.

Simon might have begun a career teaching journalism and public affairs. Chances are he would have written more history books. He could have received a political appointment or entered the media field. Instead, after a hiatus of two years, Simon succeeded in resurrecting his political career—much as he revived the *Troy Tribune*—with election to the U.S. House of Representatives from the state's southernmost congressional district. He served in that capacity during five terms from 1975 to 1985. In the world of might-have-been, Simon could have served out his political career representing the district. With tenure and a Democratic majority, he would have been a top candidate for committee leadership.

But that was not the Paul Simon people came to know. The image of serving as a legislative insider did not fit. He wanted a platform for issues and ideas, an opportunity to speak on the floor of the U.S. Senate, and a chance to tell his colleagues what was best for the nation rather than what they hoped to hear. He wanted to be "Senator Paul Simon." But wishful thinking would not get him to the House or the Senate. He needed help.

Most politicians who lose an election, and especially those who contest at the top of the ticket, never get a second chance. The losers move on to other work, preferring not to take further risks with voters. Deep down Simon wanted another shot. Fortunately, he knew what a mess he had made of the 1972 race and he vowed not to make the same mistakes. He was prepared to take responsibility for the decisions and tactics, making sure he avoided a repeat of the run for governor. That was the road to redemption.

If the stars lined up for another chance at public office, Simon had some political "money" in the bank: a reputation that almost got him to the governor's office. The public image created from 1948 to 1972 was still largely in place, thanks to a story the public knew well.

Simon's positive public image got its start during his newspaper days and was constantly reinforced by reminders of his courageous fight against crime and corruption. Although most people had forgotten the specifics, if they knew them, they had been told repeatedly of his journalistic achievements in press releases, public appearances, newspaper articles and columns, and during election campaigns. The story remained alive in the minds of Illinois journalists and ordinary citizens.

He spoke often of open government, disclosed his income annually, and battled official corruption. Through the political battles of almost twenty years, people remembered and admired the personal qualities so much a part of the public Simon. No slick political type, Simon remained the jug-eared, bespectacled guy with a bow tie who spoke convincingly about honor in public service.

Simon never gave up on his ideas about how government should operate. That made him appear different from other officials. He told people it was possible to govern an efficient cost-conscious government that took care of the needy and treated citizens with respect. These attributes, on display over time, paid steady political dividends—until he collided with the imagery of Dan Walker.

The path to resurrection was cluttered with Simon's detractors and political enemies. There was little Simon could do to remove the obstacles except wait to see how they performed without Simon present. At the top of that list was Walker, although close at hand were those who, although they never cared for Simon's self-righteous streak, did not want Walker either. The doubters applauded quietly over results of the primary. When you want a political enemy knocked off, you rarely argue with the methods, who does it, or how it is accomplished. By all precedents available, Walker had buried Simon politically.

The key to any Simon comeback was the performance of his chief nemesis: Walker. The new governor's mission was to destroy the Daley organization or render it ineffective and along the way cast aside those who Walker believed to be sympathizers with Chicago's mayor. It made no difference to Walker whether the likes of Simon, Adlai Stevenson, and Alan Dixon had built careers primarily independently of the Chicago machine. When it came to statewide office, they needed Daley and that put them in the same camp. Walker demanded purity, and he seemed to be among the few who met the standard. Walker had dispatched Simon, and if necessary he would do the same to Dixon, Stevenson, and any others who cuddled with Daley. However, he failed on his reformist mission.

When the best of intentions collide with the politics of reality in governing, something usually gives, for better or worse. As a late-bloomer in statewide politics with no previous record in elective office, Walker talked a great game—on the short term maybe better than Simon or any others—and it got him the governorship. Reality surfaced in the form of the legislature, Chicago's mayor, and a long list of Democrats who waited for an opportunity to kick Walker in the backside. The governor could not count on any help from Republicans, either. Those watching for an opening did not have to wait long.

Walker learned that image accounted for little after being elected. The challenge was to govern. Walker could not bring himself to compromise in situations where that was the only way to get a program enacted. As long as he could rule by executive order or shape a proposed budget proposal to his liking, Walker remained in control and pursued the issues and subjects that propelled his candidacy. Slowly, however, it became obvious that Walker was too stubborn to make good. When he finally realized that willingness to compromise might get needed results, it was too late. The downward spiral from victory in 1972 resulted in a single term as governor. By the time Walker's run ended, Simon thrived again.

Simon's strong standing in the state's press corps played no small role in the aftermath of 1972 and Walker's failure to maintain momentum. Observers in Springfield during the governor's four years in office acknowledged resentment among reporters for Simon's fate. In their biography of Walker, authors Taylor Pensoneau and Bob Ellis said Springfield-based reporters "never forgave [Walker] for beating Paul Simon whom they idolized."[1] They added that Walker did not seem to understand the necessity of reaching out to the press. The authors quoted Walker in a lengthy discussion of his poor relations with the press. Walker stated, "Paul had a good record, and the press in the Capitol liked him and thought he deserved or had earned the Democratic nomination for governor. Then along comes this guy Walker out of nowhere, with no elected experience in government, and he tries to take it away from Simon. The reporters in Springfield made it very clear that I did not have a chance, and further, many did not want me to have a chance." Walker said that Pensoneau and Ellis "described the inimical attitude of the Springfield press corps toward me during those years when Pensoneau was one of them."

Walker, in his autobiography, commented on treatment by the press during presentation of the governor's budget.[2] "My approach [message control] infuriated the Springfield press corps at the time . . . with continuing negative repercussions. They became and remained highly critical."

Remarkably, this is how Walker helped reverse Simon's journey to oblivion. People began to see how Walker the candidate had mesmerized them—and how Walker the governor had failed them. It resulted in voter remorse. People wondered if the outcome might have been different with Simon as governor. This change of attitude did not happen overnight but eventually laid the groundwork for Simon's rebound first to the U.S. House and finally to the U.S. Senate while Walker passed completely from the political scene.

Paul Simon called the time after finishing his term as lieutenant governor a refreshing pause. From a personal standpoint, that made sense. A more appropriate term is interregnum, an interval between two successive reigns. In that context, the use of time becomes important.

Paul and Jeanne and their children remained in a Springfield house they owned when his lieutenant governor term ended in 1973. Simon received a number of feelers about employment, including two offers that connected his favorite subjects, journalism and politics. He turned down an offer to teach at Southern Illinois University in Carbondale and took a job at Sangamon State University to maintain a Springfield base of operations, at least temporarily.[3] Practically speaking, the state capital looked better for launching a political future than Carbondale.

Sangamon State—now the University of Illinois at Springfield—was formed as a college for juniors and seniors during Simon's time as a state senator. During a process started by Governor Kerner to create new universities, Simon served as chairman of a subcommittee charged with generating a compromise proposal that would satisfy all the constituencies of higher education. The subcommittee proposed establishing Sangamon State in Springfield and Governor's State in the suburbs of Chicago.[4] The legislature and governor approved the plan. Simon felt a connection to the university in the state capital and that influenced his decision to join the faculty in September 1972 while serving out his lieutenant governor term.

The opportunity at Sangamon State was to start and manage a public affairs reporting program. It was in place without a director before Simon lost to Walker, designed and approved by the university president and Chris Vlahoplus, university public affairs officer. Vlahoplus had an impressive journalism and government background. He worked for International News Service in Chicago and was assigned to Springfield from 1958 to 1962 for United Press International. He served Governor Kerner and later Governor Shapiro as press secretary. Before joining Sangamon State, he worked briefly at the University of Illinois in Chicago. Vlahoplus left Illinois to work at the University of South Carolina in 1977.

In the early 1970s, Vlahoplus conferred with several journalism professionals about the structure of a public affairs program.[5] One of those who helped with the concept was Roy Fisher, dean of the School of Journalism at the University of Missouri and former editor of the *Chicago Daily News*. Vlahoplus, Sangamon State president Robert Spencer, and other officials developed a proposal for graduate students who had degrees other than in journalism, similar to a program at Columbia University in New York. Vlahoplus said he had no idea of hiring Simon, even after the election.

Although they had another person in mind for the position, according to Vlahoplus, university officials decided to contact Simon. The first person declined an offer. While not especially close, Simon and Vlahoplus knew each other during the Kerner and Shapiro administrations, and Vlahoplus remembered Simon as one of the "Young Turks in the legislature." Vlahoplus said, "It was a good hire. He got plenty of publicity for the program. It drew students from other colleges who had started in journalism and wanted to finish with Simon. So it was a blend of those students and grad students."

During Simon's tenure at Sangamon State, he taught and counseled journalism students who later made their marks in major media. In this way, he connected with a new generation of journalists whose careers matured during Simon's years in Congress. One major responsibility was running an intern program in public affairs reporting that drew on Simon's connections with the media. He also taught courses named "The Lawmaking Process" and "Crisis of Confidence," bringing together his familiarity with public policy and journalism.[6]

In addition to Sangamon State duty, Simon lectured for the first semester of 1973 as a fellow of Harvard's Institute of Politics at the John F. Kennedy School of Government. This placed him in a political environment as much as academic and provided contacts on a broader scale than those available in Springfield. His primary responsibility was to lecture one day a week, which left time for developing political relationships and sightseeing. The Simon family moved to the Boston area for the semester, and Simon returned to Springfield for occasional duties at Sangamon State.

At the close of Simon's fellowship at the Kennedy School, the director of the Nieman Fellows program at Harvard asked him to address a class of assembled journalists from across the country. A million-dollar grant to Harvard in 1937 had launched what became the oldest and most prestigious mid-career program for working journalists in the United States. Selection as a Nieman Fellow automatically lifted a person above the overall field of journalists in terms of achievement and promise. A fellow spent an academic year on the Harvard campus taking a variety of courses, writing, and attending seminars. Being asked to address the group was significant recognition of Simon's journalistic and writing endeavors as well as his political record. In the talk, he reflected on press coverage of state government.[7]

Using Illinois as the primary reference, Simon struck a number of themes that he repeated through the years in writing about the need for better and greater coverage of state government. He pleaded for reporters with solid knowledge of government, specifically state government, and an overall upgrade in status for the state government beat inside news organizations.

Simon set the tone with this statement: "The quality of press coverage is related to quantity. Not enough newsmen are assigned to cover state government." After making some comparisons with reporters covering Congress—he said eight reporters covered Illinois government full time—Simon observed, "We need more reporters covering the state government scene." He acknowledged that many reporters believed an assignment to Springfield was "an assignment to Purgatory." That could be changed, he stated, by improving compensation for state government reporters, making space available for state government news, and finding ways to promote statehouse reporters when better assignments are open.

He lamented that too often good reporters viewed the state assignment as an unhappy stopping place on the way to Washington or some large city assignment. He cited the experience of Tom Littlewood, a *Chicago Sun-Times* reporter who made the move from Springfield to Washington. Simon added, "I don't blame him, but when it happens, state government loses."

To make sure he did not omit comments about radio and television reporters in Springfield, Simon selected one for special mention. He said, "One of the finest reporters on the Springfield scene is a radio reporter, Bill Miller. Largely because of his leadership and aggressiveness, radio coverage in Illinois is superior to television coverage." Television stations assigned reporters for spot news events and periodically during a legislative session, but many of the reporters had little familiarity with state government, he said.

He called for a "greater sense of balance and perspective" in state government news coverage. Simon illustrated the comment by suggesting if two bills were introduced the same day in the legislature, with one assisting 50,000 non-English-speaking students of Puerto Rican and Mexican backgrounds and the other outlawing pay toilets, "I can tell you which will receive the more prominent space and the most radio, TV and press comment." This led him to another illustration of balance in news coverage. He said,

> After Daniel Walker, who walked the state of Illinois from end to end, defeated Richard Ogilvie for governor, Ogilvie told Dick Icen of the

Lindsay-Schaub newspapers "The next successful candidate for governor will cross the state swinging from limb to limb." He is not alone in lamenting the attention to gimmicks rather than substance.

Simon also spoke of the experience in the 1972 election campaign involving the income tax increase controversy that cost him dearly. Revealing that the sting of defeat lingered, he explained,

> In my recent primary contest for the Democratic nomination for governor I had the disadvantage of knowing something about state government and was not able to join my opponent in promising some sweeping reductions in taxes. I did say that I supported the philosophy of the California Serrano vs. Priest school decision (which Walker opposed) and that I favored a reduction in the real estate tax but that would mean an increase in the income tax. The Republican governor charged that my suggestion would mean a 25 percent increase in the income tax. My Democratic primary opponent said it would mean a 300 percent increase in the income tax. The more extreme—though completely unfounded—statement made most of the headlines.

He ended references to Illinois with this observation: "No state owes a greater debt to the media than do we in Illinois, where daily we see more evidence of an unhappy tradition of corruption in both parties. With a little help of the media that tradition is changing."

In later writings about the time between political campaigns, Simon did not say how often he considered future political ventures. The short-term Harvard program and the teaching assignment at Sangamon State kept Simon employed but did not answer questions about his future. Prospects were hazy. On the state level, Walker had just begun his term and would not be up for reelection until 1976. Adlai E. Stevenson, a Democrat, and Charles H. Percy, a Republican, held the two U. S. senate seats. Percy won a second term in 1972 and would not be on the ticket again until 1978. Simon's friend Alan Dixon, serving as state treasurer, was on the lookout for better things, too. None of those situations offered short-term potential for Simon.

With his connections to journalism secure, Simon kept an eye on political opportunities. When one arose, the impetus came from old friends Dixon and Callahan, confirming Richard Durbin's later observation, "All of us on the staff felt we had let Paul down, and we were determined to get him back in public service."[8]

13

The Comeback

Opportunity came like a lightning bolt in the summer of 1973 when U.S. Rep. Kenneth Gray, congressman from the southernmost district in Illinois, announced he would not seek reelection in 1974. Among Democrats, Gray had a reputation for making such announcements and then retracting the declaration and continuing his service in the district. State Treasurer Dixon suspected this announcement was firm if someone moved quickly.

Dixon and Callahan contacted Simon and urged him to enter the primary. All three friends offered different descriptions of the meeting, but they agreed on the substance. Simon wrote in his autobiography that he received a telephone call from Callahan and Dixon.[1] Callahan said in an interview that Dixon and he were attending Democrat Day at the state fair in Springfield when they heard of Gray's announcement. Callahan said they drove to the Leland Hotel where Simon had an office and told him, "You need a platform."[2] Dixon said in a separate interview that Callahan heard of Gray's announcement at lunch. Dixon explained, "I said to Gene, 'Let's go see Paul and make him run for Congress.' Callahan said they would say he is a carpetbagger. We drove straight out to Paul's house—he was taking a nap—and talked to him. He said it wouldn't be the right thing to do. We said if you go down there, you can win."[3]

However it happened, they wanted Simon to run. Simon hesitated, saying he had pledged to support Representative James D. Holloway from Randolph County if Gray retired. Callahan took the challenge and called Holloway to see if he planned to run against Gray. Holloway told Callahan he did not want to run for Congress and said he would support Simon. Still, Simon knew that opponents would label him a carpetbagger because his home in Troy was about eight miles beyond the congressional district boundary. Nevertheless, after others called to urge Simon's candidacy, and a talk with his wife Jeanne, he decided to make the run. The Simons rented a home in the district and later owned a home in Carbondale before building one in nearby Makanda.[4]

For all of those who climbed aboard in support, Simon had detractors and critics. First among them was Representative Clyde Choate of Anna, who could not forget Simon's tussles with his friend and mentor Paul Powell. He openly opposed Simon. Other Democrats in the district refused to support Simon, reflecting the candidate's mixed reputation among party members. It helped the anti-Simon crowd that his opponent was Joe Browning, a well-known local man. Although he had not held public office, he was a member of a Franklin County family and headed the sports department of a West Frankfort radio station.[5]

After urging Simon to run, friends and former staff members joined the cause. Dixon agreed to speak at the first Simon fundraiser in Marion but wondered if he should endorse his friend publicly, in fear of raising the "outsider" issue. Callahan, who advised him to make the endorsement, recalled, "It was a dynamic speech. The best speech I ever heard him give. He said, 'This is a moment of decision for Paul Simon. If he fails, his political career is over.'"[6]

Former staff members Callahan and Durbin did what they could to assist, devoting weekends to work for Simon in the district. On Fridays they drove from Springfield to Carbondale where they stayed in an apartment, out of public view. Callahan and Durbin worried about the issue of state employees working for Simon. On Saturdays they sat in on strategy meetings and stuffed envelopes, among other chores.[7]

From the outset, Simon recited his experience in public office and record of ethics in government. He denied rumors that he would not serve more than a single term if an opportunity arose to run for governor in 1976. Simon promised to disclose income, as he had done every year in office, and the sources of campaign contributions. "The integrity issue so dominates everything else," he told a reporter.[8] That statement had meaning in the year that Richard Nixon resigned the presidency.

Newspaper accounts described the contest as a "nice-guy" affair, but with memories of 1972 still fresh, Simon prepared to do what ever was necessary to win. In its endorsement of Simon, the *Southern Illinoisan* of Carbondale, the district's largest daily newspaper, addressed Simon's mood. "It is a contest in which Simon has a great deal to lose. His political future will be in doubt if he should be defeated. Simon knows the stakes and, if anything, is trying too hard. His well-oiled and widespread campaign comes off in clear but not always positive contrast to the 'just folks' Browning campaign."[9] Raising the question of Simon's political ambitions, the paper said, "While not closing the door forever to seeking some higher post, Simon has done as much as could be expected to assure that he does have a sincere interest in serving the district in Congress."

The newspaper let readers know there was no guarantee of longevity by Simon and no fair way to factor that into a voting decision. This was a new subject for residents of the district to digest given the history of the previous congressman, Kenneth Gray. He had represented the district for twenty years prior to Simon's election, denying when necessary any interest in office beyond the House. The skepticism about Simon's commitment to southern Illinois arose not just as a campaign tactic by his opponents. The question floated through the campaign in large part because of Simon's pattern over twenty years of public service as an aggressive achiever motivated by ambition.

Evidence was there for anyone to see. Simon worked six years as a newspaper editor before running for the legislature. His interest in politics first surfaced a year after he began publishing the *Troy Tribune*. After eight years in the state house, Simon ran for the state senate and won. He remained in that position six years before seeking and winning the position of lieutenant governor. Four years later, he ran for governor. With that average, he might be expected to hold a congressional seat for eight years or less.

Simon skillfully pursued upward mobility without leaving the impression of being driven solely by ambition, however. If anything, the image he created of devotion to public service made his advancement appear almost accidental, in spite of the record. In addition to his commitment to good works, Simon was an ambitious career politician. He first showed an interest in serving as a U.S. senator about 1960, and he talked about it frequently thereafter. With every term Simon served in the House, an attempt for the next step up the ladder to the Senate drew closer.

Simon defeated Browning in the primary and prepared to face the Republican nominee, Val Oshel, formerly Illinois civil defense director, mayor of Harrisburg, and unsuccessful 1968 opponent of Gray. In addition to fighting uphill in a district dominated by Democrats, Oshel waged a weak campaign against Simon's specific promises to represent the district and approaches to economic issues. Strategically, Simon disclosed his income during the general campaign, showing assets of $168,807 and liabilities of $54,943.[10] He declared an income of $20,712 as a Sangamon State University teacher. Simon buried Oshel by a margin of 34,783 votes. Back on his feet politically, Simon prepared to join new colleagues in the U.S. House of Representatives, at the bottom of the seniority list. Of eighty-four new members—including seventy-five Democrats called "Watergate babies"—Simon was eighty-first.[11]

A major advantage for Simon in the two 1974 campaigns was the large disparity between funds he accumulated versus his opponents. When Simon first ran for office in 1954, he spent $3,852, most of it out of his own pocket. Twenty years later, the campaign for congress cost Simon $227,622, the ninth largest expenditure for a House seat that year, and the fifth highest for an open (no incumbent) race.[12] While that number looks modest compared to the costs of campaigns in the twenty-first century, for 1974 it was an eye-opener. The amount allowed him to control advertising on television, radio, and in newspapers across the district, and his opposition could not compete. For example, Oshel spent $50,566. Simon had learned the importance of television exposure during the 1972 campaign, and he was determined to have plenty of money for that aspect of the campaign.

A newspaper study of 1974 costs revealed contributions to Simon's campaign of $19,500, a small percentage of the total, from seven different union organizations. In his first congressional term, Simon received a 91 percent favorable rating from the AFL-CIO and a 12 percent rating from the U.S. Chamber of Commerce. Simon denied the contributions had anything to do with his votes. Simon historically voted for labor, and labor traditionally supported him. He told a reporter, "They obviously were very helpful. There is no question I felt more comfortable with them on my side . . . I vote my conscience . . . My votes are based on my personal philosophy and the needs of my district."[13]

During the primary and general election campaigns, Simon borrowed $34,000 to cover occasional shortfalls in cash flow, an accepted practice for bridging the uneven flow of contributions. He repaid the loans before or shortly after the general election. Of interest was the source of the loans. Gerald Sinclair, executive vice president of the Salem National Bank, oversaw financing for the large expenditures and made some loans through the bank. Sinclair and his wife also loaned Simon campaign funds. Some of the loans carried no interest charges. Simon described their relationship in these words: "Jerry is one of my closest friends; we've known each other for 25 years or more."[14] Sinclair said Simon "represents everything that is good in American politics. I am happy to do all I can to help him." Simon added, "I really did not know Jerry was not charging interest. I am grateful to him, of course."

In the 1975–76 congressional session, most of the banking legislation remained in committee, and Simon was not a member. Simon and Sinclair acknowledged conversations in which the banker mentioned legislation of interest, and Simon asked his friend for counsel on bank issues. Simon said, "I respect his view." Sinclair commented, "I expect to get his attention when I call his office on matters affecting Southern Illinois. I told him recently Salem needed a new post office; our current one is too small. He always votes his conscience. He is his own man."

The published analysis of 1974 expenditures did not suggest any wrongdoing but did explore the problems inherent in raising funds for campaigns when compared to subsequent votes. Simon took a practical approach to the subject, reflecting the realities of politics whether at the state or federal level. He often commented on the importance of contributors: "If I am running late and have 20 phone messages piled up and five minutes available, I generally look down the list of callers. If I see the name of a contributor, which call do you think I will return?"[15] He usually followed that statement by saying no one could buy his vote.

Less than three months after Simon assumed the office of congressman from Illinois's twenty-fourth district, he sat at his trusty manual typewriter to write for *Illinois Issues* magazine, a publication he helped start at Sangamon State University. The magazine published the article later in the year under the heading "Mr. Simon goes to Washington."[16] He had hardly been in the capital city long enough to find the washrooms and move into his tiny office on the Hill. He devoted most of the article to contrasts between life as a state legislator and a congressman. Anecdotes sprinkled through the article gave it a real-time feel, but much of the subject matter involved processes and rules of interest mostly to political insiders. He dealt with questions of staff, the action of committees, money spent for support, the importance of seniority, demands on the time of Simon and staff members, differences in salary, and availability of research to members.

The article did not reveal anything that could not have been deduced from library books. However, content did not matter in this case. Simon wanted to remain tethered to greater Illinois, and this forum provided an early opportunity. He feared being lost in a sea of 435 House members, and thought of only as a representative for a rural portion of Illinois. During his experience as lieutenant governor, the whole state was his constituency, and he had supporters in every county and town. As carefully as Simon worked to serve the people of the district, it paid to remain in touch across the state. He resumed writing a newspaper column titled "P.S./Washington" that was circulated throughout his district and to newspapers outside the region.

After conducting business in Washington, during most weeks Simon returned to southern Illinois where he held constituent meetings. He listened patiently to people in rural outposts and small towns. If he could help with their problems, he dictated a letter to an agency or an individual. He sent a thank you letter to each person who appeared before him. Before the weekend ended, he attended community gatherings, gave talks at churches and club meetings, and made as much contact as possible in a few hours. It was the stuff of congressional reelection campaigns where one campaign began as another ended, with an endless procession of hand shaking and talk.[17]

Six months after taking office in 1975, Simon gave column readers a glimpse of his schedule during the Memorial Day "vacation" for Congress. While more than a little self-serving, it made the point that work continued during holidays for members of Congress:

> Office hours and appointments with interested citizens were conducted at all three district offices: Carbondale, West Frankfort and Mt. Vernon. More than 100 personal appointments in office with citizens and groups. Visited communities for "listening sessions" in Brookport, Ruma, Campbell Hill, Sesser, Grand Chain, Olive Branch, Cobden, Sandoval, Carterville, Rosiclare and Ridgway. Visited factory at Steeleville, helped open the Little League baseball season in Herrin. Spoke at McLeansboro high school graduation, Salem Lions Club, Methodist Men at Benton, dinner at Pinckneyville. Met with city officials, and president of UMW (United Mine Workers), rode in the Rend Lake parade at Benton. Received phone calls as early as 6 A.M., and late as 1 A.M. Met with business leaders in Gallatin and Hardin counties. Tour of Crab Orchard National Wildlife Refuge. Met with many mayors, appeared on call-in radio shows.[18]

As an aside to anyone who wondered if he spent time with the family, Simon added, "I did manage to have one dinner with my family and spend one evening with them. I also took my son to get a haircut and had a dental appointment."

In Washington, Simon participated in public policy deliberations on subjects that had little direct impact in southern Illinois. He delegated many contacts with constituents to staff people in the district and in Washington. Staff carried the word to newspapers and other media when Simon had done something of importance to the region. Meanwhile, Simon scrambled with others of little seniority for the attention of colleagues and the media. He followed this routine, with a few exceptions, for ten years in the U.S. House of Representatives, always alert to those moments when he could be lifted above the crowd. From his earliest days in Illinois, he had searched for new challenges, fresh ideas, and attention by the media. His friend and former colleague Abner Mikva caught the essence of Simon: "Paul was an absolute free agent, a crusader, chock-full of ideas . . . He took on more causes and more issues than you could shake a stick at, and he never, never ran out of gas."[19] However, in Congress there were many scrambling for attention. In Illinois, Simon had little competition.

Simon showed patience during his first year in Washington, carefully avoiding entanglements with freshmen whose agenda was headed by turning out the old—meaning those with a Watergate connection—and gaining as much publicity as possible with the Washington press. Simon appeared lost in the crowd, and it alarmed supporters in Illinois who were not accustomed to his silence. A Republican legislative aide familiar with Simon's behavior told a reporter, "Now the young Turks have fallen from favor with the Washington media, and they (the media) are looking for congressmen who seem to have more staying power and some substance. They have turned to Simon."[20] The comment followed Simon's appearance in national publications, wire service reports, and the *Washington Post*, which observed, "Some [new members] settled in easily and like Rep. Paul Simon no longer want to be identified as freshmen, but prefer to be identified with issues and stands he's taken." He received mention for his endorsement of Senator Hubert Humphrey for president in 1976, more a sign of Simon's respect toward the aging Minnesotan.

Simon still had a knack for gaining media attention, even if results were not spectacular. The Washington press acknowledged his pop-in visits to places such as the Civil Service Commission office and the U.S. Postal Service. He served on House committees—considered minor assignments—that dealt with both institutions. His favorite comment upon showing up was, "What's going on?"[21] The flabbergasted bureaucrats seemed honored and surprised. They could not remember the last time any congressman paid attention to them.

Simon made his columns for the media a priority in the first term, writing forty-eight in 1975 and thirty-nine in 1976. With a large coal mining constituency, Simon wrote about black lung proposals and strip mining laws as well as the "Peril to Small Postal Offices." In the latter, he talked about the impact on his rural constituency of a piece of legislation that was an effort to save money: "The name of the organization is Postal *Service*, not Postal Money-Maker . . . I favor an efficient post office system. But I also favor postal *service*. And if that means a few tax dollars to keep post offices in small towns, to keep newspapers and magazines flowing through the mails, I'm for it."[22]

He discussed the special problems of senior citizens, food stamps, estate taxes, school lunches, inflation, roads and bridges, and social security. Simon pursued an interest in foreign affairs and military issues, writing on "Zionism and the United Nations," "U.S. and Soviet Defenses," the foreign sale of food, and "Korea: Patience and Firmness." In all, he provided a broad choice of subjects aimed at local audiences and those with a curiosity about matters outside southern Illinois. He was feeling his way when it came to finding the right combination of subjects for audiences in the district.

In "Rural Roads and Bridges Need Help," Simon identified a major constraint on passage of legislation favoring his district. He suggested imposition of a one-cent gasoline tax strictly for rural roads and bridges but added, "Rural representatives are a minority, and it will take a coalition with urban representatives to get it done."[23] The largest town in his sprawling southern Illinois district was Carbondale with 26,000 citizens. He also suggested diverting excess money collected for the interstate highway system for use on bridges and roads.

In the columns of 1976, Simon wrote less frequently on district issues. He covered farm issues on two occasions and continued to write about deteriorating postal service. He commented on a strip mining amendment in "Compromise: Essential to Progress." With the looming national elections, he focused on the economy, the size of government, prayer in schools, and the need for a new natural gas policy and expressed concerns about Democratic candidate Jimmy Carter. The foreign policy and military subjects included wages abroad, using food as a weapon, "Thebes—and National Policy," and U.S. and Soviet defenses.

Simon returned to one of his familiar subjects from Illinois days: financial disclosure. His theme was that disclosure could help end antigovernment attitudes. He wrote, "The most popular way to run for public office this year is to run against the government. I have contended during my years in public life that the best way to win the confidence of those who elect us is to lay all of our financial dealings out on the table."[24] He mentioned distributing personal information on income and assets to media outlets and the *Congressional Record*. "If this practice had been written into law for all members of Congress and other key federal and state officials decades ago, maybe there would be more confidence in government and maybe candidates wouldn't be running against the government in our Bicentennial year."

After winning reelection, Simon's column production in 1977 topped both 1975 and 1976 output with fifty-one. The topics reflected increased attention to national and international subjects and fewer aimed directly at district issues. The plight of farmers and coal miners were exceptions. In "Income Disclosure Requirements," Simon wrote again about a favorite subject. On seven occasions he tackled foreign affairs (Panama Canal, trade, unemployment problems, China, the Mediterranean, the Middle East twice), and two times on military matters. Fans of the congressman were encouraging him to run against Senator Charles Percy in 1978, and that may have inspired more far-reaching subject matter. He declined to run, but the desire to be a U.S. senator only temporarily took a back seat.

After prolific column writing in his first three years in Washington, Simon produced only seventeen columns in 1978. With labor strife in coal mines an issue, Simon wrote "For Coal Miners, Against Violence," and "Promoting Peace in the Coal Industry." Aside from a column on Social Security coverage and care for the elderly, the remaining columns dealt with national and international matters. The low count may have reflected time spent campaigning for his third congressional term; in 1979 he rebounded to write forty-six columns. Subjects of special interest to southern Illinois included improving the postal service, a greater reliance on coal, unemployment problems, "Southern Illinois and the World," and senior citizens. On fourteen occasions he wrote about issues in foreign countries or United States foreign affairs policies.

In 1980 when Simon faced the biggest threat of defeat for reelection, he wrote twenty-eight columns, only one of which had southern Illinois content. That was about coal. Twice he wrote about a balanced budget amendment to the Constitution, one of his favorite subjects during his years in Congress. Inflation, unemployment, and concern about the MX missile program were favorite repeat subjects. Four times he discussed foreign issues.

Simon's choice of column subjects reflected his interests, not necessarily the interests of district constituents. The columns were a means of addressing matters of importance to him that may or may not have found sympathy among congressional colleagues. Simon struggled with the House system, which limited opportunities to take the floor and talk about issues and consumed time in committee hearings. He needed a means of speaking to a large audience, and that was his district column.

Frustrations for Simon in the House took several forms. In five terms, Simon never rose above chair of the subcommittee on postsecondary education. At the end of ten years, thirty-seven of the seventy-five Democrats elected in 1974 were still in the House. Most of them had positions on heavyweight committees such as Ways and Means or had become powerful subcommittee chairs. The pattern of service in the Illinois legislature, where he never had a position of organization responsibility, continued through his years in the House. He introduced large numbers of bills every session, and some passed. None shook the rafters. Simon would say that he was too independent and took positions unpopular with many in his party. He was probably right.

However, people in parts of Illinois beyond his district had not forgotten Simon. He outlasted Walker and remained on a friendly basis with reporters in the state, especially those in Washington who represented papers in Chicago and St. Louis. Believing he still had voter appeal, party officials urged him to run for governor and the senate. But Simon had experienced life in state government, and running for governor no longer appealed to him. When 1977 rolled around, speculation began about a Democratic opponent for Senator Percy, who neared the end of a second term. Naturally, that talk included Simon. Party leaders in Washington urged Simon to take the challenge. He told a newspaper in Decatur, "If ten years ago someone had told me that such an array of leaders would urge me into a Senate race and I would decline, I would not have believed it."[25] Others did not believe it either. As it turned out Percy nearly lost to businessman Alex Seith.

Another opportunity for a senate run occurred in 1980 when Adlai Stevenson decided to retire after a decade in Washington. Simon might have been tempted, but Secretary of State Alan Dixon leaped first. "It later came back to me that Paul had wanted to run, but I foreclosed him," Dixon recalled, adding that they never discussed the matter.[26] Simon said, "When Adlai Stevenson III left the Senate in 1980 there was talk again about my seeking the Senate, but Alan Dixon indicated to me he wanted to run, and both because of pragmatic reasons and because of my friendship with him over the years, I endorsed Dixon and said I would not run."[27] Dixon won easily.

As it turned out, Simon needed all the strength he could muster in the 1980 campaign for reelection to the House. Often an opponent seriously threatens a congressman in the first attempt at reelection, the assumption being that a relatively new official is most vulnerable early. Simon's district had a long history of electing Democrats to congress—Kenneth Gray served for twenty years before Simon—and that forestalled an immediate challenge. The close call came after six years. In fact, 1980 turned out to be disappointing on several counts.

Two columns during 1979 paved the way for one of the biggest controversies of his congressional tenure. The first at midyear, "A National Need, More Leadership, Less Polling," raked President Carter over the coals for his dependence on public opinion polls to determine domestic policy initiatives.[28] Simon began, "The Carter administration, to much too great a degree, has been determining policy by studying national polls rather than national needs. That does not result in effective leadership." Simon cited examples of former members of the administration who blamed polling for policy problems. He called on Carter to "extricate himself from the problem by stopping all poll-taking and simply ask himself two basic questions: What are the most pressing needs of this country? How can we in government help to meet those needs?" He speculated about the president's ability to provide answers. "Whether or not President Carter has it within himself to become an effective leader is difficult to know. He is a decent man with fundamentally good instincts, but that does not automatically translate into leadership." That commentary by itself would not have created much of a stir, but when combined with another column later that year, the local political pot boiled.

The column that may have received the highest readership, and most negative reaction, was one titled, "Why I Support Kennedy."[29] Simon's backing of Senator Edward Kennedy for president in 1980 did not set well with southern Illinoisans. His reasons for supporting Kennedy leaned heavily on the criticisms he made of Carter in the earlier column. In his 1976 run for president, Carter had built strong support in southern Illinois. Kennedy had no ballot exposure in the region.

Simon ignored warnings from associates in the district that an endorsement of the controversial Massachusetts senator would generate trouble. He might have been disinclined to listen to advice because of his close kinship with the Kennedys, dating to John F. Kennedy's election in 1960. Simon had given full support to John Kennedy and spoke and wrote admiringly on numerous occasions. Ted Kennedy had campaigned for Simon in the district.

Simon wrote a five-page single-spaced "P.S./Washington" column for district and state media—the normal length of a column was a page or two double-spaced—describing his Kennedy decision in detail. About Carter, he wrote, "He is a better president than the public recognizes. If he is the nominee of my party, I will have no difficulty supporting him over a Ronald Reagan or a John Connally. But we have the opportunity to do better." He listed four areas of greatest need including economic problems with inflation, an energy policy, White House leadership, and the need to foresee future problems. He concluded, "In all four areas Ted Kennedy has the potential to meet the needs more effectively."[30]

The endorsement sent shivers through the district. Simon's Democratic constituents saw the presidential contest differently. In the March state primary when district voters chose delegates to the Democratic National Convention, they elected a full slate of Carter supporters sponsored by former congressman Gray, and rejected Simon and the Kennedy slate. Simon admitted the Kennedy endorsement hurt him with voters and party leaders but added, "I didn't do it to gain popularity."[31] It did not help Simon that Kennedy's campaign went down in flames and Democratic convention delegates nominated Carter for a second term.

Simon then had a primary challenge for his congressional seat, a Catholic priest, Edwin Arentsen, who had resigned from active church roles. He attacked Simon for his moderate stands on abortion, the Panama Canal treaty, and the equal rights amendment (ERA).[32] While Simon won handily, Arentsen's nasty campaign left scars.

Simon's general election opponent, John Anderson, a public relations and management consultant who had run against Simon and lost in 1978 by a 2 to 1 margin, presented a conservative contrast. He favored a tax cut to deal with inflation woes, while Simon opposed a cut. Simon maintained a moderate approach to military expenditures except for elimination of proposed new weapon systems, while Anderson called for an increase. They disagreed about environmental regulations on coal burning and how to help family farms, both district issues.[33] Complicating the race was James H. Barrett, representing the Constitution Party. He voiced positions extreme to both of the mainstream candidates, taking issue in a nasty tone with virtually every stand by the incumbent congressman. Other factors that worked against Simon in the general election included Republican presidential candidate Ronald Reagan's popularity—he carried the district easily—and that Simon's opponent, John Anderson, had the same name as the Republican Illinois congressman who ran in 1980 for president as an independent.

Simon barely escaped a loss. Riding a Republican trend in southern Illinois and unhappiness with Simon, Anderson came within 2,085 votes. Barrett received over 5,000 votes, a majority of which might have gone to Anderson. In victory, Simon remained resolute, opposing many initiatives of the newly elected Ronald Reagan, some of which may have appealed to district voters. He told a reporter, "I have to live with myself. I'm just going to call the shots as I see them, or [decide] what I believe is best for my district and the nation. That's what I've done in the past, and that's what I'm going to continue to do."[34]

After returning to Washington, Simon had setbacks in the House that complicated a look at the future. As a member of the House Budget Committee, he sought the chairmanship but finished third in the voting. Gene Callahan recalled, "That was the only time I ever saw Paul really down. After that, he decided he wasn't going to be in the House very long. He knew he could never be part of the leadership. It was up or out for him."[35]

Through the 1980 campaign and beyond, officials of conservative Christian organizations nipped at his heels, taking issue with many of his moderate-to-liberal positions on issues. Leading the right-wing assault was the Moral Majority, whose objective clearly was to establish an agenda for a challenge to Simon in 1982. The organization gave Simon a zero rating on congressional issues, citing his support of the Department of Education and creation of domestic violence centers. Simon seemed amused by the challenge. "I knew I was morally imperfect, I just didn't realize the extent of my imperfection."[36] Robert Reid, a freelance columnist for papers in southern Illinois, wrote of the quarrel, "I know of no other person in Illinois or

American public life who has tried so hard, without being arrogant about it, to make morality a part of politics and to keep the interests of the average person at the center of his vision of responsibility as a politician and public servant." Moral Majority's opposition to Simon continued throughout his congressional years.

Leading up to the 1982 campaign, Simon became a target of the National Conservative Political Action Committee (NCPAC). The organization pledged funds for a campaign against Simon. He stood his ground, saying at a press conference in March that he would not be "bullied" or "bought" by radical right wing groups that had started the campaign. He said NCPAC tried to "blackmail" him into voting for President Reagan's tax program "or our voting records will be 'exposed' and they will spend vast sums of money to defeat us. This I know: The people of Southern Illinois do not want me to become a rubber stamp for any president, or any political party, or any special interest group—and certainly not to a group of self-appointed kingmakers from suburban Washington."[37] NCPAC was joined by other national organizations in opposing Simon, including the Republican National Committee. In order to fight these external forces, Simon spent $413,477 on his 1982 campaign. Concerned about the challenges, Simon hired professionals to do television work and raise money by mail.[38]

While Simon nonchalantly dismissed the 1980 election close call in public, he privately set about to gather information that would prevent a similar outcome, or worse, in 1982. He commissioned a public opinion survey early in 1981 by Peter D. Hart Research Associates, Inc., a firm that worked primarily for Democrats.[39] Responses to many questions indicated Simon's strengths, such as an overwhelmingly favorable reaction to the statement "Paul Simon really cares about people like me." Two-thirds of respondents said he kept in touch with the district and cared about helping solve problems. They rejected the statement "Paul Simon is too liberal for this area."

In its conclusions, the Hart firm identified the challenge for Simon in spite of reassuring responses. "If anything, Paul Simon has not yet communicated his position on the issues in a way that has reassured the voters of his commitment to work for them," the report said. "In general terms, there is little sense that Paul Simon has been better than mediocre in addressing the major issues." Against probable opponents, most of whom had no name recognition, he "gets barely a majority. The challenge ahead is for Simon to persuade some of the undecided vote that he is the person they need in Congress. Without a strong and early push, Simon will begin this election in a most precarious position."

The cold facts that led to such a conclusion rested largely on Simon's inability to make district voters forget the record of Congressman Gray. The "Prince of Pork," as he was fondly known, Gray earned the title by devoting his tenure to bargaining for public works. By his own count, Gray was responsible for bringing $7 billion in federal projects to southern Illinois.[40] Those included interstate highways 57, 64, and 24, the Kaskaskia River canalization project, Rend Lake, Lake of Egypt, Saline River flood control project, Devil's Kitchen Lake, and more than 120 post offices, nursing homes, hospitals, and other infrastructure improvements. District voters did not worry about Gray's national issue ideas or votes. He kept them happy with jobs and the flow of federal dollars.

Gray attributed his success to friendships he cultivated with Speaker of the House Sam Rayburn and Majority Leader Lyndon B. Johnson, who ruled Congress during Gray's early years. "Anything I wanted, they would help me get," he told a reporter.

That approach to district service and cuddling with the power brokers of Congress was not Simon's style or desire. He succeeded in saving jobs and bringing some projects to southern Illinois, but nothing in the quantity of dollars attributed to Gray. Simon worked the district from one end to another, made his presence known, listened to constituents, and did what he could to solve their problems, but no one suggested crowning him the "Prince of Pork" or anything close. When district residents told Hart pollsters they were not sure of Simon's commitment to their issues, they were resurrecting the ghost of Kenneth Gray.

Simon searched for other ways to increase visibility in the district. He asked two respected men in leadership at Southern Illinois University for outreach ideas. John Jackson and Keith Sanders responded with a memorandum titled "A Program for Strengthening Paul Simon's Relationships with Southern Illinois University."[41] They recommended more personal contacts, better written communications, improved press relations in Carbondale, more appearances in formal settings on campus, and involvement in social and civic life of the city and university. The authors reminded Simon of an earlier strategic error. "Your instincts are usually good, but you know as well as anyone that they are not infallible. For instance, a good poll might have given you a better appreciation for how extremely unpopular Senator Kennedy was in this district in late 1979 and might have made you think more carefully about the costs of endorsing him. You don't have to 'toady' to public opinion to appreciate its role and power fully."

The general election in 1982 pitted a Simon primed for another close contest against Peter Prineas, an electrical engineer from Carbondale who had opposed Simon in 1976. Prineas focused his campaign on unemployment in the district, naming Simon as the culprit. They disagreed on a range of other issues including gun control, school prayer, and abortion. Simon took the standard liberal position, while Prineas cast himself as a conservative. They debated a nuclear freeze that Simon supported as a step toward arms reduction. Although Simon ran scared after the close call in 1980, he won by a margin of 2 to 1 that included victory in twenty of twenty-one counties.

In the 1980s, a period in Simon's public life that can only be called hectic, many opportunities arose for visibility beyond Illinois. Chief among those was a constant stream of books. Simon produced nine books and coauthored two more, almost doubling his output prior to 1980. In his earlier writing, subjects ranged from Illinois history to world poverty. Looking for a broader audience during his time in Congress, Simon tackled public policy and political issues such as the foreign language crisis, Democratic party strategies for change, morality in the nation's capital, putting people to work, his race for president in 1988, Supreme Court nomination battles, and the dollar crisis (coauthored with H. Ross Perot).

Books provided a pulpit for ideas, advice to the party, and recitation of his personal experiences tied to public issues. A reporter, taking note of his prolific output, wrote, "When he feels stretched too far, Simon will pick an issue he feels most strongly about, sit down at his typewriter and write a book."[42] Simon added, "It's a discipline that forces me to learn more instead of constantly skimming the surface." Simon's wife Jeanne suggested another reason for his productivity. "I think Paul in his writings is saying, 'I know what I'm doing,'" she said, meaning that he felt compelled to prove he could do it without a college degree.[43] His ability to accommodate writing with the demands of public office astonished his staff. Even with the advent of computers, Simon preferred to pound out his manuscripts on a Royal typewriter inherited from his parents.

Toward the end of his terms in the House, Simon wrote two books. In 1980, *The Tongue-Tied American: Confronting the Foreign Language Crisis* expanded his frequently expressed concerns about the parochialism of U.S. citizens and lack of curiosity about foreign cultures.[44] He wrote, "It is one of the ironic quirks of our culture that it is often more acceptable to plead ignorance than to know." As important as the message on language, the book contained Simon's first critical essay on behavior and performance of the media. In many of his books from 1980 to his death in 2003, Simon provided commentary on the work of reporters and responsibilities of media companies. While other U.S. senators wrote books with criticism of the media, Simon preferred to call for improved coverage, better-informed reporters, and commitments to report essential information. He had the benefit of a journalism background and a deep interest in press affairs, while other elected officials mostly viewed the media with alarm.

In *The Tongue-Tied American,* he pleaded for coverage of "lesser stories" often ignored by the press. "We are more interested in a baseball strike or the latest details of a murder than in more substantial news from abroad that will ultimately have a greater impact on us," he observed. He noticed a decline in the number of reporters covering foreign news and called on editors to reverse the trend. Always conscious of the need for newspapers to turn a profit, he added, "In strict financial terms, foreign news has to be considered a loser." However, he believed the need was greater than ever for foreign news coverage.

His other book presented the clearest indication of Simon's ambition and future plans of any previous tome. They took form in a book titled *The Once and Future Democrats: Strategies for Change,* published in 1982 in advance of what became his final term as a congressman.[45] While ostensibly aimed at Democratic policy makers and party leaders, it constituted a campaign platform for the U.S. Senate. Much of the book was written during and after the near-disaster of the 1980 campaign, but little of the content was aimed at his district constituency except to say figuratively, "I am what I am, and here is how I feel about this country and its people."

Unlike his earlier books on issues such as world hunger and the need for improved foreign language skills, *Strategies for Change* spoke to a wide range of national and international policies designed to establish his point of view, while also suggesting that the Democratic party should snap out of its doldrums and adopt them. The tour de force was aimed at displaying his credentials as a spokesman on national affairs.

Across most of the pages, Simon took a broad swipe at the policies of new president Ronald Reagan and the conservative programs of the Republican party. Simon offered his ideas for the nation in direct challenge to the national political trend then in motion. His liberal tone, reminiscent of the days of Hubert Humphrey and Paul Douglas, was not designed to persuade people of southern Illinois. This was a national treatise, reaching to constituencies throughout the state, especially the large population centers.

The chapter headings read like a subject list from his newspaper columns or preparation for campaign debates: health services, education, agriculture, cities (urban problems), defense, jobs, budgets and inflation, and culture and religion. Simon labored to provide facts and figures, reflections of history, and quotes from political and intellectual leaders to bolster his arguments.

Otherwise he spoke most passionately for a renewed national commitment to education at all levels, an inclusive approach to relations with foreign nations, redirection of funds for the military away from costly weapons, and outreach to the needy.

One intriguing chapter related directly to his emotional and personal battle with the Moral Majority. The organization, in its zeal to undercut his southern Illinois constituency, had raised Simon's hackles by publicly challenging his religious background and convictions. Early in the discussion, Simon compared Moral Majority to the Ku Klux Klan:

> Political leaders find it awkward to deal with [the Moral Majority]. Like the Klan, this is in part a geographical phenomenon, primarily of great influence in the South and near south. Like the Klan Moral Majority followers embrace a strange mix of politics, religion and nostalgia. Unlike the Klan, they operate openly and have no truck with violence. And unlike the Klan, on some issues the group unquestionably voices the opinion of the majority of Americans: for example, there is too much violence on television, a position with which I personally strongly agree.[46]

Unwilling to cast a stone at everyone in the Moral Majority, Simon said members are "sincere, well-meaning people. But they are being misled." He acknowledged that the organization operated within the law and had a constitutional right to be wrong, from his perspective, on issues. He added, "Political leaders make a mistake if they go beyond that and suggest the Moral Majority is less than sincere, or that their activity violates some American tradition." Simon saved his strongest language for this description: "The Moral Majority is a political movement wrapped in a veneer of theology and the cloak of Protestant fundamentalism."

It would not have been typical of Simon to call attention to his own religious upbringing and Christian habits. If he had, sending a copy of the *Troy Tribune* of April 14, 1949, to the Moral Majority would have been an eye-opener. On that date, just before Easter in his first year of ownership of the paper, Simon devoted the entire front page to the resurrection of Jesus, retelling the story in the style of a newspaper report on the happenings.[47] The lead story opened, "Word has been received from Jerusalem in Palestine of the resurrection there of a Jew who was dead three days and whose tomb had been sealed by the Roman authorities. His small band of followers are now proclaiming him the 'Savior of the World.'" Other front-page headlines stated, "Jesus Somewhat Known for Unusual Comments," "Hope Seen for Oppressed," "Fast Trial for Jesus," "Jesus Put Stress on Self-Sacrifice," and "Jesus Only 33 at Time of Death."

Strategies for Change might have been taken as a valedictory, a summation of his attitudes and ideas covering nearly thirty years in public service. But viewing it that way would have been a mistake. This was no final flag waving. It was a statement of what Simon believed and what he would take to the Senate campaign trail in 1983 and 1984.

Full Redemption

Political opportunity for Simon knocked again in 1983 as Illinoisans speculated about Charles Percy's bid for a fourth term in the Senate. Percy looked
like an enticing target for Democrats, especially after his close call for reelection in 1978. In that election—which Simon decided not to enter—Alex
Seith, a businessman with no history of holding public office, nearly pulled
a major upset. Percy prevailed only after a furious finale to the campaign
in which the senator admitted that he had not listened to Illinois citizens.
After the election of Ronald Reagan as president in 1980, Percy, as chair of
the Foreign Relations Committee, became something of a Reagan advocate.
Democrats thought the senator's turn from positions of moderation to conservatism would make a good target in an election campaign.[1]

Eager to run, three Democrats with statewide credentials committed to
a primary election: state senate leader and Democratic party chairman Phil
Rock, State Comptroller Roland Burris, and Seith. Although he originally
decided not to run and told friends of the decision, Simon began hearing from
supporters that he should declare for a primary race that might favor him in a
split decision. While those voices helped persuade Simon, the fact remained
that he had wanted to run for the Senate since the campaign of 1962. On the
emotional side, Percy had defeated Simon's idol, Paul Douglas, in 1966.

Simon consulted his friends and colleagues, especially Dixon, Callahan,
Durbin (in his first term as a congressman), and Adlai E. Stevenson III. If
Simon wanted approval to run, he did not get it. In an interview, Dixon
said Callahan and he met with Simon and "strongly urged him not to run.
We didn't think he could win. Reagan was running for re-election and was
going to trounce [Walter] Mondale. In those days Illinois could easily go
Republican. We told Paul, 'You'll get killed, Illinoisans don't split tickets.'"[2]
Durbin recalled that the idea of Simon running against a three-term senator
who had not made any serious mistakes and putting everything on the line
in his first statewide election since the Walker loss, "made us all nervous."[3]
Stevenson acknowledged he urged Simon to remain in the House where he
had accumulated seniority. Regardless, Simon decided to run, and eventually all his friends rallied in support.[4]

During the time before Simon finally declared his candidacy, Dixon made a decision that complicated personal relations with Simon. Dixon pledged his support to Rock. Unwilling to go back on his word after Simon entered the race, he remained neutral in the primary. In the general election, Dixon gave his support to Simon but said he would not campaign against Percy. He explained, "I liked [Percy] a lot. I never said anything against Percy."[5] As early as May 1984, Simon understood the degree of involvement he could get from Dixon. Speaking to the author in Washington, Simon said he did not expect Dixon to be much campaign help. "It is difficult for one senator to campaign against another even if from different parties," Simon said.[6] He expected Dixon to make "courtesy campaign stops" in the general election.

Simon's decision to enter the race also strained relations with Rock. The two had been close enough for Simon to confide in Rock he would not run for the Senate seat. When Rock made his announcement, he assumed Simon was on the sidelines. The change by Simon infuriated Rock, causing a breech that never healed.[7]

A statewide poll before the 1984 primary showed Percy beating Simon 47 percent to 27 percent, which meant if he won the primary Simon would be the underdog in an election for the first time in thirty years. He announced his candidacy in July 1983, accusing Percy of being a Reagan acolyte and calling the senator a "rubber stamp" for policies that harmed the economy of Illinois.[8] He accepted the challenge of comparing his knowledge of foreign policy with Percy's. Simon hired Robert Perkins, a young political operative, who had done campaign work for Abner Mikva, to manage the primary campaign. It did not go well, and in October Simon announced the departure of Perkins. Simon said the lawyer from northern Cook County had "a little lack of a statewide perspective."[9]

A month earlier Simon had contacted James Wall, editor and publisher of the *Christian Century* magazine in Chicago, and asked him to take over the campaign. Wall recalled in an interview, "I said my experience was with McGovern and Carter delegate selection" not in running a campaign. Simon said he wanted Wall because "you know how to manage an organization, and you get along with the regulars."[10] The "regulars" meant the Chicago Democratic organization that eight years after the death of Richard J. Daley still had a measure of influence in party elections.

The combination of Simon and Wall had a history. The *Christian Century* published a number of articles by Simon, especially in the 1960s before Wall joined the publication. Wall and Simon met during the 1968 campaign for lieutenant governor when Wall, a United Methodist minister, held a coffee for the candidate at his home in Elmhurst. During 1972, Wall earned political recognition by recruiting candidates throughout Illinois to run as delegates for George McGovern. Wall said he tried to solicit Simon's support for McGovern but failed.[11]

In 1976, Wall again went on the road throughout Illinois recruiting delegates for Carter. Simon declined Wall's invitation to support Carter. Wall said, "He tended to go with the establishment on such occasions." During the Illinois primary, Wall earned further stripes with Chicago party regulars, especially Mayor Daley. Wall said he convinced Carter not to challenge Daley in the city with a slate of prospective delegates, believing such a move would unnecessarily anger the mayor and wouldn't gain any delegates. According to Wall, Daley appreciated the concession and that contributed to the mayor's decision for a timely endorsement of Carter in the national primary campaign.

Wall accepted Simon's invitation to manage the 1984 campaign but put a six-month limit on his direct involvement after working out a leave arrangement with the magazine. Wall went to work just before the state Democratic party central committee announced its slate of candidates. He knew the chances of a Simon endorsement were slim with Phil Rock in the race. One of Wall's first acts was to release a staff person Perkins and Simon had hired to influence the party decision. "I said it was a waste of money and we can't afford it. There was no way we were going to get the endorsement," Wall stated. He was right. Rock had all the party connections lined up, and he got the nod. Simon responded, "There is no question that if you had a secret ballot of the central committee, I would win overwhelmingly."[12] In the years since Richard J. Daley's death, the central committee's clout had faded considerably. Losing the endorsement was little more than a slap in Simon's face.

Simon the veteran campaigner and Wall the strong-willed partisan worked well together. Wall did all the media buying, hired staff, and handled press contacts, many of which he had cultivated in presidential campaigns. He remembered Simon as "idealistic, naïve, moral, and moralistic. He was a very pragmatic politician. He truly loved politics. We were very close. He knew enough about the media to help me."

The major difference between the two arose over Simon's close association with wealthy and influential members of the Chicago Jewish community. In their passion to defeat Percy, who had spoken favorably of Palestinian interests, the leadership poured money into Simon's campaign. Wall recalled, "There was a committee of seven Jewish leaders who dealt with the campaign. They asked him [Simon] to run campaign information by the committee. I had to sit down and report to them. They were the ones who backed Simon with money."

Wall feared for the strong Israel lobby's influence with Simon, but the candidate had a long history of support for Israel, and the alliance was comfortable and mutually satisfying in terms of financial assistance. When Simon's backing by Israel's supporters became an issue in the general election contest, he said, "I'm not going to kow-tow" to the Israeli lobby.[13] Percy claimed Simon entered the contest primarily because of Jewish support. Long after the contest, Simon admitted he strongly supported Israel and denied Percy's insinuation that Jewish friends had undue influence with him. He acknowledged that they had urged him to run for the Senate, however.[14]

Wall had a history of his own with the Israeli lobby in the United States. "I had been writing editorials for eleven years critical of Israel's occupation of Palestinian land," he related. This background led to an incident involving David Axelrod, a reporter for the *Chicago Tribune*. Wall knew Axelrod and had tried to bring the reporter on board the campaign. Hoping to be named political editor of the *Tribune*, Axelrod did not want to leave the paper. Wall said, "Axelrod called and said we should know [word of Wall's columns] was being circulated" and could embarrass Simon. Wall told Simon he would step down to avoid embarrassment. Simon said he could weather the situation. When the *Chicago Sun-Times* asked for comment, Wall said Simon replied, "I hired Jim Wall as my campaign manager, not my foreign policy manager."

That was not the only time Axelrod did a favor for Wall and Simon. Wall related, "Axelrod called me one day and said, 'Your man is scheduled today to go to a waste dump owned by Waste Management.'" The firm had contributed money to the Simon campaign. Axelrod said he planned to write a story the next day that would include the information, but if Simon returned the check to Waste Management it would "take the edge off the story." Wall told Simon about the call and that "Axelrod was doing us a big favor. I said he would have to return the check." Simon disagreed and refused. Wall recalled, "He said, 'They will not tell me what to do,' and said he wouldn't do any favors for the company." With Simon not budging, Wall called David Doak, a Washington-based campaign consultant who was being paid by the campaign to help shape Simon's message and strategy. He asked Doak to contact Simon and persuade him that keeping the money would be damaging. Doak made the call. "Paul paid attention to professionals; he agreed to return the check." Wall had to make the rejection call to Waste Management, "where fortunately, the executive who handled campaign contributions was an old friend from the Carter White House. He knew how the game was played. We told Alexrod the check had been returned and the item did not appear in the article."

The Israel lobby's support of Simon was not a stealth issue in the primary or general election campaigns. Newspapers identified Mideast foreign policy as a major issue. An August editorial in the *Southern Illinoisan*, the largest daily in Simon's congressional district, noted, "The fund raising drives against Percy and the media interest they have generated make this Senate race a referendum on Mideast policy."[15] Pro-Israel fundraiser Louis A. Morgan of Skokie wrote a letter for Percy's primary opponent, Republican congressman Tom Corcoran, stating, "Percy is a dangerous man. He has the power as chairman of the Foreign Relations Committee and he uses it against Israel."[16] Thomas A. Dine, at a pro-Israel workshop on politics, counted Simon among the strongest Israel supporters in Congress. "Paul Simon is a true friend. He has consistently voted for foreign aid," Dine stated.[17] An aide to Simon estimated Jewish political action committees would contribute at least $175,000 in the primary. Simon expected to receive $60,000 from labor.[18] Wall later said, "Simon owed his Senate career to the Lobby."

Simon won the primary with 31.4 percent of the party vote. Rock, supported by the state Democratic organization, finished fourth. Percy had a primary contest of his own against U.S. Representative Corcoran, who accused the senator of not being conservative enough. While the incumbent prevailed, winning all but 12 of 102 counties, the battle distracted Percy from Senate business and slowed preparation for the general election.[19]

Wall stepped down as expected after the election. Axelrod left the *Tribune*, after learning he would not be named political editor, and accepted a key role in managing media and strategy for the general election campaign, making it two journalists who contributed substantially to Simon's future in the Senate. After the election, Axelrod established a public affairs firm in Chicago and began a career that led him eventually to an essential role in Barack Obama's run for the presidency in 2008. He also worked on Simon's 1988 presidential campaign and for Chicago mayor Richard M. Daley.

Simon never underestimated the challenge of unseating Percy. In a letter to a supporter, he wrote, "Percy will be a tough opponent in the general election . . . Percy has run good campaigns in the past and I assume this time will be no different. He is a good fundraiser and, as a wealthy individual, can spend his own money as well."[20] On a more practical note, a report for the Democratic Senatorial Campaign Committee on May 1 cited weak support for Percy by labor, Jewish, and black voters, "which will go to Simon this time, and Simon's outstanding record with Illinois voters make this one of our most promising races."[21]

For the first time as a candidate, Simon in 1983 ceased writing his column for newspapers in order to concentrate on the primary. Within a few weeks of the general election, he resumed the column and charged the cost to his campaign. This gave him license to use the writings as campaign material and attack Republicans at will. He also kept his ideas afloat in public with a timely new book titled *The Glass House: Politics and Morality in the Nation's Capital*.[22] It had the characteristics of many "campaign books" with a scattering of stories about his personal journey, contemplative moments, and ideas for directions of government. For the man colleagues called "Reverend," the topic seemed appropriate. Simon talked primarily to members of Congress, the executive branch, and the national media, and those who might like what they read enough to contribute campaign funds.

Typical of Simon, some of his ideas seemed to clash with his actions. One example was about campaign financing. He outlined in detail a plan for federal financing of campaigns with caps on spending. During Simon's campaign for the presidency in 1987, the *Washington Post* observed that Simon's book called for a crackdown on political action committee contributions, while his campaign for the Senate in 1984 collected $904,054 in PAC donations.[23] Never intimidated by such reporting, Simon always felt comfortable telling people what was best for them while proceeding apace under current regulations. This was the practical Simon at work.

Simon reaffirmed his unhappiness with trends of the Republican-led federal government, especially President Reagan and the Senate. In a chapter headed "Inappropriate Responses to World Hunger and Nuclear Threat," he spoke of the need for foreign economic aid. He acknowledged that some members of Congress opposed aid, but he questioned the reasons. If someone voted no because the appropriation was inadequate, Simon could understand. On the other hand, if a member disagreed with any aid that was another matter. He wrote, "If a legislator stands before an audience and says, 'Let's stop sending money to other countries; let's spend it on our problems,' it is likely that he or she is using a convenient and surefire way to get votes, one that ignores the long-range best interests of the nation."[24]

On the nuclear arms race, Simon argued against a further buildup of weapons and for a nuclear freeze, and called for dialogue to solve differences with the Soviet Union. He believed a reduction in arms could be achieved by diplomatic talks. He wrote, "We should be trying to build a much broader understanding between the Soviet Union and the United States in particular, and among nations in general." He acknowledged the difficulty for members of Congress to vote against increased military spending. "A vote to cut any defense expenditure will generally result in more negative editorials than favorable ones, though that varies from district to district and state to state . . . There are times, however, when morality is visible in the decision-making process. In an arms race, whether the motivation is moral or merely a selfish desire to survive, any move toward a world more likely to avoid nuclear holocaust is desirable."

He wrote at length on the subject of religion, expressing his concern for the direct influence on public policy while acknowledging the personal side and its importance. He used one example to demonstrate his unease with religion in political campaigning: "Before an election there usually are special invitations to visit certain churches in my district, sometimes with an invitation to speak. A year before an election I am pleased to accept until four weeks before an election when I feel uneasy and usually decline, unless it is an occasion such as that offered by Calvary Baptist Church in Marion, Illinois, which invites all candidates to say a word or two."

He had little ambivalence about the initiatives of the Moral Majority in affairs of government. The book continued his war with the organization, its leader Jerry Falwell, and its attempt to dictate decisions on national affairs. He drew the distinction between acceptable religious behavior and that of the Moral Majority with these words: "Most who try to apply the tenets of faith to the world of politics do so with the recognition that the application of religious principles to life is a somewhat uncertain business, and there is a possibility of being wrong. But there are some in both the liberal and conservative camps who take rigidly dogmatic stands, and charge that those who disagree are morally inferior. Foremost among these is the Moral Majority, headed by the Reverend Jerry Falwell."[25]

This was a personal battle for Simon, reflecting attempts by the Moral Majority and its political kin to condemn Simon for his position on public policies and defeat him at the polls. He mentioned how the organization rated him a zero out of a possible 100 percent on "key moral issues." The Moral Majority criticized Simon for opposing prayer in schools, voting against an amendment that would have prevented the Internal Revenue Service from taking tax-exempt status away from private schools that racially discriminate, voting against a proposal that would have stopped school busing for integration, and other issues that brought them in conflict. He argued, "This is the same group that does not touch on the subject of world hunger, but says a member of Congress has cast an immoral vote if he or she wishes to slow down the arms race."

Simon wrote at length about the weaknesses of Washington reporting and his own attitudes toward the press. He began by declaring the intentions of his office toward the media. "My office has standing instructions: reporters get priority." He acknowledged when the media takes up an issue "it will mean a commitment of time in our office, whether the subject is intrinsically important or not." Simon never went far into comments about the press without reminding readers of his journalistic background. He said, "Reporters look to Congress and see our faults, usually with a fair amount of accuracy and discernment. As a former newsman now serving in Congress let me suggest what I sense are the five basic weaknesses of congressional coverage." His list, paraphrased by the author:

- Trivial items often get more attention than matters of substance (which he also mentioned in the foreign language book).
- There is an appalling insensitivity to the international dimension in both stories and editorials. This continued his cry for more foreign news coverage.
- Political commentators lack a sense of perspective. He made an exception of columnists David Broder and George Will.
- Editorials are too flabby. He praised the editorials of the *St. Louis Globe-Democrat*, with which he often disagreed, as having "punch. There is no question where the editors stand. Its vigorous positions, whether you agree or not, should be applauded."
- Journalists need to keep alive at least a small flame of optimism.

Ranging beyond these points, Simon expressed frustration about the increasing concentration of newspaper ownership in the hands of fewer people. While newspaper chains often improved properties they bought, they also paid too much attention to profits. He stated, "Newspapers—and legislators—ought to provide more courageous leadership, and I fear chain ownership diminishes that possibility."[26] In the 1970s and 1980s, chain ownership accelerated, putting an end to much private ownership and introducing widespread corporate consolidation.

Simon's campaign book made clear the issues on which he planned to run against Senator Percy and the Republican party while presenting a thoughtful treatise on behavior in Washington.

Simon had learned his election lessons the hard way in the Walker debacle. Leaving no room for a repeat, he took the 1984 fight directly to Percy with an aggressive campaign designed to paint the incumbent as a born-again conservative who supported a president with whom Simon did not agree on many issues. Percy stood his ground as a Reagan convert, calling him "my president." Percy believed the president's likely reelection in November would help him in Illinois. Meanwhile, the senator turned his verbal guns on Simon, repeatedly calling him a liberal. The contest was unlike any Simon had run in terms of ferocity and name-calling. Gone was the "turn the other cheek" approach. Simon's television ads were particularly biting, and during debates between the two he challenged the incumbent relentlessly. Simon explained his approach in 1984: "Whenever anyone took out after me after that, I didn't hesitate about coming right back at them."[27] At one point, he demanded that Percy disclose his income tax returns to show how much he had benefited from tax cuts pushed through by Reagan. As a House member, Simon had voted against all the tax cuts.

Because of the high-profile aspect of the contest, national media gave it a close look, pointing to accusations by both sides and the intensity of claims. Because Simon had not been in a tight race since the Walker contest, the press noticed changes in his approach. A *Wall Street Journal* profile mentioned an independent expenditure against Percy by a California real estate developer, Michael Goland. Simon told a reporter he wrote Goland twice asking him to stop the negative advertising. The reporter wrote, "But he did little to publicly disavow it until late in the campaign."[28]

The Simon campaign knew primary and general election opponents would focus on his legislative record in the House. In readiness for that eventuality and in preparation for speeches, press releases, and campaign materials, Simon's longtime press relations person David Carle pulled together a memorandum for internal use titled "Paul Simon Achievements Summary."[29] Carle included Simon's efforts to influence and direct legislation for his district and a national audience. Noticeably, it ran heavily to subjects he supported, proposed, argued for or against, task forces and studies in which he participated, activity in federal jobs programs, and cosponsorship of bills and amendments in education, energy, postal service issues, and coal. The summary provided a snapshot of an active member of Congress with a few legislative victories related to his committee assignments.

The general election Senate battle brought together two candidates with records as "Mr. Clean" in Illinois and national politics. Neither had the slightest smell of corruption or questionable ethics. This factor had special meaning just a decade after the scandals of Watergate. That may have influenced the campaigns to do what they could through advertising and public statements to cast the opponent in the "worst" ways possible: "conservative" or "liberal."

The race went to the wire. On election night, Dixon appeared as a commentator with columnist Mike Royko on a Chicago television station. He recalled, "The screen flashed that Percy had won. Mike said that confirmed what people were expecting. I said it might not be correct. I had knowledge of voting patterns in Will County, a Republican county, and I could see that in those precincts Paul was doing well. I said to Royko, 'I don't think they analyzed that correctly.' Royko said, 'You heard it here folks.'"[30] Dixon left the show and went to Simon's hotel in Chicago where they watched the finale. Dixon stated, "It was a miracle that Paul won."

Simon's margin of victory was 89,000 out of 4.7 million votes cast, although Percy won the counties 61 to 41.[31] Reagan won the state by 600,000 votes. Simon stated with pride, "I became the first United States senator elected from deep southern Illinois in 147 years." Richard M. Young, a native of Kentucky, practiced law in Jonesboro, Illinois, before being chosen U.S. senator in 1837. A Jacksonian Democrat, he held a single six-year term.[32]

While Simon's victory again affirmed his overall popularity in Illinois, there were other factors in the victory. Voting returns by county revealed that Simon won because of strength in Democratic urban county strongholds of Cook, St. Clair, Madison, Peoria, Macon, and Rock Island, not because of statewide voter choice.[33] Percy's strength was concentrated in the northern half of the state and along the eastern border, areas with few voters. With the exception of suburban Chicago areas that Percy carried, large numbers of the counties he won provided a plurality of only a few hundred votes. Simon succeeded in keeping matters close where Percy should have racked up large pluralities and obviously gained from an erosion of moderate Republican support for Percy. In spite of his longtime downstate credentials, Simon rode to victory on the Democratic party's traditional strengths, helped immeasurably by his boost from the Israeli lobby and education and union interests. To no one's surprise, Simon won handily in areas constituting his congressional district.

Percy's standing among conservative Republicans, the core of state partisans, was never high and had weakened noticeably with election victories in 1972 and 1978 against much lesser known opponents. Conservatives never thought he leaned sufficiently in their direction on issues. They also remembered that he had supported Gerald Ford's candidacy for president in 1976 rather than Ronald Reagan.[34] As the conservative movement gained strength nationally leading to Reagan's presidential victory in 1980, there was no reason to bow to Percy, a reluctant Reagan backer. Percy's conservative rhetoric during the campaign failed to convince the party core. Also, the fact that conservatives challenged Percy in the 1984 primary did not help the incumbent.

Percy learned that he could not make the liberal label stick to Simon, in spite of the challenger's voting record. The tactic never worked for Simon's opponents. Percy may have looked at Simon's election record since the loss in 1972 and concluded that congressional opposition was weak. Percy was not the first opponent to underestimate Simon. Those miscalculations by Percy made Simon's aggressive campaign more effective.

The impact of Simon's victory on the short-term political history of Il-linois was substantial. After the 1984 victory, which put the two U.S. senate seats in Democratic hands, Republicans elected a senator for only one six-year term through the 2008 election.

After the bitter campaign, during which Simon accused Percy of lying to the people of Illinois, the two candidates managed to form a civil relation-ship. The odor lingered, however, with those close to Percy. Carter Hendren, Percy's campaign manager, called Simon a hypocrite, "a very successful hypocrite, and as dangerous a man as there exists in politics," for inferring Percy helped spread cancer by voting against increased funding for toxic chemical cleanup.[35] Hendren also cited a brochure distributed in black areas that boasted of Simon's record in support of civil rights. It featured a photo of Simon surrounded by black faces in a parade. A Simon brochure distributed in white areas used the same photo without black faces. When this accusa-tion arose during the 1988 presidential campaign involving Simon, Axelrod responded. He said having two different versions was "a graphic design decision. There were two different brochures for two different purposes."[36] Axelrod added, "I think Hendren is groping for an excuse for losing."

The United States Senate. This is where Paul Simon wanted to be more than anywhere in a long political career. If he could not send Everett Dirksen to retirement at least he succeeded in ending the career of Charles Percy, a three-term Republican senator. The victory made Simon a giant in the eyes of friends, loyal supporters, and diehard Illinois Democrats. But those accolades cheered him only momentarily. Now he could trot out those long-held beliefs about reaching out to foreign countries and leaders, help-ing domestic needy, a balanced budget amendment, and open government initiatives. Before the campaign with Percy, he told a reporter why the Senate had such great appeal: "I'm a generalist. In the Senate I'll be able to speak on anything I like."[37]

There were personal moments, too. As if someone had revised an old movie script, the downstate Illinois boy wonders—friends for thirty years—Simon and Dixon were back within frequent sight of each other. However, even with the proximity, they found the playing field different. Dixon already had four years seniority in the Senate and was working the inner sanctum of the Democratic caucus for leadership responsibilities. Simon wanted to be a senator in order to advance policy ideas. Dixon acknowledged being "more conservative" during the Senate years. As a member of the Armed Services Committee and chairman of the subcommittee responsible for 40 percent of the Department of Defense budget, Dixon said, "I supported

Reagan's buildup. Paul voted against military buildups. I was more a Truman Democrat, and he was a Kennedy Democrat."[38] Gene Callahan, knowing the two well, said this about their styles: "Dixon was a domestic issue senator who worked hard on Illinois issues. Simon did his share on Illinois issues, but he had a great interest in national and international affairs."[39]

Senate leaders placed Simon on two major committees, the normal limit, but thanks to a special waiver Simon became a member of four. His duty on the House Budget Committee earned him a seat on the Senate Budget Committee. Although he did not have a law degree, or any college degree, he received assignment to the Judiciary Committee. The other committees were Labor and Human Resources and Foreign Relations. Simon had a full plate but not more than he wanted.

Protocol for new senators was to be seen and not heard for a period of time deemed necessary to understand the chamber's rules, make the acquaintance of members and Senate leaders, and stand in line patiently. Some called this process an unspoken initiation rite. That also meant not grabbing headlines and not stepping on the toes of colleagues. In spite of staff urgings, Simon went along with tradition. In November 1985 the *Wall Street Journal* in an article about the freshman class in the Senate stated, "Simon of Illinois is widely rated the class of the class."[40]

Simon's cautious approach did not go unnoticed. It resulted in opportunities to work with Republican senators, who held the majority. During the Ronald Reagan administrations, and when Republicans controlled the flow of legislation in the Senate, crossing the aisle in bipartisanship was about the only practical way to have influence.

An unabashed advocate of a balanced budget amendment to the Constitution, Simon received an invitation to work with Republican senator Orrin Hatch of Utah to sponsor an amendment proposal. Hatch told a reporter, "Paul Simon's presence says to liberals: 'Don't be afraid of the balanced-budget amendment.'"[41] To accommodate Simon, Hatch sent two amendment proposals to the floor, one that Simon requested. He wanted no limits placed on congressional authority to raise taxes. A balanced budget amendment never passed during Simon's tenure.

On another occasion, Simon submitted an antiterrorism amendment to a supplemental appropriations bill, reflecting concern over a hostage crisis involving Trans World Airlines. Senator Nancy Kassebaum of Kansas, who headed the aviation subcommittee, asked Simon to withhold his amendment so she could incorporate it in her plan for a larger airport security bill. It meant Simon did not get credit for the idea. He told a reporter, "Now it's a Kassebaum bill, not a Simon bill, but we're getting the job done."[42]

A Republican senator with whom Simon developed a strong personal and professional relationship was Alan Simpson of Wyoming. They first met in 1970 at a gathering of state legislators and elected officials chosen for their promise of future leadership, where they spent four days exchanging notes and ideas. The two maintained contact through the years until they both were members of the Senate. Simpson was elected in 1978. When Simon entered the Senate, they had a basis for working together. Simpson told an interviewer, "You cannot serve effectively in the Senate without working with the other side of the aisle . . . If you only work with members of your own party you won't get anything done."[43] He found Simon shared that opinion.

Simon and Simpson served together on the Judiciary Committee, with Simpson holding the chairmanship of the Subcommittee on Immigration and Refugee Policy during most of the Reagan years. Simpson helped with the selection of Simon to the committee and to the subcommittee along with Simon's friend Ted Kennedy, the other Democrat on the subcommittee. "Simon said he didn't know anything about immigration," Simpson explained, "but I told him we had good staff of people to help him learn. And he learned quickly."

Simon developed an interest in uncovering fraudulent marriage and financial arrangements to obtain permanent resident immigration status. He asked Simpson to schedule a subcommittee hearing and call witnesses who could help craft legislation to prevent this fraud. Simpson told Simon his schedule was too full at that time. Simon asked if he alone could arrange a hearing. "Remember, minority members of a subcommittee don't have the power to set the agenda," Simpson explained. "But Simon worked hard to understand the problem. I conferred with committee members of both parties, and told them Simon would preside. That was a most unusual agreement for a senator from the minority party." Simon chaired the hearing and worked with the staff to schedule time and select witnesses.

The relationship between Simpson and Simon was based in large part on mutual respect. "He was a doer," Simpson said of his friend. "He was tolerant and collaborative. If Paul Simon told you something you believed it." They maintained the friendship and mutual interest in issues until Simon's death in 2003. Simpson shared the eulogy at Simon's funeral services.

William A. "Bud" Blakey, a staff member who worked with Simon in the House and Senate on education issues, gave high marks for Simon's bipartisanship. "He was very effective. He worked with Republicans on education issues and subcommittees, when Democrats were in leadership and when the Republicans were."[44] Blakey cited one specific example of

Simon's success in working with Republicans. Simon and Representative E. Thomas Coleman, Republican of Missouri, served together as members of the House Subcommittee on Special Education. When Simon chose to move on and serve as chairman of the Subcommittee on Postsecondary Education, Coleman switched too, "because he enjoyed working with Paul," Blakey said. Simon's willingness to work with Republicans did not always sit well with Democrats. "Some Democrats thought Paul worked too well with Republicans," Blakey added.

Simon hardly had adjusted to the manners of the Senate cloakroom and working with Republicans when another career opportunity opened just two years after becoming the junior senator from Illinois. With Ronald Reagan's two terms as president coming to an end, political chatter about his successor started early in 1987. Vice President George Bush appeared likely to win the Republican nomination, but the Democratic contest was wide open. Early mention of names by columnists and in news articles included Simon, although he had little recognition beyond Illinois. Two other prospects interested Simon and he deferred to their potential candidacies: New York governor Mario Cuomo and Senator Dale Bumpers of Arkansas. In February, Cuomo bowed out, and Simon called a press conference to announce support of Bumpers.[45] In March, Bumpers said he would not run.

In the meantime, Simon continued conversations with union leaders and others familiar with his political record. He also consulted longtime associates and friends, some of whom doubted the political advantages of a long-shot race for president. After spending a week in Florida with Jeanne to discuss the ramifications of a presidential run, Simon announced his candidacy on May 18. He said he was not intrigued by living in a big white house or hearing the band play "Hail to the Chief." He added, "I have been in politics long enough to know how empty those things can be." Simon wanted an opportunity "to lead and inspire and give the nation a vision of the kind of tomorrow we can build for future generations."

The New York Times account of the announcement observed that at age fifty-eight he was the oldest Democrat in the race. It prominently mentioned his background as a newspaper editor and author of eleven books, adding "he would be the first President since Harry Truman, and only the second in this century, who did not graduate from college."[46] Simon's remarks prompted the Times to report on his "unabashed advocacy of traditional Democratic values at a time when many younger Democrats are pressing their party to move away from New Deal policies. He is known for his support of jobs programs, civil rights and arms control." Underscoring its comments about Simon clinging to the past, the reporter added, "For 40 years he has used an old manual typewriter, which he refuses to replace with a computerized word processor."

Simon jumped the gun on what he expected media writers to say about his appearance. He said, "To become fashionable some people tell me to get rid of my bow tie and my horn-rimmed glasses, and most of all to change my views. Harry Truman wore a bow tie and horn-rimmed glasses, and he didn't knuckle under to pressure to change his views as he fought for working and retired Americans." Simon's physical appearance—mostly his ears and hair style—also drew frequent comments, some in jest, others not so.

Media skeptics called Simon a "long shot," adding, "He doesn't have a presidential appearance" followed by "little appeal to young people." Simon joined a large field of possibilities for the nomination: Senator Gary Hart of Colorado, the Reverend Jesse Jackson, Senator Albert Gore Jr. of Tennessee, Governor Michael Dukakis of Massachusetts, Senator Joseph Biden of Maryland, former governor Bruce Babbitt of Arizona, and Representative Richard Gephardt of Missouri. None had run a national campaign.

Simon began the labors of a presidential candidate during the summer and early fall, raising money, hiring a staff, and campaigning in Iowa and New Hampshire. As the first primaries of 1988 approached, Simon's poll numbers improved dramatically in the caucus state of Iowa. This caused increased interest by reporters and columnists across the nation who wrote at length about Simon, his background, public service, and the ideas he offered as a presidential candidate.

The image of Simon as a "gentlemanly liberal," as the *Washington Post* said, as a "boy scout, of undeniable intelligence" as the *Wall Street Journal* put it, or as a person of unchallenged integrity, as the *Seattle Times* mentioned, echoed for weeks in the fall. The avalanche of newspaper profiles generated so much press attention that Simon's staff borrowed an extra van for transporting reporters in Iowa.[47] Almost every article repeated Simon's biography, the choice item relating to his days as a crime-fighting journalist. One *Washington Post* profile began, "Back in his days as a crusading young newspaper editor, Democratic Sen. Paul Simon commented almost weekly on the great political figures of the day in the columns of the Troy Tribune."[48] Although something of an exaggeration, the flavor of the lonesome weekly editor pounding his typewriter with the truth about good and bad people made the rounds in one form or another. Reporters repeated stories of Simon's attachment to Adlai Stevenson, Paul Douglas, and Harry Truman as evidence that Simon was preaching an old-time religion on the presidential trail.

Occasionally, someone in the press ranks told a more pertinent story about Simon's career. One who did was David S. Broder, political columnist for the *Washington Post*. In a November column, Broder sifted through comments by several political analysts about Simon as a tough campaigner who spoke candidly about his beliefs in an effort to connect with voters.[49] Broder added, "Simon's beliefs are a bit of a hodgepodge. Alone among 1988 candidates, he voted against all the tax cutting of the Reagan years and still asserts it was wrong. Not even [Jesse] Jackson is matching Simon's proposal to make the federal government the employer of last resort for all long-term layoff victims. And no one else has echoed his promise to have a plan for financing long-term health care costs ready within 60 days of taking office." The columnist mentioned the differences between "Simon's liberal House voting record and his independent-sounding stump speeches." Broder and a few other columnists began trying to pin Simon down on the costs of his proposals—without much luck.

As Simon moved to the front of the pack in Iowa polls, another article in the same time period as Broder's column raised more questions about what a reporter called "his elusive philosophy." David Shribman of the *Wall Street Journal* observed that Democratic party activists questioned whether Simon's proposals for jobs, healthcare, and a balanced budget were workable. Shribman also commented on the imagery of Simon's campaign and how it did not always match reality. He wrote, "His image as the modest country editor of a half-century ago isn't his only incongruity, however. He is a vigorous champion of the labor movement and yet he believes a split minimum wage providing for a lower rate for young people is worth trying as an experiment. He calls himself a 'pay-as-you-go Democrat' but, besides the Rev. Jesse Jackson, Mr. Simon is the only Democrat who is a strong advocate for major new domestic spending."[50]

Shribman quoted Simon in response to the critics: "People want someone who is going to play it straight, to level with them. People understand I'm not just holding my fingers to the wind, that there's a base of conviction."

One of Simon's campaign brochures translated the candidate's words into shorthand for issues he believed would reach a national audience. The brochure was titled "The Wisdom to See What is Right. The Courage to Fight for It. Paul Simon does not run from a tough fight."[51] These were the points raised in the brochure:

- Fighting organized crime: young Paul Simon took them on. And won.
- Paul Simon is fighting to protect America's environment. Because he believes we have an obligation to preserve it. Not a right to destroy it.
- Paul Simon believes we should not license any new nuclear plants until all the questions about safety and nuclear waste storage are answered.

- The key to seeing America grow: invest in education for Americans.
- It's plain common sense: you don't export arms to Iran. Or jobs to Japan.
- Caring for older Americans: it's time to provide long-term care.
- Giving our children a chance for peace: we must seize responsible opportunities to end the arms race.
- Paul Simon is fighting for working families and senior citizens. In the great Democratic tradition of Roosevelt, Truman and Kennedy.

Before the Iowa caucuses, Senator Biden and Senator Hart left the field. Hart dropped out upon revelations of a sexual affair. Biden's campaign ended with disclosure of plagiarism. Hart later attempted a comeback that took the wind out of Simon's sails but did little else. By caucus day, polls showed Simon running third behind Dukakis and Gephardt, but he surprised everyone with a strong second-place finish. He received 27 percent of the vote to 31 percent for Gephardt.[52] However, Iowa was literally costly for Simon. A shortage of money meant he could do little radio or television advertising in New Hampshire, the next challenge. "There is a money problem in my campaign," Simon admitted. Dukakis, governor of nearby Massachusetts, won the New Hampshire primary, with Simon finishing third.[53]

Simon's momentum came to a virtual stop before the Super Tuesday contests in February because of a shortage of funds. Jackson, Dukakis, and Gore took most of the delegates with Simon a no-show. He resurrected the campaign a bit by winning his home state's March primary, giving rise to speculation that Simon was back in the hunt.[54] After finishing fourth in Wisconsin, he suspended the campaign in April.[55] Dukakis went on to win the party nomination and lost in the general election to George H. W. Bush.

Simon wrote a book about his experiences in the campaign titled *Winners and Losers: The 1988 Race for the Presidency—One Candidate's Perspective.* The book received mixed reviews, including one in the *New York Times* that said dryly, "Most of these comments could have been made after any election during the last quarter-century."[56] On the positive side, the *Times* stated the book "offers tough, though sporadic, criticism of his own campaign . . . There would have been a terrific book had Senator Simon only stuck to his subtitle and realized that 'one candidate's perspective' implies more than one candidate's opinions, however judicious."

The book contained a full chapter of observations about press coverage that repeated complaints and praise mentioned in earlier books, such as "More attention should be paid to the issues, less to the horse race," and "Less attention should be paid to the trivia."

Media aside, Simon took a hard look at his own campaign and gave it a less than sterling grade. He took the blame for poor issue ads but noted that David Axelrod and Associates "is still relatively new in the field."[57] In Simon's kindly approach to Axelrod's work, he really meant the firm's work left much to be desired.

In a critique of his speeches, Simon pulled no punches, saying that they did not reflect his thoughts or personality. "I rarely read a speech, but I certainly am not going to read one that is dull and mediocre, that does not reflect me, not only in substance but in style." The speeches produced by many writers, including Axelrod, "did not quite fit me."[58] Toward the end of the campaign, Simon found writers "who sensed a little better than others what I needed." Among those were Jim Broadway, a former Illinois newspaper reporter.

Simon found moments for levity in the book, including fun he had at a Rotary Club meeting in Waterloo, Iowa. They sang a song to Simon to the tune of "R-O-T-A-R-Y, That Spells Rotary":

> B-O-W-T-I-E, that spells bow tie.
> B-O-W-T-I-E, Paul Simon is the guy.
> He's his own man, it's plain to see;
> He wears his tie with dignity.
> B-O-W-T-I-E, that spells bow tie.[59]

Typical of his upbeat personality, Simon could see personal growth from the presidential effort although it took time and energy from his Senate duties. Still, questions remained as to why the campaign was not more successful. There were practical considerations, such as a shortfall of money that generally kills well-intentioned primary candidates. For whatever reasons, he was unable to capitalize on his generally positive press and a solid showing in Iowa. He managed to save some face with his victory in Illinois.

The imagery that worked so well for so long in Illinois did not connect on a national level or with reporters who had little knowledge of his strengths and successes. They skimmed the showy pieces of background and repeated them but rarely explored how those experiences fit with the desire to be president. As soon as writers exhausted the "Simon story," they began picking at his proposals, asking questions about the cost and practicality. They found the ideas mostly warmed-over liberalism and concluded they did not work for 1988.

In Illinois, Simon had the benefit of thirty years' work on his reputation and image, but it all seemed weak when mentioned as a presidential qualification for a national audience. Reporters in Illinois did not probe as deeply as those covering national politics. In the end, reporters and commentators looked with skepticism at what one columnist called "his hickish, odd-duck appearance while suggesting he was not one of those 'slickly packaged' politicians" and his proposals that looked as if they might break the national bank.[60] In the final analysis, Simon's image as a politician of ideas, independence, and decency did not build a following in the harsh national political environment of the late 1980s.

Always on the lookout for statements that seemed to capture the essence of a moment or lift the candidate's spirits after a disappointment, Simon recited a favorite from the end of his presidential effort in his autobiography. It was spoken by Bob Krueger, Simon's Texas co-chair: "Like Truman and Lincoln, Paul Simon is outwardly undistinguished. But the real strength of leadership always comes from inner qualities. A president cannot lead a nation without first finding direction within himself. Paul Simon could. He is a man of heart."[61]

More than three years into his first term as a senator, Simon returned to business in Washington and the looming bid for reelection in 1990. The senator might have looked vulnerable to a strong Republican candidate. After all, his first two years in the Senate, 1985–87, were devoted to getting feet on the ground in a chamber encrusted with seniority and history. In 1987–88, Simon devoted most of his attention to the failed presidential campaign. Illinois Republicans nominated Lynn Martin of Rockford, a former member of the state house and senate and a five-term member of Congress. With a conservative voting record and generally positive marks as a legislator, she faced Simon, a Democratic party institution with a public record covering nearly four decades.

Compared to some of Simon's election campaigns, this one created little fire. After more than three decades in politics, his lagging enthusiasm for the rigors of campaigning and raising money may have begun to surface. He ran a "you know me" campaign designed mostly to rest on laurels, name recognition, and incumbency. Beneath the surface was the prospect of the first woman in Illinois history to sit in the U.S. Senate. It made Simon nervous and cautious in his campaign. He chose to ride the tide rather than attack the challenger. She, on the other hand, made his record the issue. Simon was too liberal, his programs would cost the taxpayers too much money, and he had not been especially attentive to Illinois issues during the Senate term, she claimed. From the mouth of a more dynamic campaigner with a strong record, the words might have given Simon a legitimate scare.

She discovered that none of his opponents had ever made the "spendthrift liberal" label stick.

There were moments during the campaign that gave Simon cause for worry. A sign of Simon's nervousness appeared while assessing his standing with the Chicago press. He asked friend and colleague Alan Dixon for help by "loaning" Gene Callahan, an expert in press relations, for a week to work in the city. Dixon said to Callahan, "Go ahead." Callahan had provided previous services for Simon while a member of Dixon's staff.[62]

During the campaign, Simon signed a petition calling for discontinuance of Chief Illiniwek as mascot at the University of Illinois on the grounds of it being a racist symbol. When made public, his sympathy for the cause created a clatter across the state as alumni of the university rose to defend the mascot and its famous halftime war dance at athletic contests. Simon never backed down and if anything stuck his chin out further. At the Illinois-Michigan football game that fall, his opponent sponsored an airplane to fly over the stadium with a banner reading "Keep the Chief, Dump Simon."[63] While many thought this would end Simon's career, the controversy passed as a campaign issue, although it continued to rage in the state for decades more.

Simon's record offered a mixture of heartland conservatism and liberal dogma. He repeatedly called for a balanced budget amendment and was outspoken in criticism of violence on television. Well-known were his arguments for reductions in defense spending and raising taxes on the wealthy with more money for education. In an attempt to label Simon a has-been, Representative Martin stated, "His time is past." But she was wrong. Simon crushed her on election day, taking 65 percent of the vote. In what became Simon's last election campaign, he raised $8.4 million in contributions.

Settling in for a second six-year term, Simon remained a member of the Judiciary Committee, one duty of which was to consider presidential nominations for the Supreme Court. During Simon's first term, the committee and full Senate approved Anthony Kennedy and David Souter with little argument. The consideration of Robert Bork, a defiant conservative, was another matter. Simon voted against Bork in committee, and the full Senate later rejected the nomination as Simon prepared for his presidential campaign in 1987. When President George H. W. Bush presented Clarence Thomas for approval as an associate justice in 1991, Simon appeared front and center.[64]

The Thomas nomination became one of the most acrimonious processes in modern Court and Senate history. The controversy involved a statement by Anita Hill, a law professor at the University of Oklahoma, accusing Thomas of sexual harassment. Before the statement by Hill and her testimony at a second round of hearings, Simon had decided to vote against Thomas. The media turned its attention on Simon outside the hearing room when Hill's affidavit, which she insisted be held in confidence by the committee, was leaked to the press. Simon was accused of the deed, although he denied being the culprit from that time forward in public statements and books.[65]

Eventually, the nomination came to the Senate floor for a vote. Thomas won a seat on the court 52 to 48, the closest vote for a Supreme Court nominee in more than a century. Simon voted against Thomas. Eleven Democrats voted for Thomas, including Simon's Illinois colleague, Alan Dixon. Both senators felt the strain on their friendship. Dixon said later, "That was a little touchy."[66]

Much of Simon's second term in the Senate passed without great notice or controversy. He committed time and energy to a myriad of issues of interest to him, especially in the field of education. He fought for many proposals that failed in the Senate, such as the balanced budget amendment. Ultimately, that idea struck a dead end with Democratic Senate powerhouses Robert Byrd and Majority Leader Tom Daschle.

One of Simon's greatest triumphs in Congress came in the Senate on the subject of literacy, an initiative that had failed to catch the attention of Congress until Simon came along. He held hearings on the need for attention to literacy while in the House. As a senator, he sponsored the National Literacy Act that established the National Institute for Literacy. One of his strongest supporters for the law was Barbara Bush, the president's wife.[67] A public critic of obscenity and violence on television, Simon encouraged adoption of the V-chip in television sets that allowed parents to monitor programs watched by their children.

Simon also voiced active opposition to domestic programs that he believed were not in the best interest of the nation. He was one of twenty-one senators, all Democrats, who voted against the Personal Responsibility and Work Opportunity Act, otherwise known as welfare reform, that was signed by President Clinton.[68] Simon was lead sponsor of Clinton's effort to reform the student loan program. He also opposed federal mandatory prison sentences in an article that appeared in a national magazine as his second term came to an end.[69]

Simon continued work on education issues and support of minorities that began during his days in the House of Representatives. He supported legislation to build endowments for small colleges, worked on behalf of education for children with disabilities, proposed legislation for a database to help find lost children, was a continuing advocate for foreign language studies, and offered ideas for new school-to-work opportunities. Colleagues and staff members who worked with Simon praised his support of antidiscrimination legislation, proposals to assist black colleges, and advocacy for American Indian colleges. A pragmatist when it came to political achievements, Simon did not always expect to win when he made an amendment or proposal, and he realized that in many cases it took several attempts to pass bills or to get the attention of members.

The Illinois reelection contest in 1992 involving his friend Alan Dixon provided some fireworks en route to Dixon's primary loss to Carol Moseley-Braun. Simon worked hard for his friend's reelection, but his wife Jeanne, irked at Dixon's vote for Clarence Thomas as an associate justice of the Supreme Court, campaigned for the election of Moseley-Braun. While it is likely Dixon felt wounded by Jeanne's opposition at the time, in an interview years later he was philosophical. "You don't control everything your wife does," Dixon said. "You see differences, and you accept them."[70]

Another embarrassment for Simon during the 1992 primary involved David Alexrod, Simon's campaign director in 1984 and media consultant in the 1988 presidential campaign. As the primary campaign unfolded in 1991, Axelrod handled media for Democrat Albert F. Holfield, a wealthy Chicago lawyer with a plentiful supply of personal money for advertising, whose entry in the contest probably cost Dixon a victory. Axelrod led a television campaign for Holfield that blistered Dixon as a tool of lobbyists. This caused Simon to publicly defend his friend by endorsing him on TV and campaigning across the state. In a conversation with a reporter for the *National Journal,* Axelrod responded by calling Simon, who he had praised as an honorable public servant on any number of occasions, "an aspiring hack trapped in a reformer's body."[71]

In a 2007 interview with the *Chicago Tribune,* Axelrod, then a strategic adviser to Barack Obama, said of that comment, "If I go back in my whole public life, I don't think there is anything I regret more than that comment." He did not take anything back about Dixon, however, adding, "I felt that Sen. Dixon had made some very bad and harmful decisions, and I felt they were antithetical to Paul's progressive principles." Axelrod said Simon never mentioned the comment, and although Axelrod's name was mentioned frequently in Simon's books and his autobiography, he never spoke of the episode.

Whatever tension existed between Simon and Axelrod, their relationship formed one of several links for Simon when Barack Obama began a meteoric rise in Illinois politics en route to the presidency. Other connections were Abner Mikva, who became a friend and early adviser to Obama, and Senator Richard Durbin. Associates of Simon recall some contact between the two as early as when Obama was a student at Harvard. When Obama served in the Illinois Senate, an initiative of the SIU Public Policy Institute headed by Simon increased the personal contact. As part of an effort for campaign finance reform in state statutes, Simon created an advisory group that included Obama. The relationship was casual, and friends believe Simon never was an insider with the 2004 Obama campaign for the U.S. Senate. Days before Simon died in December 2003, he told friends of his plan to endorse Obama for the Senate. After Simon's death, his daughter Sheila made a television commercial for Obama. On the road to the presidency, Obama made occasional references to Simon's public service.

As the time approached for Simon to think about seeking a third term in the Senate, he decided not to run. He later acknowledged the signs of waning enthusiasm and a desire for a change of personal direction. He did not look forward to raising millions of dollars for another campaign. The statement on November 14, 1994, announcing his decision did not speak to those issues. Instead he said:

> I have discussed this with Jeanne and our children and reached a careful but firm decision. I have an obligation to the people of Illinois, to the Senate, and to myself to leave the Senate while I am still eager to serve, not after I tire of serving. The citizens of Illinois and my supporters elsewhere in the nation have been generous to me through the years, and I am grateful to them beyond anything words can express. I have tried to repay that confidence by working hard and by leading, and when the causes were not popular my friends have been patient and tolerant. My family has loyally put up with the long hours and frequent discomforts of public life . . . I have no personal plans beyond 1996. I have served in public life to make a difference, not to hold a title, and I know there will be opportunities in private life to make a difference after retirement from the Senate.[72]

A final show of affection from all his Senate colleagues, Democrats and Republicans, occurred on the floor of the chamber just days before his retirement. All members—men and women—appeared wearing blue polka dot bow ties or scarves tied as bow ties. Simon described the surprise scene in these words: "Jeanne, and my son Martin and my staff, all of whom knew about it in advance, sat in the gallery. Everyone enjoyed the occasion, no one more than I did. Small things in life make a difference."[73] That from a man whose public life contained countless small—and large—things.

Other senators remembered that day as something special, too. Alan Simpson of Wyoming, who ended his Senate career at the same time as Simon, told an interviewer, "I had never seen anything like it before or after. It was a special day."[74] In remarks to the Senate, Senator Christopher Dodd of Connecticut called the display "an appropriate tribute to a man as unique and distinctive as Paul Simon."[75]

Simon had many opportunities for work after his term ended in 1997, some offering large amounts of money. He chose Illinois, where he started a public policy institute at Southern Illinois University and served as a professor. Serious changes occurred in Simon's life relatively soon after committing to southern Illinois. In 2000 Jeanne Simon died after a fight with brain cancer, and in 2001 Simon married Patricia Derge, the widow of David Derge, once a president of SIU. He watched his children's achievements with pride. Sheila, the older child, settled in Carbondale after earning a law degree and joined the law school faculty at Southern Illinois University. She served on the Carbondale city council but lost a 2007 bid for mayor of the community. Martin, his son, was a respected and successful photographer in the Washington area, whose works appeared in national publications and drew high praise.

Simon built the public policy institute from scratch and devoted its work to many of the ideas that drove his interests in public life. He brought a wide variety of participants to the campus for discussions, speeches, and events and raised millions of dollars for an endowment to assure the institute's longevity. Simon continued to write books—the world water crisis, an autobiography, and *Our Culture of Pandering* among others—and traveled abroad. He occasionally wrote opinion pieces for newspapers and appeared on radio and television shows. It all was an extension of his life and public image begun a half century earlier. He died after surgery on December 9, 2003, and the institute took his name and continued his work, with Mike Lawrence, former journalist and close associate of Simon, as director.

Conclusions

Many of the superlatives spoken about Paul Simon at the end of his life ring true, especially after weighing his triumphs and achievements against failures, controversies, and contradictions. The judgment is influenced by the character and moral convictions that drove his personal and professional life for more than a half century in the public eye.

Much can be learned about Simon's success from his newspaper career, brief as it was. There are few businesses more demanding and subject to public viewing than running a weekly newspaper in a small town. From 1948 to 1955, including nearly two years of Army service, Simon took the responsibilities of a newspaper editor seriously, and with them the occasional sting of criticism. He discovered the courage it took to face readers and defend the paper's decisions up and down the town's main street, in places of business, and at the newspaper office after every issue of the *Troy Tribune*. In a small community, there is no escape route.

He also felt the rush that accompanies acceptance from subscribers and esteem among peers. He thrilled at seeing his name and photograph in major newspapers and national news magazines. Simon seemed perfect for a political stage from the earliest days in Troy. Moreover, he found that acclaim made the hard work worthwhile. During the crusade against crime and corruption in Madison County, Simon built the ground floor of an image that lodged firmly in the minds of the public for more than fifty years.

Simon continued newspaper editing and ownership into the mid-1960s, but he found a special voice in those first few years at the *Tribune*. This was the gift that kept giving, the public awareness that paid far more in political dividends than in cold cash or profits. Born and reared in a time when the printed word was the essential carrier of news and opinion, he never stopped writing: newspaper stories, columns, editorials, speeches, newsletters, magazine articles, and books. He amazed people with his productivity but even more with his range of interests and ideas.

"Journalist" is the title he cherished most, and there is no question that he deserved it. He easily met the standards of journalist for his era. He was self-taught in the image of thousands of newspaper people in the 1940s and

1950s. His reputation as a crusader resonated with fellow journalists and gave him credibility in the media for which other politicians would willingly have paid a fortune. That might have been enough for many who yearned to own and operate a successful weekly newspaper. Simon could have made it his life work. But he wanted more. He discovered that the lessons learned on newspapers could be transferred to politics. That is when the shift in ambition occurred from newspapers to politics.

There is a level of self-confidence that comes with repeated cheers from audiences. It leads people to assume they can climb any mountain under any circumstance. Many do not survive the public glare and slip into arrogance. Through all the praise, and considering the inevitable contradictions, Simon remained self-effacing and genuine. Among colleagues, friends, and associates his word was golden, a trait uncommon in politics. And climb he did. Combined with a streak of rectitude developed from his family roots, the appeal of public approval and the mission of doing good drove Simon to politics as a career.

The streak of independence that characterized Simon's political career was born at the *Troy Tribune*. However, it reached full expression in public office. From the first campaign for state legislator, Simon declared his political independence as an outspoken advocate of morality, ethics, openness, and honesty in government. It was a conversation he insisted on having with the public. Although there were many facets to his public policy interests, including helping the needy and caution with public finances, his political purity stuck in spite of the practicalities of winning elections.

Ironically, the voice he developed that so many voters admired and respected led down a path of no return. Few doubted his ability to lead others in a legislative setting. He had the intelligence, touch of common sense, public appeal, energy, and the ability to communicate. Simon demonstrated a knack for proposing legislation that became law, in some cases years after he left office. But the reality of politics in Illinois in the 1950s and 1960s was that independence of thought and open criticism of policies and people who failed to meet Simon's standards meant he would not become an insider with the opportunity to directly influence the course of state government. Leadership in the legislature—state or federal—meant cutting deals, trading favors, and voting for an occasional proposal that did not deserve passage. It is no less so today. There is no way Simon could have written all those newspaper columns about a wide range of public policy, or the infamous *Harper's* article, if he had held a leadership position. He could have continued a campaign for open government and ethical standards from the inside but not by publicly condemning the action or inaction of colleagues or quarreling with policies of the Democratic Central Committee. Right or wrong, these were the rules of engagement.

Simon, not others, chose the path. Early in his legislative career, he discovered the realities. He could have shifted gears and laid claim to a role as insider, as did his friend Alan Dixon. Simon might have succeeded. However, the longer he continued as an independent voice, the fewer options he had. Periodically—especially during his terms as a congressman—he sought an insider role while maintaining an independent position on a range of national and international issues. It never quite worked. In Congress, Simon made progress on issues by working across the party aisles. He refused to give up the public image of Paul Simon so carefully developed over the Illinois years. Rather than languish and grow stale, he jumped repeatedly at career opportunities, using the image to greatest advantage and feeding a healthy ambition. He did not wait for others to give him the breaks. An amazing election record built his reputation as a high-risk politician. The verdict is that he proved to be more than a risk taker; he was a risk winner.

Simon did not need the coattails of governors and presidents to prevail. He built a successful election record by establishing personal loyalty with many voters across the state. Democratic party strength in Madison County provided all the protection he needed against political winds at the upper levels for his legislative victories. He won easily whether the governor was a Republican or Democrat. Running statewide for the first time in 1968, he succeeded in spite of Richard Nixon's and Richard Ogilvie's victories in Illinois. The safety of a Democratic congressional district provided protection for Simon even though the Ronald Reagan tide of 1980 made his race close. In the triumphant 1984 U.S. Senate race against Charles Percy, Simon overcame Reagan's huge numbers in the state. In every statewide race, the votes generated in Chicago and the Metro-East regions gave him a huge advantage, but the record also shows he ran better than other Democrats in traditionally Republican precincts. On election nights Simon drew well among split-ticket voters.

At first glance, Simon's forty years in office looks like a seamless journey, interrupted only by a two-year break out of office. A closer look reveals two distinct periods in his career, linked by image and personality but differing in environments and results. Those who watched his climb in Illinois government might have wondered if he was the same person who spent twenty-two years in Washington. The environments were dramatically different, and Simon had to make adjustments. Even so, he continued to find his voice outside the chambers of government through books, newspaper columns, public statements, and media appearances as means to influence the legislative agenda.

In the Illinois years up to 1973, Simon's voice and image lifted him easily above the state's governing mediocrity, which was tainted by corrupt behavior. With some luck, his star rose steadily and with it support at all levels of society and across the state. These were the years during which his lasting image developed.

The years in Congress leave a somewhat different impression. He no longer was the only class act. His voice often was just another sound at the national level, although he retained standing at home. The further he moved beyond Illinois, the more he struggled for success, in spite of his energy, ideas, and willingness to work with Republicans. It appeared to some that he grew cautious and more mainstream. Still, the state electorate looked less at his standing in Washington than his lasting reputation in Illinois.

Just or unjust, one standard of achievement in the state legislature and in Congress was influence in the creation, and especially the passage, of laws. Simon proposed many laws, and some passed. He knew how to fight for causes and work with others of a similar mind, regardless of party. Few doubted his intelligence and grasp of important public policies. However, final judgment of the effort rests with others, not with the public official's biographical statements.

The insiders who saw Simon in action gave mixed reviews. Those who used the term "Conscience of the Senate" to describe him were not necessarily affirming his impact on the Senate's work. One colleague characterized Simon as determined to take a favorite issue to the floor of the Senate even if it got only six votes. Members and staff people with whom he worked closely on projects constituted his cheering section. Simon knew precisely where he stood on the issues, regardless of the votes. But counting votes is what defines a master legislator. Nonetheless, he racked up impressive achievements in Congress, as acknowledged by staff members with whom he worked and Democratic and Republican colleagues.

Across the decades there was much to admire, most notably his record of winning elections and his determination to act on principle and take unpopular stands. His memory remains strong for the right reasons: words, thoughts, ideas, and caring for others. He is also remembered well for what he had to say about the responsibilities of individuals and governments.

Any final judgment must acknowledge Simon's high moral standards, willingness to turn the other cheek even against the nastiest of charges, and relentless commitment to help citizens in need. He made compromises, some that failed and others that kept his political career moving. Simon never apologized for being ambitious. He fought fiercely to win elections. Simon's public relations machine amazed his political opponents. Practically speaking, he had a natural touch and feel for politics. When viewed across more than five decades, and compared to public officials serving then and now, Paul Simon set a standard of life worth imitating.

Notes

Bibliography

Index

Notes

Part One. Newspaper Years, 1948–55

1. A Youthful "Ink-Stained Wretch"

1. Paul Simon, *P.S.: The Autobiography of Paul Simon* (Chicago: Bonus Books, 1999), 1–18. Simon covers his years and family background until he got his first newspaper job. Simon's background appeared in print throughout the years with minor alterations.

2. Arthur Simon interview with author, 23 Apr. 2008.

3. Ibid. The story varied. Arthur was quoted as saying Paul mentioned newspaper work at age eight; others remember the story as occurring in grade school.

4. *P.S.*, 18–19.

5. "Troy Weekly Devotes Front Page to Easter Story," *St. Louis Lutheran*, 30 Apr. 1949.

6. *P.S.*, 19–21.

7. William Allen White set a standard for national acclaim achieved by few as editor and publisher of the *Emporia (Kan.) Gazette*. His story is best told in *The Autobiography of William Allen White* (New York: Macmillan, 1946).

8. Ronald Steel, *Walter Lippmann and the American Century* (Boston: Little, Brown, 1980).

9. *P.S.*, 28.

10. Ibid., 25.

11. Ibid., 91.

12. Jarvis did not sell the *Call* name to Simon, so Simon changed the name to *Tribune*. The Jarvis family operated newspapers in Troy from the earliest years. The Simon purchase story was repeated frequently during his life, *P.S.*, 29.

13. James W. Jarvis, "The Early History of Troy," *Troy Tribune*, 25 July 1957. This history was published as part of the town's centennial. See also *History of Madison County, Ill.* (Edwardsville: W. R. Brink, 1882), which provides greater coverage of the founding Jarvis family, and "Troy History," http://www.65.61.129.114/troy/History.htm. This brief history from the town website confirms the early sources.

14. George R. Stewart, *U.S. 40: Cross Section of the United States of America* (Boston: Houghton Mifflin, 1953), 117–19.

15. "This event always attracted considerable attention," *History of Madison County*, 442.

16. Ibid., 443, called the publication *The Commercial Bulletin*.

17. *U.S. 40*, 120.

18. *P.S.*, 29. Simon signed a note for $3,500 at Troy Security Bank. James Watson, president of the bank, was a Lions Club member.

19. "22-Year-Old Troy (Ill.) Publisher Finds Editor's Task a Busy One," *St. Louis Post-Dispatch*, 24 Jan. 1951, also "Troy Publisher's War on Gaming Keeps Him Busy," *East St. Louis Journal*, 28 Jan. 1951, *Metro-East Journal* clipping morgue, Louisa H. Bowen University Archives and Special Collections, Southern Illinois University–Edwardsville (hereafter cited as Bowen Archives).

20. Arthur Simon interview.

21. Paul Simon, "Trojan Thoughts," *Troy Tribune*, 17 Aug. 1961. Hereafter, Simon's name will not be used with the column title.

22. "Troy Weekly Devotes Front Page to Easter Story."

23. Mike Lawrence interview with author, 28 May 2008.

24. *P.S.*, 32.

25. Simon's *Troy Tribune* column continued under the name "Trojan Thoughts" until he entered the Illinois General Assembly in 1955. Thereafter, when writing only for the *Tribune* the column title was "P.S. by P.S." or "P.S. by Paul Simon."

26. *P.S.*, 35.

27. Ibid., 34.

2. Crusader and Politician

1. "The Case against Dallas Harrell," *Troy Tribune*, 15 Mar. 1951, also *P.S.*, 35–36. Much of the author's research for Simon's crusade against corruption was completed for "Paul Simon, Crusading Editor from Troy, Illinois," published in the *Journal of Illinois History* (Spring 2005). Portions of that article are included in this text with permission of the Illinois Historic Preservation Agency, publisher of the magazine.

2. Elliott M. Rudwick, *Race Riot at East St. Louis, July 2, 1917* (Carbondale: Southern Illinois University Press, 1964), 4–5, 197.

3. Carl Baldwin, "East St. Louis," *Journal of the St. Clair County Historical Society* 3, no. 8 (1983): 8–17; 3, no. 9 (1984): 19–25; Hartley, unpublished manuscript about criminal activity in St. Clair and Madison counties, Illinois.

4. Taylor Pensoneau, *Brothers Notorious: The Sheltons— Southern Illinois' Legendary Gangsters* (New Berlin, Ill.: Downstate, 2000). Pensoneau has written the definitive work on the outlaws. See also John Bartlow Martin, *Butcher's Dozen and Other Murders* (New York: Harper, 1950). In *Investigation of Organized Crime in Interstate Commerce*, "Gangland Murders in St. Louis and East St. Louis Areas" (Washington: Government Printing Office, 1951), Exhibit 50, 812–18, and "Summary of Certain Evidence Now in Records Prior to Dec. 10, 1950," Exhibit 40, 209–19.

5. *Investigation of Organized Crime*, "Department of Police, City of St. Louis," 819. See also "Frank (Buster) Wortman Dies; East Side Hoodlum Gang Boss," *Metro-East Journal*, 4 Aug. 1968.

6. Charles O. Stewart, "Signs Indicate Major Invasion Materializing," *East St. Louis Journal*, 28 Sept. 1947. From 1946 to 1950, *Journal* reporters wrote frequently about links between Capone and Wortman, citing no sources. Federal Bureau of Investigation reports spoke of the connections as if they were fact, FBI File 92-2810, 26 Aug. 1959, and *Chicago Tribune*, 24 July 1957.

7. Walter E. Moehle, interview with author, 24 June 1989. FBI Agent Moehle was assigned to the East St. Louis office during the 1950s.

8. Continuous newspaper battles against crime and corruption had been waged in St. Clair and Madison counties since the 1920s. While St. Louis papers focused considerable attention on Illinois, daily newspapers in East St. Louis and Alton often used local sources to provide specific examples.

9. Ted Link began his newspaper career covering activities of the Shelton gang. He joined the *Post-Dispatch* in 1939. Charles Stewart began reporting for the *Journal* in 1946. He was a full-time crime reporter until the early 1960s.

10. Adlai E. Stevenson, speech at Department of Soldiers and Sailors Reunion, Salem, Ill., 27 July 1948, 3, Adlai E. Stevenson Papers, Department of Rare Books and Special Collections, Princeton University Library, Princeton, N.J.

11. John Bartlow Martin, *Adlai Stevenson of Illinois: The Life of Adlai E. Stevenson* (New York: Doubleday, 1976), 336.

12. Howard W. Allen and Vincent A. Lacey, eds., *Illinois Elections, 1818–1990: Candidates and County Returns for President, Governor, Senate, and House of Representatives* (Carbondale: Southern Illinois University Press, 1992), 63.

13. Stevenson to Dilliard, 20 Aug. 1949, in Walter Johnson, ed., *The Papers of Adlai E. Stevenson* (Boston: Little, Brown, 1974), 3:144.

14. Simon to Stevenson, 23 July 1949; Mulroy to Simon, 29 Aug. 1949; Simon to Mulroy, 3 Sept. 1949; Mulroy to Simon, 6 Sept. 1949; and Simon to Mulroy, 12 Sept. 1949; all in box 124, folder 3—Gambling, K-M—Adlai E. Stevenson Papers, Abraham Lincoln Presidential Library, Springfield, Ill. (hereafter cited as Stevenson Papers).

15. Simon to Mulroy, 3 Sept., and Mulroy to Simon, 6 Sept.

16. Simon became an outspoken ally of Adlai E. Stevenson II from the early encounters of 1949 until Stevenson's death in 1965.

17. *Troy Tribune*, 20 Oct. 1949.

18. "Vice Organized in Many County Spots," *Troy Tribune*, 27 Oct. 1949.

19. "Trojan Thoughts," 27 Oct. 1949.

20. *Troy Tribune*, 3 Nov. 1949.

21. "Trojan Thoughts," 3 Nov. 1949.

22. *Troy Tribune*, 10 Nov. 1949.

23. "'Closed' 200 Club Now Operating Again," *Troy Tribune*, 17 Nov. 1949.

24. "A Questionable Policy," *Troy Tribune*, 17 Nov. 1949.

25. "Trojan Thoughts," 1 Dec. 1949.

26. A review of Simon's columns through his term as lieutenant governor of Illinois reveals he endorsed few Republicans for office.

27. James O. Monroe to Simon, 8 Dec. 1949, Paul Simon Papers, Abraham Lincoln Presidential Library, box 15 A, 1949–1957, (hereafter cited as Simon Papers–ALPL).

28. Simon to Benjamin Adamowski, 21 Nov. 1949, Simon Papers–ALPL, box 15 A, 1949–1957.

29. Stevenson, radio broadcast, 2 Jan. 1950, in Johnson, 3:212–14. See also, "Stevenson Calls Gambling Biggest Headache in State," *Troy Tribune*, 5 Jan. 1950.

30. "Gambling in Illinois," *St. Louis Globe-Democrat*, 4 Jan. 1950.

31. "'Common Sense' Lets More Gamblers into Our County," *Troy Tribune*, 2 Mar. 1950. See also "Hard Times Hit East Side Bookies Due to Squeeze on Capone Gang," *St. Louis Post-Dispatch*, 4 Feb. 1950.

32. Gordon Schendel, "Illinois Shakedown: The Little Guys Lose," parts 1 and 2, *Collier's*, 15 and 22 Apr. 1950.

33. Simon to Mulroy, 2 May 1950, quoted in Johnson, 3:270.

34. Mulroy to Simon, 4 May 1950, Simon Papers–ALPL, box 16, Stevenson.

35. "Big County Gambling Places to Be Closed," *Troy Tribune*, 11 May 1950. A week later, "Trib Scoops Other Papers," 18 May 1950.

36. "Hyde Park Club, 200 Club Closed: 3 Operators, 48 Helpers Booked," *St. Louis Post-Dispatch*, 13 May 1950.

37. "Trojan Thoughts," 18 May 1950.

38. *St. Louis Post-Dispatch*, 15 May 1950.

39. "Governor Has Hour-Long Talk with Troy Tribune Editor," *Troy Tribune*, 25 May 1950.

40. "Trojan Thoughts," *Troy Tribune*, 20 July 1950.

41. "Simon Pure," *Newsweek*, 12 Feb. 1951, 48.

42. Simon insisted on being called "Paul" as long as he served in public office. On the cover of a book, his name was "Senator Paul Simon."

43. "Up to Austin Lewis," *Troy Tribune*, 15 June 1950.

44. Mulroy to Simon, 17 June 1950, Simon Papers–ALPL, box 16, Stevenson.

45. "Trojan Thoughts," 22 Nov. 1950.

46. "Tribune Editor Takes Legal Steps Against Dallas Harrell," 25 Jan. 1951. The letter from Simon to Charles B. Stephens appeared in full with the article announcing action against Harrell and Lewis by Simon.

47. Ibid., 25 Jan. 1951; also "Editor Requests Jury Probe of Dallas Harrell," *East St. Louis Journal*, 22 Jan. 1951, Bowen Archives.

48. "Troy Gets Publicity Galore on Story," *Troy Tribune*, 25 Jan. 1951.

49. Charles Klotzer, "Searchlight," *Troy Tribune*, 25 Jan. 1951.

50. "22-Year-Old Troy (Ill.) Publisher," *St. Louis Post-Dispatch*, 28 Jan. 1951.

51. "G-U-T-S," *Mounds Independent*, reprinted in *Troy Tribune*, 1 Feb. 1951.

52. "Trojan Thoughts," 1 Feb. 1951.

53. Tom Duffy, "An Open Letter to Paul Simon," *East St. Louis Journal*, 28 Jan. 1951, Bowen Archives.

54. "Simon Pure," *Newsweek*.

55. "Trojan Thoughts," 22 Feb. 1951.

56. *Investigation of Organized Crime*, "Testimony of Paul Simon, Madison County, Ill.," 4-A:781. Unofficially the media referred to the committee as the "Senate Crime Committee" or the "Kefauver Committee."

57. Kefauver Committee, 4-A, 781–82.

58. "Testimony of Dallas Harrell," Kefauver Committee, 4-A:150–54, 726–33.

59. "Sidelights from Kefauver Hearing," *Troy Tribune*, 1 Mar. 1951.

60. "Case against Dallas Harrell."

61. "Trojan Thoughts," 22 Mar. 1951.

62. "Grand Jury reports Harrell 'Not Guilty,'" *Troy Tribune*, 19 Apr. 1951.

63. "Trojan Thoughts," 26 Apr. 1951.

64. Simon was smitten with foreign travel during his Army tour. In the 1950s and 1960s, he traveled frequently to Europe and Asia.

65. *P.S.*, 49.

66. "Agreement," signed by Ray Johnsen, stated $1,300 would be paid on 1 Aug. 1951 for a 12' x 18' printing press. Payments would continue until 1 Aug. 1958, Simon Papers–ALPL, box 97, folder 24, Bids and Estimates.

67. "Simon in Army; 'Liz' Takes Over," *Troy Tribune*, 17 May 1951.

68. "Trojan Thoughts," 9 Aug. 1951.

69. Ibid., 11 Oct. 1951.

70. "Why Retreat," *Troy Tribune*, 4 Oct. 1951.

71. The FBI declared Frank Wortman a "top hoodlum" on 25 Sept. 1953. Thomas J. Jones to author, 24 May 1991. In 1989 interviews with the author, State Police Capt. Emil Toffant and FBI Agent Moehle acknowledged that they provided information in secret to reporters as a method of keeping pressure on organized crime suspects.

3. Elective Office Beckons

1. "Trojan Thoughts," 8 May 1952.

2. Ibid., 25 Sept. 1952.

3. "Club Prevue Still Operating Full Blast," *Troy Tribune*, 20 Aug. 1953.

4. "Trojan Thoughts," 21 Aug. 1953.

5. Ibid., 3 Sept. 1953.

6. "Young Editor Scores in Gaming War," *East St. Louis Journal*, 9 Sept. 1953, Bowen Archives.

7. "Paul Simon Announces Candidacy for Nomination as State Representative," *Troy Tribune*, 17 Dec. 1953.

8. "Young Editor Seeks Post in Legislature," *East St. Louis Journal*, 17 Dec. 1953, Bowen Archives.

9. *P.S.*, 56.

10. "Trojan Thoughts," 17 Dec. 1953.

11. John Clayton, compiler, *The Illinois Fact Book and Historical Almanac, 1673–1968* (Carbondale: Southern Illinois University Press, 1970), 290–321 (Harris), 300–323 (Kennedy).

12. *P.S.*, 59.

13. *East St. Louis Journal*, 5 Feb. 1954, Bowen Archives. Reporter Charles Stewart wrote at length about Simon's campaign.

14. Arthur Simon interview.

15. Ibid., and *P.S.*, 59.
16. Ibid.
17. *P.S.*, 60.
18. *East St. Louis Journal*, 14 Apr. 1954.
19. *Alton Evening Telegraph*, 14 Apr. 1954.
20. *St. Louis Post-Dispatch*, editorial, 15 Apr. 1954.
21. Gross income figures were included in "General Facts," a draft document that outlined future operations for the *Troy Tribune*. It included policies to begin 1 Jan. 1954 and contained no signatures, Simon Papers–ALPL, box 97, corporation.
22. Elmer Fedder email to author, 12 June 2007.
23. The proposed agreement dated 28 Dec. 1954 for *Tribune* operations had a name block for Simon and Johnsen but no signatures, Simon Papers–ALPL, box 97, corporation.
24. Simon joined the International Typographical Union while publisher and editor of the *Tribune* for reasons of principle and because it could help hire a Linotype operator or printer on short notice. When teaching at a university, he affiliated with the teachers' union. He did not insist on other executives or employees belonging to unions, *P.S.*, 48.
25. Arthur Simon interview.
26. Paul Simon to H. R. Fischer, 28 Dec. 1954, Howard K. Long collection, Brigham Young University manuscript, 1690, box 14, folder 28.
27. Biographical information is taken from Irving Dilliard manuscript collection, Western Historical Collection, University of Missouri, St. Louis, online at http://www.unsl.edu/whmc/guides/whjm0491.htm.
28. Daniel W. Pfaff, *No Ordinary Joe: A Life of Joseph Pulitzer III* (Columbia: University of Missouri Press, 2005), 233.
29. Ibid., 231.
30. Simon to Irving Dilliard, 23 June 1949, Simon Papers–ALPL, box 15, folder 9, Irving Dilliard.
31. Simon to Dilliard, 7 Oct. 1949, Simon Papers–ALPL.
32. Dilliard to Simon, 21 Feb. 1950, Simon Papers–ALPL.
33. Dilliard could have sent this note after Simon's election victory in 1954, Simon Papers–ALPL.
34. Dilliard to Simon, 14 Mar. 1950, Simon Papers–ALPL.
35. Simon to Dilliard, 19 Apr. 1951, Simon Papers–ALPL.
36. Simon to Dilliard, 9 Feb. 1955, Simon Papers–ALPL.
37. Simon to Dilliard, 8 Feb. 1960, Simon Papers–ALPL.

Part Two. Climbing the Political Mountains, 1955–66

4. Racetrack Runaround

1. For the purposes of this book, the author read all columns Simon wrote from 1948 to 1973. The first "Sidelights from Springfield" column appeared 3 Feb. 1955.
2. "Sidelights from Springfield," *Troy Tribune*, 27 June 1957.
3. *P.S.*, 61–62, also "Sidelights," 27 June 1957.
4. Jeanne Simon to author, 14 Sept. 1971. She proudly proclaimed her husband "the father of the open meeting bill."
5. "Sidelights," 9 May 1957.
6. Anthony Scariano memoir, vol. 1, Archives/Special Collections, University of Illinois at Springfield, 109.
7. Robert E. Hartley, "'Almost Like Brothers': The Friendship of Alan Dixon and Paul Simon," presented 19 Oct. 2007 at the annual Conference on Illinois History sponsored by the Illinois Historic Preservation Agency.
8. Richard Durbin interview with author, 2 July 2007.

9. Alan Dixon interview with author, 30 Jan. 2007.

10. Ibid. Dixon shared his recollections of Simon, including his own experiences with political victories in St. Clair County.

11. Dixon interview with author, 24 May 2005.

12. Dixon interview, 2007.

13. Ibid.

14. Scariano memoir, 110.

15. Ibid.

16. Durbin interview.

17. Dixon interview, 2007.

18. Dixon interview with author, 18 Sept. 1990.

19. Dixon interview, 2005.

20. Dixon interview, 1990.

21. Dixon's 2007 review of his relationship with Simon ended with this comment: "We were different, but we loved each other in a special way. I am grateful for the friendship. It made me a better man."

22. *P.S.*, 63.

23. *P.S.*, 64.

24. Robert E. Hartley, *Paul Powell of Illinois: A Lifelong Democrat* (Carbondale: Southern Illinois University Press, 1999), 87–94.

25. Ibid., 97.

26. Adlai E. Stevenson, Illinois State Budget Report, 1949, Paul Powell Papers, ALPL (hereafter cited as PP Papers).

27. Illinois House and Senate Committee roll call votes; final votes of House and Senate, Illinois State Archives, PP Papers.

28. "Complete Roster of Stockholders," *Chicago Daily News*, 22 Aug. 1951.

29. Hartley, *Paul Powell*, 106.

30. Ibid., 109.

31. Ibid., 110.

32. "Powell Track Fees Tied to Ex-Convict," *Chicago Today*, 4 July 1969, PP Papers.

33. Hartley, *Paul Powell*, 119–22.

34. Affidavit, 14 July 1966, attesting to purchase of land trust units and common stock shares, PP Papers.

35. Hartley, *Paul Powell*, 124.

36. David Kenney, *Political Passage: The Career of Stratton of Illinois* (Carbondale: Southern Illinois University Press, 1990), 127–29.

37. Hartley, *Paul Powell*, 54.

38. Ibid., 127.

39. *P.S.*, 63.

40. Ibid.

41. Paul Powell to V. Y. Dallman, 31 Mar. 1958. In this letter, Powell provides votes for the mud guard bill and Simon's participation, Simon Papers–ALPL, box 16, folder 7, Paul Powell.

42. *P.S.*, 67.

43. Simon to Dallman, 3 Apr. 1958, Simon Papers–ALPL, box 16, folder 7, Paul Powell.

44. Simon to Clement A. Nance, secretary, Illinois Racing Board, 31 July 1958, Bowen Archives, "Buster Wortman." See also "P.S. by Paul Simon," *Troy Tribune*, 7 Aug. 1958, and "Racing Board Standards Questioned," *East St. Louis Journal*, 1 Aug. 1958.

45. Simon's letter stated the Munie quote was from the *East St. Louis Journal* of 18 Feb. 1958.

46. Simon's letter stated the Delbartes quote was from the *Journal* of 27 Feb. 1958.

47. "P.S. by Paul Simon," 18 Sept. 1958.

48. "Sidelights from Springfield," 30 Apr. 1959.

49. "Sidelights," 21 Feb. 1957.

50. Simon to Milburn P. Akers, 29 Nov. 1956, Simon Papers–ALPL, box 15 A, 1949–1957.

51. Taylor Pensoneau and Bob Ellis, *Dan Walker: The Glory and the Tragedy* (Evansville, Ind.: Smith-Collins, 1993), 39, in "The Young Turks."

52. Powell to Dallman.

53. Simon to Dallman.

54. "Sidelights," 30 Apr. 1959.

55. Clyde Lee, oral history memoir, University of Illinois–Springfield, 1988, 190–98, vol. 2, session 8, 9.

56. Lee said Powell suggested the quip, 196.

57. Lee, 195. He read from a roll call on HB 884.

58. Ibid., 190.

59. Ibid., 346, session 16.

60. Simon interview with author, 20 Feb. 1998.

61. Simon to Bill Boyne, 14 Apr. 1958, Simon Papers–ALPL, box 16, folder 7, Paul Powell.

62. Boyne to Simon, 12 May 1958, Simon Papers–ALPL.

63. Simon interview.

64. Ibid.

65. Simon to Powell, 5 Nov. 1962, Simon Papers–ALPL, box 16, folder 7, Paul Powell.

66. "P.S. by P. S.," *Troy Tribune*, 26 July 1956. Simon explained his votes against Hodge's appropriations requests in this column. Simon also mentioned Powell's role in *P.S.*, 243.

67. Simon said, after declining to have his vote changed, "I certainly don't regret my action now," in "P.S. by P.S.," 26 July 1956.

68. "Sidelights from Springfield," 14 Mar. 1957.

69. *Political Passage*, 137–51. Kenney provides a fine summary of the Hodge affair and Stratton's role. See also Robert P. Howard, *Illinois: A History of the Prairie State* (Grand Rapids: Eerdmans, 1972), 549–51.

70. "Sidelights," 14 Mar. 1967.

71. *P.S.*, 243.

5. Corruption in Springfield

1. *P.S.*, 64. "I respected Al [Balk] and felt that the problems would be exposed, even if it meant the end of my political career."

2. Simon to Alfred W. Balk, 11 May 1964, Simon Papers–ALPL, box 99, folder 39, Harper's article 1964.

3. *P.S.*, 64.

4. Simon and Alfred Balk, "The Illinois Legislature: A Study in Corruption," *Harper's*, 74–78, Simon Papers–ALPL, box 95, folder 35.

5. "Corruption," 74.

6. Ibid., 75–76.

7. Robert E. Hartley, *Charles H. Percy: A Political Perspective* (Chicago: Rand McNally, 1975), 73–74.

8. "Corruption," 76.

9. Ibid., 77.

10. Ibid.

11. Ibid., 78.

12. Paul Simon, "Follow-Up Report on Illinois," a draft article submitted to Marion K. Sanders at *Harper's* on 7 July 1965. Excerpts are from the edited draft, Simon Papers–ALPL, box 99, folder 16.

13. John Dreiske, "The New Assembly Faces Purity Test," *Chicago Sun-Times*, 7 Dec. 1964.

14. "Follow-Up," 2, see also *P.S.*, 68, and Pensoneau, *Powerhouse: Arrington from Illinois* (Baltimore: American Literary Press, 2006), 179.

15. Ibid., 3.

16. Ibid.

17. "1965 Report of the Illinois Crime Investigating Commission," report to Gov. Otto Kerner and the Seventy-fourth General Assembly of Illinois, 1965; and "Creation and Composition of the Commission," 3, Illinois State Archives, GA R1, 1965.

18. "Report of the Illinois Crime Investigating Commission re Charges of Corruption in the Illinois General Assembly," June 1965, "The Nature and Scope of the Investigation," 2–3, Illinois State Archives, GA R1, 1965.

19. Simon to Charles Siragusa, 22 Jan. 1965, Simon Papers–ALPL.

20. Hartley, *Paul Powell*, 111–12.

21. "Report," 4–6.

22. Ibid., 6.

23. "Sidelights," 24 June 1965.

24. "Statement of Prentice H. Marshall and Harlington Wood Jr., re Charges of Corruption in the Illinois General Assembly," no date, Harlington Wood Jr. collection, box 11, 1965, clippings, 5, Illinois History and Lincoln Collections, University of Illinois.

25. Ibid.

26. Ibid., 6.

27. *P.S.*, 67.

28. "Another Midwesterner Trying to Put on Harry Truman's Shoes," *Washington Post National Weekly Edition*, 7 Dec. 1987.

29. "Dan Walker: The Long Road to Springfield," *Chicago Tribune Magazine*, 12 Mar. 1972, 23.

6. Newspaper Mogul

1. Ray Johnsen, interview with author, 7 Mar. 2008.

2. *Editor and Publisher International Yearbook* (New York: Editor and Publisher), 1962–65, weekly newspaper listings, Morgan Library, Colorado State University, Ft. Collins.

3. "The Herald Goes to Young Hands," *Carterville Herald*, 18 Apr. 1958.

4. "New Editor Takes Charge Tomorrow," *Carterville Herald*, 2 May 1958.

5. "On Dave Saunders," editorial, *Troy Tribune*, 13 July 1961.

6. *P.S.*, 48.

7. David Saunders to Mr. and Mrs. John D. Saunders, 5 June 1961, Simon Papers–ALPL, box 99, folder 6, Carterville Herald, 1961–64.

8. Saunders to Simon, 9 June 1961, Simon Papers–ALPL, box 99, folder 6.

9. John and Orena Saunders to Mr. and Mrs. Paul Simon, 11 June 1961, Simon Papers–ALPL, box 99, folder 6.

10. "The Carterville Herald Has New Editor," *Carterville Herald*, 7 Sept. 1961.

11. "Saunders Honored," *Troy Tribune*, reprinted from *Southern Illinoisan*, 10 Oct. 1962, written by Ben Gelman.

12. "A Statement of Principle," editorial, *Carterville Herald*, 27 Sept. 1962.

13. "Scrapbook," *Carterville Herald*, 4 Oct. 1962.

14. "P.S. by Paul Simon," *Carterville Herald*, 11 Oct. 1962.

15. Simon, "Montgomery Looks Forward," *Christian Century*, Simon Papers–ALPL, box 99, folder 6.

16. Simon to Saunders, 22 Oct. 1962, Simon Papers–ALPL, box 99, folder 6.

17. "Scrapbook," 25 Oct. 1962.

18. "P.S. by Paul Simon," 25 Oct. 1962.

19. "Scrapbook," 1 Nov. 1962.

20. Saunders to Simon, 5 Nov. 1962, Simon Papers–ALPL, box 99, folder 6.

21. "Saunders Honored."

22. "Herald Is Sold to Group of Four Men, Effective June 30," *Metamora Herald*, 20 June 1958.

23. *Editor and Publisher Yearbook*, weekly newspaper listings, *Metamora Herald* circulation, 1962.

24. Dixon was a minor stockholder and never had any management role. He provided banking contacts and made personal loans to principals.

25. "Retiring Editor of Herald Gets Writeup in Daily Pantagraph," Bloomington, Illinois, reprinted in *Metamora Herald* 4 July 1958, also *Metamora Herald* editorial, 29 Apr. 1965.

26. "P.S. by Paul Simon," *Metamora Herald*, 25 July 1958.

27. "The Leader Sold to Group of Four Men," *Washburn Leader*, 26 Jan. 1961.

28. Walter I. Shockey to Ray Johnsen, 5 Jan. 1961, Simon Papers–ALPL, box 97, folder 40, Abingdon.

29. "Announcement," signed by Paul Simon, *Avon Sentinel*, 20 Apr. 1961.

30. *Editor and Publisher*, 1962.

31. Simon to Robert Edmiston, 28 Apr. 1962, Simon Papers–ALPL, box 97, folder 40, Abingdon. Simon had just won the Democratic party primary nomination for state senator.

32. "Newspaper Properties Sold Effective September 1," *Williamsfield Times*, 3 Sept. 1964.

33. *Editor and Publisher*, 1966.

34. "Record Has New Owners, Oct. 1," *Roodhouse Record*, 26 Sept. 1962.

35. G. E. Shipton, "Swan Song," *Record*, 26 Sept. 1962.

36. Elmer Fedder email to author, 18 Nov. 2007.

37. "Record Has New Owners."

38. "Dear Readers," *Winchester Times*, 12 July 1963.

39. "Proud to Be Part of Your Area," *Winchester Times*, 19 July 1963.

40. Fedder remained as owner and editor of the Roodhouse, Winchester, and White Hall, Illinois, papers until his retirement in 1999.

41. "Register-Republic Is Sold," *White Hall Register Republic*, 19 Apr. 1965.

42. *Editor and Publisher*, 1963.

43. *P.S.*, 74.

44. Gene Callahan, interview with author, 4 Jan. 2007.

45. "Paul Simon, Tribune Founder, Sells Ownership," *Troy Tribune*, 6 Jan. 1966.

7. Spreading His Words

1. Sid Landfield to Simon, 25 Mar. 1961, Simon Papers–ALPL, box 82, folder 26, Newsmen.

2. Chuck Hayes to Simon, 30 Dec. 1958, Simon Papers–ALPL, box 100, folder 8, state column. Simon answered in a letter to Hayes, 5 Jan. 1959.

3. "Sidelights from Springfield," appearing in the *Flanagan Home Times*, 6 July 1961, Simon Papers–ALPL, box 100, folder 8. Simon answered editor Joseph J. Cullen in a letter, 18 July 1961.

4. "Sidelights," 28 Feb. 1957.

5. Ibid., 12 Mar. 1959.

6. Ibid., 14 Mar. 1963.

7. Ibid., 12 Feb. 1950; also 2 Feb. 1961.

8. Ibid., 4 Feb. 1965.

9. Ibid.

10. Ibid., 5 Feb. 1959.

11. Ibid., 9 Feb. 1961.

12. Ibid., 9 May 1957.

13. Ibid., 5 Mar. 1959.

14. Ibid., 24 Jan. 1963.

15. Ibid., 21 Jan. 1965.

16. Ibid., 28 Mar. 1963.

17. Ibid., 6 July 1961.

18. "P.S. by P.S.," 1 Nov. 1956.

19. Simon to Sen. Paul Douglas, 13 Sept. 1950, Simon Papers–ALPL, box 156, Douglas, 1950–1970.

20. "P.S. by Paul Simon," 3 July 1958.

21. Ibid., 2 Oct. 1958.

22. *P.S.*, 75.

23. "A New Nation Grows in Africa," *Troy Tribune*, 3 Oct. 1957.

24. "Protestant Has Audience with Pope," *Troy Tribune*, 10 Oct. 1957.

25. "Lands That Breathe Tension," *Troy Tribune*, 24 Oct. 1957.

26. "Time Can Work for, against Free World," *Troy Tribune*, 12 Dec. 1957.

27. "P.S. by Paul Simon," 15 Oct. 1959.

28. *P.S.*, 378.

29. Simon said *Lovejoy* was the least read of his books but the most fascinating, *P.S.*, 379.

30. *P.S.*, 244.

31. "'Where Did All the People Come From?' Former President Truman Asks as He Rides Through Troy," *Troy Tribune*, 2 Aug. 1962.

32. Simon, "Personal Memories of John F. Kennedy," *Troy Tribune*, 28 Nov. 1963. Simon supported Kennedy for president in 1960 only after getting Adlai Stevenson's assurances that he would not be a candidate.

33. *P.S.*, 248.

34. Simon with Jeanne Simon, *Protestant-Catholic Marriages Can Succeed* (New York: Association Press, 1967).

35. *P.S.*, 246.

36. Ibid., 75.

37. John Manion to Simon, 13 Mar. 1961. Simon thanked Manion for his support in a letter of 30 Mar.; Simon Papers–ALPL, box 82, folder 26, Newsmen.

38. Chuck Hayes to Simon, 22 May 1961, Simon Papers–ALPL, box 82, folder 26, Newsmen.

39. Simon to James McCulla, 19 July 1961, Simon Papers–ALPL, box 82, folder 26, Newsmen. In a note to Simon with the editorial, Chuck Hayes called McCulla, "one of us."

40. Irving Dilliard to Dale L. Gonemeier, 1 July 1961, Simon Papers–ALPL, box 15, folder 9, Irving Dilliard.

41. Simon to Godfrey Sperling Jr., 9 Aug. 1961, Simon Papers–ALPL, box 15, folder 9, Newsmen.

42. "Paul Simon Makes Bid for U.S. Senate," *Troy Tribune*, 31 Aug. 1961, also "Simon Boosted for U.S. Senate," *Carterville Herald*, 31 Aug. 1961.

43. Hartley, *Paul Powell*, 63.

44. Ibid., 64.

45. Callahan interview with author, 27 Dec. 2007.

46. "Troy's First State-Wide Candidate Withdraws from U.S. Senate Race," *Troy Tribune*, 11 Jan. 1962.

47. *P.S.*, 46. Simon called O'Neill's candidacy "a sacrifice he lived to regret."

48. "The Charges and the Facts," 5 Apr. 1962.

49. "Look at the Record and Vote for Paul Simon for State Senator," *Troy Tribune*, 5 Apr. 1962.

50. "An Urgent Appeal," Simon Papers–ALPL, box 97, folder 24, Bids and Estimates.

51. "If," *Troy Tribune*, 5 Apr. 1962.

52. "Official Vote Is Announced," *Troy Tribune*, 26 Apr. 1962, also *P.S.*, 77.

53. *Troy Tribune*, 1 Nov. 1962.

54. "Troy's First State Senator Elected," *Troy Tribune*, 8 Nov. 1962.

55. "Trojan Thoughts," *Troy Tribune*, 28 Jan. 1956.

56. "Look at the Record," *Troy Tribune*, 1 Nov. 1956.

57. "Trojan Thoughts," 10 Feb. 1956.

58. "Financial Statement of Paul Simon," 6 July 1956, Simon Papers–ALPL, box 97, folder 27, corporation.

59. News release to editors, no date, 1962 income statement, Simon Papers–ALPL, box 97, folder 31.

60. "Sen. Simon Lists Income at $17,312," *Metro-East Journal*, 23 Mar. 1966, Bowen Archives.

61. Edmund P. Doyle, editor, *As We Knew Adlai: The Stevenson Story by Twenty-Two Friends* (New York: Harper and Row, 1966), 129.

62. Walter Johnson, editor, and Carol Evans, assistant editor, *The Papers of Adlai E. Stevenson Governor of Illinois, 1949–1953*, vol. 3 (Boston: Little, Brown, 1974), 339, also *P.S.* 53.

63. Stevenson to Simon, 25 Aug. 1952, Simon Papers–ALPL, box 16, Stevenson.

Part Three. Rapid Rise, Sudden Fall, 1966–72

8. The Big Bounce

1. Dixon interview, 2007.

2. Howard W. Allen and Vincent A. Lacey, eds., *Illinois Elections 1818–1990: Candidates and County Returns for President, Governor, Senate, and House of Representatives* (Carbondale: Southern Illinois University Press, 1992), 64, 67, 73.

3. Editors' Service press releases and order forms, Simon Papers–ALPL, box 100, folder 6, Sidelights from Springfield 1967.

4. "Paul Simon customers as of Sept. 19 [1966]," Simon Papers–ALPL, box 99, folder 52, Howard Long.

5. "Draft Revision Desirable," Editors' Service, no. 13, no date, Simon Papers–ALPL, box 99, folder 52.

6. "A Tribute to a Newsman," Editors' Service, no. 34, no date, Simon Papers–ALPL, box 99, folder 52.

7. Simon to Howard Long, November 1966, Brigham Young University, Provo, Utah, Howard R. Long collection, manuscript 1690, box 14, folder 29, Harold B. Lee Library.

8. Long to Simon, 26 Nov. 1966, Simon Papers–ALPL, box 99, folder 52, Howard Long.

9. "Where Will the Money Come From?" Sidelights from Springfield, *Winchester Times*, 19 Jan. 1967.

10. "Sidelights," *Winchester Times*, 15 June 1967.

11. "Not All Anti-Crime Bills Are Good," Sidelights, *Winchester Times*, 2 Feb. 1967.

12. "Ethics Legislation: Will It Survive?" Sidelights, *Winchester Times*, 9 Feb. 1967.

13. "Open Housing: An Emotion-Packed Issue," Sidelights, *Winchester Times*, 16 Mar. 1967.

14. "Journalist's Questions Get No Response from North Vietnam," *Winchester Times*, 31 Aug. 1967.

15. Gene Callahan to Simon, 30 Oct. 1966, Simon Papers–ALPL, box 15, folder 4, Gene Callahan.

16. Poll for Lerner Newspapers, *Glenview Life*, 21 Jan. 1968, also "Altorfer, Simon Top State Poll," *Winchester Times*, 22 Feb. 1968.

17. Jack Mabley, *Chicago American*, 12 Feb. 1968.

18. "An Important Vote on April 12th," P.S. by Paul Simon, *Troy Tribune*, 31 Mar. 1960.

19. Bob Estill, "Gibbs Advised: Change Target," *Illinois State Journal*, 2 Jan. 1968.

20. "Demo Hopefuls Run Gauntlet," *Illinois State Journal*, 24 Feb. 1968.

21. "Clark Gets Top Billing on Democrats' '68 Slate," *Illinois State Journal*, 28 Feb. 1968.

22. Ken Watson, "Demo Slate Cheers GOP," *Illinois State Journal*, 29 Feb. 1968.

23. *P.S.*, 85–86.

24. Ibid., 86.

25. Harold R. Piety, "Independents Elect Democrat Paul Simon," *Focus/Midwest* 69, 14 (Sept. 1969): 33. Piety worked on Simon's 1968 campaign staff.

26. "Delegates Blast Daley," *Decatur Review*, 29 Aug. 1968.

27. "Lessons from the Chicago Convention," Simon column, no date, Simon Papers–ALPL, box 104, memos and notes.

28. Simon for Lieutenant Governor press release, 15 Sept. 1968, Simon Papers–ALPL, box 104, folder 3.

29. Arthur Simon interview.

30. Paul Simon interview, 1998.

31. As related in Piety, "Independents," 24. The editor was the author Robert E. Hartley.

32. "Proposal for Weekly Policy Speeches," draft campaign document, no date, Simon Papers–ALPL, box 104, folder 3; also "Suggested Outline of Proposed Meeting on Issues," Simon Papers–ALPL, box 104, folder 3.

33. Editorial, *Chicago Tribune*, 1 Nov. 1968.

34. "Lieutenant Governor: Simon," editorial, *Decatur Sunday Herald and Review*, 20 Oct. 1968.

35. "Paul Simon Is the Man," editorial, *Winchester Times*, 17 Oct. 1968.

36. Piety, "Independents," 25.

37. *P.S.*, 88.

38. Richard Icen, "Ogilvie, Simon Become Unlikely Pair," *Decatur Sunday Herald and Review*, 10 Nov. 1968, 47.

39. Ibid.

40. "Split Government in Illinois—Will It Work?" From the Statehouse by Lt. Gov. Paul Simon, *Winchester Times*, 6 Feb. 1969.

41. *P.S.*, 88.

9. An Agent of Great Change

1. Ray Johnsen interview. Johnsen worked almost continuously with Simon from 1951 to 1994.

2. Michael Brown and Richard E. Cohen, *The Almanac of American Politics, 2006* (Washington: National Journal Group, 2006), 555–57.

3. Callahan interview, 4 Jan. 2007.

4. "The Lieutenant Governor," editorial, *Cairo Evening Citizen*, 7 Feb. 1969.

5. Simon to Martin Brown, 18 Feb. 1969, Simon Papers–ALPL, box 26, Cairo.

6. Taylor Pensoneau, *Powerhouse: Arrington from Illinois* (Baltimore: American Literary Press, 2006), 297–300. Pensoneau provides a balanced look at the office grab by Arrington and Simon's refusal to take the bait.

7. Callahan interview, 27 Dec. 2007.

8. "Our Ombudsman at Work," *News from Paul Simon*, winter 1969.

9. Paul Simon, "The Ombudsman in Illinois: An Experiment in Government," June 1970, 2, Simon Papers–ALPL, box 95, folder 35, Magazine Articles.

10. Robert E. Hartley, "Some Solons Playing Politics with Simon's Budget, Ombudsman Use," *Decatur Sunday Herald and Review*, 13 Feb. 1969.

11. "Ombudsman?" *Winchester Times*, 13 Feb. 1969.

12. Ibid.

13. "The Ombudsman in Illinois," 4.

14. Ibid., 3.

15. Ibid., 5.

16. Ibid., 2.

17. "Ombudsman?"

18. "Cairo, Ill., Divided by Racial Conflict; City Fears Future," *New York Times*, 23 June 1969, 1.

19. "Militants Fail to Provoke Calling Out 'White Hats,'" *Cairo Evening Citizen*, 1 Apr. 1969.

20. *P.S.*, 93.

21. Callahan interview with author, 19 Mar. 2008.

22. "Simon Opens Investigation of Conditions in Cairo," *Citizen*, 18 Apr. 1969.

23. "No Instant Solution," editorial, *Citizen*, 21 Apr. 1969.

24. Paul Simon, "Recommendations regarding Cairo, Illinois, 22 April 1969," Simon Papers–ALPL, box 26, Cairo.

25. The Illinois House of Representatives approved a resolution on 14 Apr. 1969 calling for an investigation, *Citizen*, 15 Apr. 1969.

26. "Thanks, Paul Simon," editorial, *Citizen*, 23 Apr. 1969.

27. *P.S.*, 94–95.

28. "Charges Asked in Cairo Case," *Metro-East Journal*, 29 Apr. 1969. A day after the House hearing, Governor Ogilvie ordered a National Guard company to Cairo. See also "State Panel Fails in First Effort to Initiate Cairo Peace Talks," *St. Louis Post-Dispatch*, 10 May 1969.

29. Editorial, *Marion Republican*, 19 May 1969.

30. Simon to Oldham Paisley, 13 May 1969, Simon Papers–ALPL, box 30, folder 8.

31. "Simon Sends Staff Member to Cairo to Consult with Community Leaders," *Citizen*, 25 June 1969.

32. Dick Durbin to Simon, memorandum, "Recent Cairo Visit," no date, but shortly after 25 June 1969, Simon Papers–ALPL. Durbin reported that the new police chief was ineffective, and that *Citizen* editor Brown was looking for work.

33. "Simon Offers New Proposal to End Cairo Racial Strife," *Alton Evening Telegraph*, 22 Sept. 1969, Paul Simon Papers, Special Collections Research Center, Southern Illinois University Carbondale, family scrapbook 1 1928–1957 (hereafter cited as Simon Papers–SIU).

34. "Simon Muddying Waters," *Illinois State Journal*, 15 Aug. 1969.

35. Durbin to Simon, memorandum, no date, discusses plan for no advance publicity, Simon Papers–ALPL, box 26, Cairo clippings.

36. Simon to editor, *Tri-State Informer*, 30 Mar. 1970, Simon Papers–ALPL, box 26, Cairo correspondence, January–April 1970.

37. Darrell E. Kirby to Simon, 28 Apr. 1970, Simon Papers–ALPL, box 26, Cairo correspondence, May–December 1970.

38. "The Ombudsman in Illinois," 4.

39. Robert E. Hartley, "Simon Should Report," *Decatur Sunday Herald and Review*, 26 Apr. 1970.

40. "The Ombudsman in Illinois," 7. Hartley wrote approvingly of the report in "Ombudsman's Need Proved," *Decatur Sunday Herald and Review*, 21 June 1970.

41. Jason Stacy, "'I Do Not Think We Can Keep Universities Open with Bayonets,'" *Journal of Illinois History*, winter 2006, 283–306. Stacy provides in-depth coverage and analysis of the riot.

42. Simon to Brian Whalen, 13 May 1970, Simon Papers–ALPL, box 46, folder 1, Southern Illinois University 1968–1970. The editor to which Simon referred was John C. Gardner.

43. John C. Gardner, email to author, 21 Apr. 2008.

44. The Lieutenant Governor's Committee on Southern Illinois University issued recommendations in a report, "A Practical Study of Campus Problems," on 20 Sept. 1970, Simon Papers–ALPL, box 46, folder 6.

45. "From the Statehouse," October 1970, Simon Papers–ALPL, box 99, folder 30, columns 1970.

46. Simon, "Southern Illinois University: The Challenges of 1970," Simon Papers–ALPL, box 99, folder 16, Articles Written by Paul Simon. The undated copy of the article appears to have been distributed before September 1970 when the committee report appeared.

47. The eight-page report, "A Practical Study of Campus Problems," contained six pages of recommendations, and attached were reports from five subcommittees.

48. Hartley, *Paul Powell*, 144–77. The story of Powell's death and aftermath are contained in the chapter, "Hide and Seek: The Story of $800,000."

49. *P.S.*, 105.

50. Simon interview, 1998.

51. Like many others, Simon believed the money had originally been kept in Powell's office safe and was transferred to his apartment at the St. Nicholas Hotel in Springfield the night of his death. Simon said, "I think Paul was too conservative just to leave money in the closet in the hotel. That just doesn't make sense to me," 1998 interview.

52. Simon, interview with author, 24 Jan. 1997.

53. Hartley, *Paul Powell*, 171–73.

10. A Louder Voice

1. Gene Callahan, press aide during the lieutenant governor years, said Simon treated most column subjects in a general fashion, unless he had a passion for the subject. One of those was Gov. Ogilvie's plan to issue bonds for transportation projects.

2. "Ogilvie Budget: Some Changes Needed," From the Statehouse, 7 May 1969, Simon Papers–ALPL, box 99, folder 27, Columns 1969.

3. "State Tax Increase: The Wrong Answer," From the Statehouse, 1969, Simon Papers–ALPL, box 99, folder 27.

4. Simon to "Editorial writers of the state," press release 6 May 1969, Illinois State Archives, Office of Lieutenant Governor, Paul Simon Administrative files, series 102.041, folder "Highway bond issue, House Bill 443" (hereafter cited as State Archives).

5. Statement by Simon at news conference, 28 May 1969, State Archives.

6. Statement by Simon, 6 June 1969, State Archives.

7. Statement by Simon, 9 July 1969, with attached letter from Simon to Atty. Gen. William J. Scott, State Archives.

8. Scott statement of 9 July 1969 as copied and distributed in the capital pressroom by Shelby Vasconcelles, State Archives; and "Simon Reverses on Highway Bill," *Daily Pantagraph*, Bloomington, Illinois, 10 July 1969, Simon Papers–ALPL, box 97, folder 5, bond issue.

9. "Ogilvie's Road Bond Issue Ruled Unconstitutional," *Illinois State Journal*, 24 Mar. 1970, State Archives.

10. "Taxpayers Give Thanks to Illinois Court," From the Statehouse, 1970, Simon Papers–ALPL, box 99, folder 30, Columns 1970.

11. "A Dangerous Bond Issue Proposal," and "A Dangerous Proposal Still Lurks," From the Statehouse, 1971, Simon Papers–ALPL, box 99, folder 28, columns 1971.

12. "Aid to Non-Public Schools—A Necessity," From the Statehouse, January 1970, Simon Papers–ALPL, box 99, folder 30, columns 1970.

13. "Important Questions—Important Answers," From the Statehouse, January 1970, Simon Papers–ALPL, box 99, folder 30.

14. "Income Disclosure: The Time Has Come," From the Statehouse, 9 Sept. 1971, Simon Papers–ALPL, box 80, folder 39.

15. "Public Aid—Are Costs Excessive?" From the Statehouse, *Winchester Times*, 27 Feb. 1969.

16. *News from Paul Simon, Lt. Governor of the State of Illinois*, winter 1969, Simon Papers–ALPL, box 41, folder 17, Newsletters 1970–72.

17. *News from Paul Simon*, winter 1970, Simon Papers–ALPL, box 41, folder 17.

18. Robert Wiedrich, "Tower Ticker," *Chicago Tribune*, 16 Oct. 1969.

19. "Complete Income Disclosure by Lieutenant Governor Paul Simon and His Administrative Assistants," memorandum to the press, 19 Apr. 1971.

11. Reaching for the Ring

1. "Paul Simon to Run for Governor Only," *Chicago Daily News*, 28 Sept. 1971.

2. For a full story of Walker's achievements in his own words, *The Maverick and the Machine: Governor Dan Walker Tells His Story* (Carbondale: Southern Illinois University Press, 2007).

3. Walter Jacobson, "The Organization Man (Don't Call It a Machine)," *Chicago Sun-Times Midwest Magazine*, 19 Mar. 1972, 9.

4. Robert Weinberger to Simon, "The Walker Candidacy," 18 Nov. 1970, Simon Papers–SIU, provisional box 1688, Walker Campaign Research.

5. *P.S.*, 109.

6. Victor de Grazia to Gene Callahan, 13 Apr. 1971, Simon Papers–ALPL, box 84, folder 28, Gene Callahan.

7. *P.S.*, 108.

8. *The Maverick*, 108–69. Walker delivers a blow-by-blow account of the walk.

9. "The Organization Man," 11.

10. Ibid., 13.

11. Clifford Terry, "Dan Walker: The Long Road to Springfield," *Chicago Tribune Magazine*, 12 Mar. 1969, 25.

12. Jeanne Simon to author, 22 Aug. 1971.

13. "Mudge Flies Second Campaign Mission in Prosecutor Race," *East St. Louis Journal*, 8 Apr. 1956, Bowen Archives.

14. "P.S. by P.S.," *Troy Tribune*, 17 July 1957.

15. Jim Wiggs, "Metro-East Portrait," *Metro-East Journal*, 16 Feb. 1963, Bowen Archives.

16. "Prosecutor in Race Against Demo Leader," *East St. Louis Journal*, 21 Jan. 1958, Bowen Archives.

17. "P.S. by Paul Simon," *Troy Tribune*, 3 Nov. 1960.

18. "Hits Chicago Machine," letter to the editor, *Tribune*, 15 Mar. 1962.

19. "Mudge: Mayor Daley Is a Humiliating Experience," *Metro-East Journal*, 8 Sept. 1968, Bowen Archives.

20. Editorial, *Metro-East Journal*, 15 Mar. 1970, Bowen Archives.

21. "Another Midwesterner," 7 Dec. 1987.

22. "Paul Simon's Credentials," *Chicago Daily News*, 6 Nov. 1971, Simon Papers–ALPL, box 89, folder 68.

23. Simon to Hartley, 29 Dec. 1971.

24. Ibid.

25. "The Long Road," 24.

26. Durbin interview.

27. *The Maverick*, 177. Walker explains how he capitalized on Simon's tax proposal in *P.S.*, 112.

28. "You're Right, but Don't Say It," Simon statement accompanying annual income disclosure, 6 Mar. 1972, Simon Papers–ALPL, box 99, folder 29, Columns 72–1.

29. "Complete Income Disclosure by Lieutenant Governor Paul Simon and His Administrative Assistants," press release, 6 Mar. 1972, Simon Papers–ALPL, box 95, folder 35, News releases.

30. Callahan interview, 27 Dec. 2007.

31. "Nomination of Paul Simon Recommended," *Decatur Sunday Herald and Review*, 12 Mar. 1972.

32. *P.S.*, 113.

33. "My Thanks," Simon column, 30 Apr. 1972. Simon Papers–ALPL, box 99, folder 29. In the column, Simon repeated his concession statement.

34. Ibid.

35. Draft of article for *Chicago Sun-Times*, no date. Obviously written after his loss to Walker, Simon Papers–SIU, provisional box 1688, Illinois Legislation.

Part Four. Beyond Defeat, 1973–97

12. Interregnum

1. *Dan Walker: The Glory and the Tragedy*, 246–47.

2. *The Maverick*, 227.

3. *P.S.*, 125.

4. Ibid.

5. Chris Vlahoplus interview with author, 22 Apr. 2008.

6. Deborah K. Gill, email to author, 10 Apr. 2008.

7. Simon article draft based on talk to Neiman Fellows, no date, Simon Papers–ALPL, box 95, folder 35, Magazine Articles.

8. Durbin interview.

13. The Comeback

1. *P.S.*, 127.

2. Callahan interview, 4 Jan. 2007.

3. Dixon interview, 2007.

4. Sheila Knop interview with author, 28 May 2008.

5. "Veteran versus Newcomer," *Southern Illinoisan*, 12 Mar. 1974.

6. Callahan interview, 4 Jan. 2007.

7. Durbin interview, and Callahan interview, 4 Jan. 2007.

8. Karen Rothe, "Simon, Browning Wage 'Nice Guy' Campaign," *Southern Illinoisan*, 20 Jan. 1974.

9. "Simon and Gaffner Endorsed," editorial, *Southern Illinoisan*, 17 Mar. 1974.

10. "Paul Simon Makes Full Disclosure," *Southern Illinoisan*, 23 Apr. 1974.

11. "P.S./Washington," 2 Feb. 1975, Simon Papers–SIU, provisional 96–0399, 1975–78, 1975 column no. 1.

12. "Simon's Campaign Spending Raises Questions about Money in Politics," *Decatur Sunday Herald and Review*, 22 Aug. 1976. From 22 to 25 Aug. 1976 Lindsay-Schaub newspapers in central and southern Illinois ran a series of articles titled, "The Money Connection." Reporter Carol Alexander conducted months of research into the 1975 election campaign of Simon and disclosed financial information.

13. "Simon More Comfortable with Labor on His Side," *Decatur Herald and Review*, 22 Aug. 1976.

14. "Banker Sinclair a Friend Indeed in Simon Campaign," *Herald and Review*, 24 Aug. 1976.

15. "Sam Stern, among Simon Contributors, Asks a Kind Smile," *Herald and Review*, 25 Aug. 1976.

16. "Mr. Simon Goes to Washington," *Illinois Issues*, August 1975, http://www.lib.niu.edu/ipo/1975/ii750822.html.

17. Patricia O'Brien, "Impact of a Congressman: Behind Closed Doors with Rep. Paul Simon," *Akron Beacon-Journal*, 10 Oct. 1982.

18. "That Congressional 'Vacation,'" P.S./Washington, 8 June 1975, Simon Papers–SIU.

19. "Another Midwesterner," 7 Dec. 1987.

20. Hartley, "Simon Gaining Attention for 'Staying Power,'" *Decatur Sunday Herald and Review*, 21 Dec. 1975.

21. *P.S.*, 135.

22. "The Peril to Small Post Offices," P.S./Washington, 23 Feb. 1975, Simon Papers–SIU, provisional 96–0399, 1975–78, 1975 no. 4.

23. "Rural Roads and Bridges Need Help," P.S./Washington, 17 Aug. 1975, Simon Papers–SIU, 96–0399, 1975–78, 1975 no. 29.

24. "Financial Disclosures Would Help End Anti-Government Attitudes," P.S./Washington, 16 May 1976, Simon Papers–SIU, 96–0399, 1975–78, 1976 no. 20.

25. "Simon's Decision Simple," editorial, *Decatur Herald*, 4 Nov. 1977.

26. Dixon interview, 30 Jan. 2007.

27. *P.S.*, 154.

28. "A National Need: More Leadership, Less Polling," P.S./Washington, 20 July 1979, Simon Papers–SIU, provisional 5n3b8b, Columns 1978–80, 1979 no. 30.

29. "Why I Support Kennedy," P.S./Washington, 20 Nov. 1979, Simon Papers–SIU, provisional 5n3b8b, Columns 1978–80, 1979 no. 42.

30. Ibid.

31. "Simon to Support Carter and Work for Party Unity," *Southern Illinoisan*, 13 Aug. 1980.

32. *P.S.*, 153.

33. "Spicy 24th District Race Pits Three Distinct Views," *Southern Illinoisan*, 26 Oct. 1980.

34. "Simon Reflective after Narrow Escape," *Southern Illinoisan*, 8 Nov. 1980.

35. "Another Midwesterner," 7 Dec. 1987.

36. Robert D. Reid, "Simon Doesn't Deserve Moral Majority Barbs," *Southern Illinoisan*, 22 Mar. 1981.

37. Press release, 27 July 1981, Simon Papers–SIU, provisional box 6s4b12b, 1982 Campaign.

38. Simon, *The Once and Future Democrats: Strategies for Change* (New York: Continuum, 1982); also Hartley, "Paul Simon's New Book on Ideas: A Thirty-Year Veteran of Illinois Politics Tells Us What's Going On above the Bow-Tie," *Illinois Times*, 25 Aug. 1982.

39. Survey of Voters, 24th Illinois District, Peter D. Hart Research Associates, Inc., Simon Papers–SIU, provisional 6s4a12c, Campaign Resources.

40. "'Prince of Pork' Earned Title," *The Southern*, 8 June 2008.

41. John Jackson and Keith Sanders, memorandum, "A Program for Strengthening Paul Simon's Relationships with Southern Illinois University," Simon Papers–SIU, 97–0002, 1982 campaign.

42. "Impact of a Congressman."

43. "Some of That Old-Time Religion," *Time*, 16 Nov. 1987.

44. Simon, *The Tongue-Tied American: Confronting the Foreign Language Crisis* (New York: Continuum, 1980).

45. *Strategies for Change*. Simon said voters favored Republicans in the 1980 elections because of questions about inflation, unemployment, and leadership, not philosophical differences, 5.

46. Ibid., 88.

47. *Troy Tribune*, 14 Apr. 1949, also, "Troy Weekly Devotes Front Page to Easter Story," *St. Louis Lutheran*, 30 Apr. 1949, Simon Papers–SIU, scrapbook 1, 1927–1955.

14. Full Redemption

1. Robert D. Reid, "The Perils of Paul," *Illinois Times*, 12 May 1983.

2. Dixon interview, 2007.

3. Durbin interview.

4. "Stevenson Says Endorsement Is 'Right if Not a Duty,'" *Southern Illinoisan*, 5 Oct. 1983.

5. Dixon interview, 2007.

6. Simon, conversation with author, 9 May 1984.

7. Mike Lawrence, conversation with author, 27 May 2008.

8. "Simon Launches Senate Bid," *Southern Illinoisan*, 18 July 1983.

9. "Rep. Simon, Opponent Rock Change Campaign Managers," *Southern Illinoisan*, 5 Oct. 1983; also James Wall, interview with author, 25 Apr. 2008.

10. Wall interview.

11. Wall worked with William Singer of Chicago in unseating the delegates committed to Mayor Richard J. Daley at the 1972 Democratic National Convention. Wall ended up as cochairman of the delegation, Hartley, "Wall, Choate, Singer Made Unity Look Easy," *Decatur Herald*, 16 July 1972.

12. "Democrats Back Rock," *Southern Illinoisan*, 22 Nov. 1983.

13. "Percy: I Won't Bow to Pro-Israel Lobby," *Southern Illinoisan*, 14 Aug. 1983.

14. *P.S.*, 156.

15. "Senate Race Links Illinois and Israel," *Southern Illinoisan*, 14 Aug. 1983.

16. "Percy Faces Jewish Bloc in Re-election Campaign," *Chicago Tribune*, 7 Aug. 1983.

17. Thomas A. Dine, "Illinois: A Key to Campaign 1984," 16 Oct. 1983, Simon Papers–SIU, provisional 6s2b11c, Middle East.

18. Carter Eskew to Forrest Claypool, 1 Nov. 1983, Simon Papers–SIU, provisional 6s2b11c, Campaign Strategy.

19. Election results by county, printout, *Associated Press*, 21 Mar. 1984.

20. Simon to Jerome Grossman (Council for a Livable World), 10 Nov. 1983, Simon Papers–SIU, provisional 6s2b11c, Endorsements.

21. "1984 Senate Candidate Update," Democratic Senatorial Campaign Committee, 1 May 1984, Simon Papers–SIU, provisional 6s2b11c, General Campaign Information.

22. Simon, *The Glass House: Morality in the Nation's Capital* (New York: Continuum, 1984).

23. "Another Midwesterner," 7 Dec. 1987.

24. *Glass House*, 63.

25. Ibid., 88.

26. Simon's acquisition of fourteen weekly newspapers in Illinois would constitute a "chain" in the minds of many.

27. "Another Midwesterner."

28. "Paul Simon Pins His Presidential Aspirations on His Liberal Policies and 'Boy Scout' Image," *Wall Street Journal*, 2 Oct. 1987, also *P.S.*, 158.

29. David Carle to Bill Knapp, Carter Eskew, David Doak, memorandum, "Paul Simon Achievements Summary," 8 Feb. 1984, Simon Papers–SIU, provisional 6s4a12b, Voting Record Categories.

30. Dixon interview, 2007.

31. Election results by county, printout, *Associated Press*, 9 Nov. 1984.

32. David Kenney and Robert E. Hartley, *An Uncertain Tradition: U.S. Senators from Illinois, 1818–2003* (Carbondale: Southern Illinois University Press, 2003), 22.

33. Election results by county, 9 Nov. 1984.

34. Former governor Richard B. Ogilvie and Percy worked diligently to assure Gerald R. Ford the majority of Illinois delegates in spite of Reagan's efforts.

35. "Another Midwesterner."

36. Ibid.

37. "Has a Traditionalist Found the Keys to the Senate?" *Wall Street Journal*, 6 Mar. 1984.

38. Dixon interview, 2007.

39. Callahan interview, 4 Jan. 2007.

40. *Wall Street Journal*, 27 Nov. 1985.

41. "Paul Simon of Illinois Makes a Mark in Senate by Turning Its Customs to His Own Advantage," *Wall Street Journal*, 1 Aug. 1985.

42. Ibid.

43. Alan Simpson interview with author, 4 Nov. 2008.

44. William A. Blakey interview with author, 16 Oct. 2008.

45. Simon, *Winners and Losers: The 1988 Race for the Presidency—One Candidate's Perspective* (New York: Continuum, 1989), 9.

46. "Simon Declares, Embracing Democrats' Activist History," *New York Times*, 19 May 1987.

47. "'Ugly Duckling' Simon Becoming Attractive to Democrats," *Seattle Times*, 25 Oct. 1987.

48. "Another Midwesterner."

49. David S. Broder, "Simon Not a Candidate to Take too Lightly," *Seattle Times*, 18 Nov. 1987.

50. David Shribman, "Simon Is Drawing More Voters—and Criticism—as His Elusive Philosophy Comes Under Scrutiny," *Wall Street Journal*, 13 Nov. 1987.

51. "The Wisdom to See What Is Right. The Courage to Fight for It," Paul Simon for President, 1988 campaign brochure.

52. *Winners and Losers*, 22–27.

53. "Simon and Gephardt Are Forced to Go Hunting for Money," *Seattle Post-Intelligencer*, 11 Feb. 1988, also *Winners and Losers*, 30.

54. "Democratic Fight Seems Likely to Go Distance," *New York Times*, 20 Mar. 1988.

55. "I have no illusions that the nomination will come my way," Simon told a press conference, *Associated Press* and *United Press International*, 7 Apr. 1988.

56. Book review, *New York Times*, 5 Feb. 1989.

57. *Winners and Losers*, 137.

58. Ibid., 182.

59. Ibid., 196.

60. In his book *Winners and Losers*, Simon criticized shallow reporting during the campaign.

61. *P.S.*, 220.

62. Callahan interview, 4 Jan. 2007.

63. *P.S.*, 167–69.

64. Simon, *Advice and Consent: Clarence Thomas, Robert Bork, and the Intriguing History of the Supreme Court's Nomination Battles* (Washington: National Press Books, 1992). Simon discusses his involvement in the Thomas controversies.

65. Ibid., 105–7.

66. Dixon interview, 2007.

67. *P.S.*, 169–71.

68. U.S. Senate roll call vote, 104th Congress, 2nd Session, H. R. 3734.

69. "Restore Flexibility to U.S. Sentences," *National Law Journal*, 16 Dec. 1966.

70. Dixon interview, 2007.

71. "The Agony and the Agony," *Chicago Tribune*, 24 June 2007, http://www.chicagotribune.com/news/local/chi-0706209axelrod.

72. Statement of Paul Simon, 14 Nov. 1994, issued by his Senate office.

73. *P.S.*, 207.

74. Simpson interview.

75. Sen. Christopher Dodd tribute to Paul Simon, 30 Sept. 1996.

Bibliography

Manuscript Sources

Paul Simon Papers, Abraham Lincoln Presidential Library, Springfield, Illinois. (Simon Papers–ALPL)

Paul Simon Papers, Special Collections Research Center, Morris Library, Southern Illinois University, Carbondale, Illinois. (Simon Papers–SIU)

Paul Simon, Lieutenant Governor Administrative files, Illinois State Archives.

Adlai E. Stevenson II Papers, Abraham Lincoln Presidential Library, Springfield, Illinois. (Stevenson Papers)

Howard R. Long Collection, L. Tom Perry Special Collections, Harold B. Lee Library, Brigham Young University, Provo, Utah.

Metro-East Journal files, Louisa H. Bowen University Archives and Special Collections, Lovejoy Library, Southern Illinois University, Edwardsville, Illinois. Cited as Bowen Archives.

Paul Powell Papers, Abraham Lincoln Presidential Library, Springfield, Illinois.

Newspapers and Wire Services

Abingdon (Ill.) Argus

Alton (Ill.) Evening Telegraph

Associated Press

Avon (Ill.) Sentinel

Bellevue (Wash.) Journal-American

Cairo (Ill.) Evening Citizen

Carterville (Ill.) Herald

Chicago American

Chicago Daily News

Chicago Sun-Times

Chicago Tribune

Christian Science Monitor

Decatur (Ill.) Herald and Review

East St. Louis (Ill.) Journal (Metro-East Journal)

Elmwood (Ill.) Gazette

Farmington (Ill.) Bugle

Flanagan (Ill.) Home Times

Illinois Journal Register (Springfield)

London (Ill.) Times

Metamora (Ill.) Herald

Mt. Sterling (Ill.) Democrat-Messenger

New York Times

Newsweek

Paddock Publications (Arlington, Ill.)

Roodhouse (Ill.) Record

Seattle Post-Intelligencer

Seattle Times

Southern Illinoisan (Carbondale, Ill.)

Springfield (Ill.) State Journal

St. Louis Globe-Democrat

St. Louis Post-Dispatch

Time

Tri-State Informer (Cairo, Ill.)

Troy (Ill.) Tribune

Wall Street Journal

Washington Post

White Hall (Ill.) Register-Republican

Wichita (Kans.) Eagle-Beacon

Williamsfield (Ill.) Times

Winchester (Ill.) Times

Books

Allen, Howard W., and Vincent A. Lacey, eds. *Illinois Elections, 1818–1990: Candidates and County Returns for President, Governor, Senate and House of Representatives.* Carbondale: Southern Illinois University Press, 1992.

Barnhart, Bill, and Gene Schlickman. *Kerner: The Conflict of Intangible Rights.* Urbana: University of Illinois Press, 1999.

Barone, Michael, and Richard E. Cohen. *The Almanac of American Politics (2006).* Washington: National Journal Group, 2006.

Clayton, John, compiler. *The Illinois Fact Book and Historical Almanac, 1673–1968.* Carbondale: Southern Illinois University Press, 1970.

Editor and Publisher International Yearbook. New York: Editor and Publisher, annual issues 1960–66.

Hartley, Robert E. *Charles H. Percy: A Political Perspective.* Chicago: Rand McNally, 1975.

———. *Paul Powell of Illinois: A Lifelong Democrat.* Carbondale: Southern Illinois University Press, 1999.

History of Madison County, Illinois. Edwardsville: W. R. Brink, 1882.

Howard, Robert P. *Illinois: A History of the Prairie State.* Grand Rapids: William B. Eerdmans, 1972.

Johnson, Walter, ed., and Carol Evans, assistant ed. *The Papers of Adlai E. Stevenson, Governor of Illinois, 1949–1953.* Boston: Little, Brown, 1974, vol. 3.

Kefauver, Estes. *Crime in America.* New York: Doubleday, 1951.

Kenney, David. *A Political Passage: The Career of Stratton of Illinois.* Carbondale: Southern Illinois University Press, 1990.

Kenney, David, and Robert E. Hartley. *An Uncertain Tradition: U.S. Senators from Illinois, 1818–2003.* Carbondale: Southern Illinois University Press, 2003.

Martin, John Bartlow. *Adlai Stevenson of Illinois: The Life of Adlai E. Stevenson.* New York: Doubleday, 1976.

———. *Butcher's Dozen and Other Murders.* New York: Harper, 1950.

Pensoneau, Taylor. *Brothers Notorious: The Sheltons, Southern Illinois' Legendary Gangsters.* New Berlin, Ill.: Downstate Publications, 2002.

———. *Powerhouse: Arrington from Illinois.* Baltimore: American Literary Press, 2006.

———. *Richard Ogilvie: In the Interest of the State.* Carbondale: Southern Illinois University Press, 1997.

Pensoneau, Taylor, and Robert Ellis. *Dan Walker: The Glory and the Tragedy.* Evansville, Ind.: Smith-Collins, 1993.

Pfaff, Daniel W. *No Ordinary Joe: A Life of Joseph Pulitzer III.* Columbia: University of Missouri Press, 2005.

Rudwick, Elliott M. *Race Riot at East St. Louis, July 2, 1917.* Carbondale: Southern Illinois University Press, 1964.

Simon, Paul. *Advice and Consent: Clarence Thomas, Robert Bork, and the Intriguing History of the Supreme Court's Nomination Battles.* Washington: National Press Books, 1992.

———. *Freedom's Champion: Elijah Lovejoy.* Carbondale: Southern Illinois University Press, 1994.

———. *The Glass House: Politics and Morality in the Nation's Capital.* New York: Continuum, 1984.

———. *The Once and Future Democrats: Strategies for Change.* New York: Continuum, 1982.

———. *P.S.: The Autobiography of Paul Simon.* Chicago: Bonus Books, 1999.

———. *The Tongue-Tied American: Confronting the Foreign Language Crisis.* New York: Continuum, 1980.

———. *Winners and Losers: The 1988 Race for the Presidency—One Candidate's Perspective.* New York: Continuum, 1989.

Steel, Ronald. *Walter Lippmann and the American Century.* Boston: Little, Brown, 1980.

Stewart, George R. *U.S. 40: Cross Section of the United States of America.* Boston: Houghton Mifflin, 1953.

Walker, Dan. *The Maverick and the Machine: Governor Dan Walker Tells His Story.* Carbondale: Southern Illinois University Press, 2007.

White, William Allen. *The Autobiography of William Allen White.* New York: Macmillan, 1946.

Selected Sources

Alexander, Carol. "The Money Connection." *Lindsay-Schaub Newspapers,* 22–25 Aug. 1976.

Baldwin, Carl. "East St. Louis." *Journal of the St. Clair County Historical Society,* no. 8 (1983) and no. 9 (1984).

Hartley, Robert E. "'Almost Like Brothers': The Friendship of Alan Dixon and Paul Simon." Presented in October 2008 at the Illinois Historic Preservation Agency's Conference on Illinois History.

———. "The Boy Wonders Are Back Together." *Illinois Times,* 14 May 1981.

———. "Chairman Chuck." *Illinois Times,* 18 Nov. 1980.

———. "Charles O. Stewart's Journalistic Fight Against Crime in East St. Louis, 1945–1965." Presented at the 1989 Illinois History Symposium, Illinois State Historical Society, December 1989.

———. "Paul Simon, Crusading Editor from Troy, Illinois." *Journal of Illinois History* (Spring 2005): 2–24.

———. Unpublished history of criminal activity in St. Clair and Madison counties, Illinois.

Jacobson, Walter. "The Organization Man (Don't Call It a Machine)." *Chicago Sun-Times Midwest Magazine,* 19 Mar. 1972.

Jarvis, James W. "The Early History of Troy." *Troy Tribune,* 25 July 1957.

Lee, Clyde. Oral history. University of Illinois–Springfield, recorded 1988.

Marshall, Prentice H., and Harlington Wood Jr. "Charges of Corruption in the Illinois General Assembly." Minority report to the "Report of the Illinois Crime Investigating Commission re Charges of Corruption in the Illinois General Assembly," 1965.

O'Brien, Patricia. "Impact of a Congressman: Behind Closed Doors with Rep. Paul Simon." For Knight-Ridder newspapers, in the *Akron Beacon-Journal,* 10 Oct. 1982.

"Obit: Paul Simon." *Illinois Issues,* 10 Dec. 2003.

Piety, Harold. "Independents Elect Democrat Paul Simon." *Focus/Midwest/69,* 7, no. 46 (1969): 22–25.

"Practical Study of Campus Problems, A." Lieutenant Governor's Committee on Southern Illinois University, 1970.

Reid, Robert D. "The Perils of Paul." *Illinois Times,* 12 May 1983.

———. "Simon Doesn't Deserve Moral Majority's Barbs." *Southern Illinoisan,* 22 March 1981.

"Report of the Illinois Crime Investigating Commission." For Gov. Otto Kerner and the Seventy-fourth General Assembly of Illinois, 1965.

"Report of the Illinois Crime Investigating Commission re Charges of Corruption in the Illinois General Assembly." State of Illinois, 1965.

Schendel, Gordon. "Illinois Shakedown: The Little Guys Lose." *Collier's,* parts 1 and 2, 15 and 22 Apr. 1950.

Simon, Paul. "Follow-up Report on Illinois." Draft article submitted to *Harper's,* 7 July 1965.

———. "Montgomery Looks Forward." *Christian Century,* 22 Jan. 1958.

———. "Mr. Simon Goes to Washington." *Illinois Issues,* http://www.lib.niu.edu/ipo/1975/117508227.html.

———. "The Ombudsman in Illinois: An Experiment in Government." Office of the Lieutenant Governor, 1970.

———. "Personal Memories of John F. Kennedy." *Troy Tribune,* 28 Nov. 1963.

———. "Southern Illinois University: The Challenges of 1970." Article, 1970.

Simon, Paul, and Alfred Balk. "The Illinois Legislature: A Study in Corruption." *Harper's,* September 1964.

Terry, Clifford. "Dan Walker: The Long Road to Springfield." *Chicago Tribune Magazine,* 12 Mar. 1969.

United States Senate. Special Committee to Investigate Organized Crime in Interstate Commerce. Proceedings of hearings 23–24 Feb. 1951 in St. Louis, Missouri, Parts 4, 4A, 4A exhibits, 5. Washington: Government Printing Office, 1952.

Index

Robert E. Hartley has written about Illinois politics and history for more than four and a half decades. He is the author of six previous books about the state, including political biographies of Charles H. Percy, James R. Thompson, and Paul Powell. He wrote about the six months Lewis and Clark lived on Illinois soil in 1803–4 and is coauthor with David Kenney of books about U.S. senators from Illinois and coal mine disasters at Centralia and West Frankfort. His works include articles for Illinois history magazines and papers for history symposia and programs. Hartley worked from 1962 to 1979 for Lindsay-Schaub newspapers in Illinois.